SOCIAL SECURITY LEGI
SUPPLEMENT 201(

General Editor
David Bonner, LL.B., LL.M.

Commentary by
David Bonner, LL.B., LL.M.
Professor of Law, University of Leicester
Formerly Member, Social Security Appeal Tribunals

Ian Hooker, LL.B.
Formerly Lecturer in Law, University of Nottingham
Formerly Chairman, Social Security Appeal Tribunals

Richard Poynter B.C.L., M.A. (Oxon)
District Tribunal Judge,
Judge of the Upper Tribunal

Mark Rowland, LL.B.
Judge of the Upper Tribunal

Robin White, M.A., LL.M.
Professor of Law, University of Leicester,
Judge of the Upper Tribunal

Nick Wikeley, M.A. (Cantab)
Emeritus Professor of Law, University of Southampton,
Judge of the Upper Tribunal

David W. Williams, LL.M., Ph.D., C.T.A.
Judge of the Upper Tribunal,
Honorary Professor of Tax Law,
Queen Mary College, London

Penny Wood, LL.B., M.Sc.
District Tribunal Judge

Consultant to Vol.II
John Mesher, B.A., B.C.L., LL.M.
Professor Associate of Law, University of Sheffield,
Judge of the Upper Tribunal

Consultant Editor
Child Poverty Action Group

SWEET & MAXWELL　　　　**THOMSON REUTERS**

Published in 2011 by
Sweet & Maxwell, 100 Avenue Road, London NW3 3PF
Part of Thomson Reuters (Professional) UK Limited
(Registered in England & Wales, Company No 1679046.
Registered Office and address for service:
Aldgate House, 33 Aldgate High Street,
London EC3N 1DL)

Typeset by Interactive Sciences Ltd, Gloucester
Printed in Great Britain by
Ashford Colour Press, Gosport, Hants

For further information on our products and services,
visit www.sweetandmaxwell.co.uk

No natural forests were destroyed to make this product.
Only farmed timber was used and re-planted.

A CIP catalogue record for this book is
available from the British Library

ISBN 978-0-414-04736-5

PREFACE

This is the combined Supplement to the 2010/11 edition of the four-volume work, *Social Security Legislation*, which was published in September 2010.

Part I of the Supplement contains new legislation (Acts and Regulations), presented in the same format as the main volumes. This will enable readers to note very quickly new sets of legislation. The key set here is the "Migration Regulations": The Employment and Support Allowance (Transitional Provisions, Housing Benefit and Council Tax Benefit) (Existing Awards) (No.2) Regulations 2010 (SI 2010/1907) (as amended). These govern the process whereby existing recipients of incapacity benefit, income support and severe disablement allowance will be re-examined against the stricter limited capability for work assessment under Employment and Support Allowance to see whether they can be "migrated" to that benefit or, if not, lose title to their existing award, and left reliant, most commonly, on Jobseeker's Allowance. These key regulations are the subject of an explanatory General Note and will be more fully annotated in the next edition of *Social Security Legislation*. They also effect for the purposes of "migration" decisions a number of modifications of existing legislation. Where appropriate these are noted in the updating material, as are permanent amendments effected by them.

Parts II, III, IV and V contain the updating material—a separate Part for each volume of the main work—which amends the legislative text and key aspects of the commentary so as to be up to date as at December 8, 2010. Part VI, the final section of the Supplement, gives some notice of changes forthcoming between that date and the date to which the main work (2011/12 edition) will be up to date (mid-April) and some indication of the April 2011 benefit rates, and takes account of changes known to us as at December 8, 2010.

As always we welcome comments from those who use this Supplement. Please address these to the General Editor, David Bonner, at the School of Law, The University, Leicester LE1 7RH.

David Bonner
Ian Hooker
John Mesher
Richard Poynter
Mark Rowland
Robin White
Nick Wikeley
David W. Williams
Penny Wood
December 15, 2010

CONTENTS

USING THE UPDATING MATERIAL IN THIS SUPPLEMENT

The amendments and updating contained in Parts II–V of this Supplement are keyed in to the page numbers of the relevant main volume of *Social Security Legislation 2010/11*. Where there have been a significant number of changes to a provision, the whole section, subsection, paragraph or regulation, as amended, will tend to be reproduced. Other changes may be noted by an instruction to insert or substitute new material or to delete part of the existing text. The date the change takes effect is also noted. Where explanation is needed of the change, or there is updating to do to existing annotations but no change to the legislation, you will also find commentary in this Supplement. The updating material explains new statutory material, takes on board Upper Tribunal or court decisions, or gives prominence to points which now seem to warrant more detailed attention.

This Supplement amends the text of the main volumes of *Social Security Legislation 2010/11* to be up to date as at December 8, 2010.

David Bonner
General Editor

PAGES OF MAIN VOLUMES AFFECTED BY MATERIAL IN THIS SUPPLEMENT

VOLUME II

Pages of Main Volumes Affected by Material in this Supplement

Pages of Main Volumes Affected by Material in this Supplement

TABLE OF ABBREVIATIONS USED IN THIS SERIES

1978 Act	Employment Protection (Consolidation) Act 1978
1979 Act	Pnumoconiosis (Workers' Compensation Act 1979
1998 Act	Social Security Act 1998
2002 Act	Tax Credits Act 2002
2004 Act	Child Trust Funds Act 2004
(No.2) Regulations	Statutory Paternity Pay (Adoption) and Statutory Adoption Pay (Adoptions from Overseas) (No.2) Regulations 2003
AA	Attendance Allowance
AA 1992	Attendance Allowance Act 1992
AA Regulations	Social Security (Attendance Allowance) Regulations 1991
AAC	Administrative Appeal Chamber
AACR	Administrative Appeals Chamber Reports
AAW	Algemene Arbeidsongeschiktheidswet (Netherlands General Act on Incapacity for Work)
A.C.	Law Reports Appeal Cases
A.C.D.	Administrative Court Digest
ADHD	Attention Deficit Hyperactivity Disorder
Adjudication Regs	Social Security (Adjudication) Regulations 1986
Admin L.R.	Administrative Law Reports
Administration Act	Social Security Administration Act 1992
AIDS	Acquired Immune Deficiency Syndrome
AIP	assessed income period
All E.R.	All England Report
All E.R. (E.C.)	All England Reports (European Cases)
AMA	Adjudicating Medical Authority
ANW	Algemene Nabestaandenwet (Netherlands law of 21 December 1995 on General Insurance for Surviving Dependants)
AO	Adjudication Officer
AOG	*Adjudication Officers' Guide*
AOW	Algemene Ouderdomswet (Netherlands law on the General Scheme for Old-age Pensions)
APG	Austrian General Pensions Act of 18 November 2004

art.	article
ASPP	Additional Statutory Paternity Pay
ASVG	Allgemeines Sozialversicherungsgesetz (Austrian Federal Act of 9 September 1955 on General Social Insurance)
A.T.C.	Annotated Tax Cases
Attendance Allowance Regulations	Social Security (Attendance Allowance) Regulations 1991
BA	Benefits Agency
BAMS	Benefits Agency Medical Service
Benefits Act	Social Security Contributions and Benefits Act 1992
B.C.L.C.	Butterworths Company Law Cases
B.H.R.C.	Butterworths Human Rights Cases
B.L.G.R.	Butterworths Local Government Reports
Blue Books	*The Law Relating to Social Security*, Vols 1–11
B.M.L.R.	Butterworths Medico Legal Reports
B.P.I.R.	Bankruptcy and Personal Insolvency Reports
BSVG	Bauern-Sozialversicherungsgestez (Austrian Federal Act of 11 October 1978 on social security for farmers)
B.T.C.	British Tax Cases
BTEC	Business and Technology Education Council
B.W.C.C.	Butterworths Workmen's Compensation Cases
C	Commissioner's decision
C&BA 1992	Social Security Contributions and Benefits Act 1992
CAA 2001	Capital Allowance Act 2001
CAB	Citizens Advice Bureau
CAO	Chief Adjudication Officer
CBA 1975	Child Benefit Act 1975
CBJSA	Contribution-Based Jobseeker's Allowance
C.C.L. Rep.	Community Care Law Reports
CCM	Claimant Compliance Manual
CCN	New Tax Credits Claimant Compliance Manual
C.E.C.	European Community Cases
CERA	Cortical Evoked Response Audiogram
CESA	Contributory Employment and Support Allowance

Ch.	Chancery Division Law Reports
Child Benefit Regulations	Child Benefit (General) Regulations 2006
CJEU	Court of Justice European Union
Claims and Payments Regulations	Social Security (Claims and Payments) Regulations 1987
Claims and Payments Regulations 1979	Social Security (Claims and Payments) Regulations 1979
CMEC	Child Maintenance and Enforcement Commission
C.M.L.R.	Common Market Law Reports
C.O.D.	Crown Office Digest
Commencement order	Welfare Reform Act 2007 (Commencement No.12) Order 2010
Com. L.R.	Commercial Law Reports
Commissioners Procedure Regulations	Social Security Commissioners (Procedure) Regulations 1999
Computation of Earnings Regulations	Social Security Benefit (Computation of Earnings) Regulations 1978
Computation of Earnings Regulations 1996	Social Security Benefit (Computation of Earnings) Regulations 1996
Consequential Provisions Act	Social Security (Consequential Provisions) Act 1992
Const. L.J.	Construction Law Journal
Contributions and Benefits Act	Social Security Contributions and Benefits Act 1992
Convention	Human Rights Convention
Council Tax Benefit Regulations	Council Tax Benefit (General) Regulations 1992 (SI 1992/1814)
CP	Carer Premium
CP	Chamber President
CPAG	Child Poverty Action Group
C.P.L.R.	Civil Practice Law Reports
CPR	Civil Procedure Rules
C.P. Rep.	Civil Procedure Reports
Cr. App. R.	Criminal Appeal Reports
Cr. App. R. (S.)	Criminal Appeal Reports (Sentencing)
CRCA 2005	Commissioners for Revenue and Customs Act 2005
Credits Regulations 1974	Social Security (Credits) Regulations 1974
Credits Regulations 1975	Social Security (Credits) Regulations 1975
Crim. L.R.	Criminal Law Review
CRU	Compensation Recovery Unit

Table of Abbreviations used in this Series

CSA 1995	Child Support Act 1995
CSIH	Inner House of the Court of Session
CSOH	Outer House of the Court of Session
CS(NI)O	Child Support (Northern Ireland) Order 1995
CSO	Child Support Officer Act 2000
CSPSSA 2000	Child Support, Pensions and Social Security Act 2000
CTA	Common Travel Area
CTB	Council Tax Benefit
CTC	Child Tax Credit
CTC Regulations	Child Tax Credit Regulations 2002
DAT	Disability Appeal Tribunal
DCA	Department for Constitutional Affairs
DCP	Disabled Child Premium
Decisions and Appeals Regulations 1999	Social Security Contributions (Decisions and Appeals) Regulations 1999
Dependency Regulations	Social Security Benefit (Dependency) Regulations 1977
DfEE	Department for Education and Employment
DHSS	Department of Health and Social Security
Disability Living Allowance Regulations	Social Security (Disability Living Allowance) Regulations
DLA	Disability Living Allowance
DLA Regulations	Social Security (Disability Living Allowance) Regulations 1991
DLAAB	Disability Living Allowance Advisory Board
DLAAB Regs	Disability Living Allowance Advisory Board Regulations 1991
DLADWAA 1991	Disability Living Allowance and Disability Working Allowance Act 1991
DM	Decision Maker
DMA	Decision-making and Appeals
DMG	Decision Makers Guide
DMP	Delegated Medical Practitioner
DP	Disability Premium
DPTC	Disabled Person's Tax Credit
D.R.	European Commission of Human Rights Decisions and Reports
DSDNI	Department for Social Development, Northern Ireland
DSS	Department of Social Security

DTI	Department of Trade and Industry
DWA	Disability Working Allowance
DWP	Department of Work and Pensions
DWPMS	Department of Work and Pensions Medical Services
EAA	Extrinsic Allergic Alveolitis
EAT	Employment Appeal Tribunal
EC	European Community
ECHR	European Convention on Human Rights
ECHR rights	European Convention on Human Rights rights
ECtHR	European Court of Human Rights
ECJ	European Court of Justice
E.C.R.	European Court Report
ECSMA Agreement	European Convention on Social and Medical Assistance
EC Treaty	European Community Treaty
EEA	European Economic Area
EEC	European Economic Community
EESI	Electronic Exchange of Social Security Information
E.G.	Estates Gazette
EHIC	European Health Insurance Card
E.H.R.L.R.	European Human Rights Law Review
E.H.R.R.	European Human Rights Reports
E.L.R.	Education Law Reports
EMA	Education Maintenance Allowance
EMO	Examining Medical Officer
EMP	Examining Medical Practitioner
Employment and Support Allowance Regulations	Employment and Support Allowance Regulations 2008
ERA	Employment, Retention and Advancement Scheme
ERA	Evoked Response Audiometry
ERA 1996	Employment Rights Act 1996
ER(NI)O	Employers Rights (Northern Ireland) Order 1996
ES	Employment Service
ESA	Employment and Support Allowance
ESA Regulations	Employment and Support Allowance Regulations 2008
ESA Regulations	Employment and Support Allowance (Transitional Provisions, Housing Benefit and Council Tax Benefit) (Existing Awards) (No.2) Regulations 2010 (SI 2010/1907)

ESA WCAt	Employment and Support Allowance Work Capability Assessment
EU	European Union
Eu.L.R.	European Law Reports
EWCA Civ	Civil Division of the Court of Appeal in England and Wales
FA 1990	Finance Act 1990
FA 1996	Finance Act 1996
FA 2000	Finance Act 2000
FA 2004	Finance Act 2004
F(No.2) A 2005	Finance (No.2) Act 2005
Family Credit Regulations	Family Credit (General) Regulations 1987
Fam. Law	Family Law
FAS	Financial Assistance Scheme
F.C.R.	Family Court Reporter
FIS	Family Income Supplement
Fixing and Adjustment of Rates Regulations 1976	Child Benefit and Social Security (Fixing and Adjustment of Rates) Regulations 1976
F.L.R.	Family Law Report
Former regulations	Employment and Support Allowance (Transitional Provisions, Housing Benefit and Council Tax Benefit) (Existing Awards) Regulations 2010
FSVG	Bundesgesetz über die Sozialversicherung freiberuflich selbständig Erwerbstätiger (Austrian Federal Act of 30 November 1978 on social insurance for the self-employed in the liberal professions)
FTT	First-tier Tribunal
GA	Guardians Allowance
GA Regulations	Social Security (Guardian's Allowance) Regulations 1975
General Benefit Regulations 1982	Social Security (General Benefit) Regulations 1982
General Regulations	Statutory Maternity Pay (General) Regulations 1986
GMP	Guaranteed Minimum Pension
G.P.	General Practitioner
GRA	Gender Recognition Act 2004
GRP	Graduated Retirement Pension
GSVG	Gewerbliches Sozialversicherungsgestez (Austrian Federal Act of 11 October 1978 on social insurance for self-employed persons engaged in trade and commerce)
G.W.D.	Greens Weekly Digest
HASSASSA	Health and Social Services and Social Security Adjudication Act 1983

HB	Housing Benefit
HCD	House of Commons Debates
HCWA	House of Commons Written Answer
HESC	Health, Education and Social Care
H.L.R.	Housing Law Reports
HMIT	Her Majesty's Inspector of Taxes
HMRC	Her Majesty's Revenue & Customs
HNCIP	(Housewives') Non-Contributory Invalidity Pension
Hospital In-Patients Regulations 1975	Social Security (Hospital In-Patients) Regulations 1975
Housing Benefit Regulations	Housing Benefit (General) Regulations 1987
HPP	Higher Pensioner Premium
HRA 1998	Human Rights Act 1998
H.R.L.R.	Human Rights Law Reports–UK Cases
HSE	Health and Safety Executive
IAP	Intensive Activity Period
IB	Incapacity Benefit
IB/IS/SDA	Incapacity Benefits' Regime
IBJSA	Incapacity Benefit Job Seekers Allowance
IB PCA	Incapacity Benefit Person Capability Assessment
IB Regs	Social Security (Incapacity Benefit) Regulations 1994
IB Regulations	Social Security (Incapacity Benefit) Regulations 1994
IBS	Irritable Bowel Syndrome
ICA	Invalid Care Allowance
ICA Regulations	Social Security (Invalid Care Allowance) Regulations 1976
ICA Unit	Invalid Care Allowance Unit
I.C.R.	Industrial Cases Reports
ICTA 1988	Income and Corporation Taxes Act 1988
I(EEA) Regulations	Immigration (European Economic Area) Regulations 2006
IFW Regulations	Incapacity for Work Regulations
IIAC	Industrial Injuries Advisory Council
Imm. A.R.	Immigration Appeal Reports
Immigration and Asylum Regulations	Social Security (Immigration and Asylum) Consequential Amendments Regulations 2000

Table of Abbreviations used in this Series

Incapacity for Work Regulations	Social Security (Incapacity for Work) (General) Regulations 1995
Income Support General Regulations	Income Support (General) Regulations 1987
Increases for Dependants Regulations	Social Security Benefit (Dependency) Regulations 1977
IND	Immigration and Nationality Directorate of the Home Office
I.N.L.R.	Immigration and Nationality Law Reports
IO	Information Officer
I.O.	Insurance Officer
IPPR	Institute of Public Policy Research
IRC	Inland Revenue Commissioners
IRESA	Income Related Employment and Support Allowance
I.R.L.R.	Industrial Relations Law Reports
IS	Income Support
ISAs	Individual Savings Accounts
IS Regs	Income Support Regulations
ITA 2007	Income Tax Act 2007
ITEPA	Income Tax (Earnings and Pensions) Act 2003
ITEPA 2003	Income Tax (Earnings and Pensions) Act 2003
I.T.L. Rep.	International Tax Law Reports
ITS	Independent Tribunal Service
ITTOIA	Income Tax (Trading and Other Income) Act 2005
IVB	Invalidity Benefit
IWA 1994	Social Security (Incapacity for Work) Act 1994
IW	Incapacity for Work
IW (Dependants) Regs	Social Security (Incapacity for Work) (Dependants) Regulations
IW (General) Regs	Social Security (Incapacity for Work) (General) Regulations 1995
IW (Transitional) Regs	Incapacity for Work (Transitional) Regulations
Jobseeker's Regulations 1996	Jobseekers Allowance Regulations 1996
J.P.	Justice of the Peace Reports
JSA	Jobseeker's Allowance
JSA 1995	Jobseekers Allowance Act 1995
JSA Regs 1996	Jobseekers Allowance Regulations 1996
JSA Regulations	Job Seekers Allowance Regulations

Table of Abbreviations used in this Series

JSA (Transitional) Regulations	Jobseeker's Allowance (Transitional) Regulations 1996
JS(NI)O 1995	Jobseekers (Northern Ireland) Order 1995
J.S.S.L.	Journal of Social Security Law
J.S.W.F.L.	Journal of Social Welfare and Family Law
J.S.W.L.	Journal of Social Welfare Law
K.B.	Law Reports, King's Bench
K.I.R.	Knight's Industrial Law Reports
L.& T.R.	Landlord and Tenant Reports
LCWA	Limited Capability for Work Assessment
LEL	Lower Earnings Limit
L.G.R.	Local Government Law Reports
L.G. Rev.	Local Government Review
L.J.R.	Law Journal Reports
Ll.L.Rep	Lloyd's List Law Report
Lloyd's Rep.	Lloyd's Law Reports
LRP	Liable Relative Payment
L.S.G.	Law Society Gazette
LTAHAW	Living Together as Husband and Wife
Luxembourg Court	Court of Justice of the European Communities (also referred to as ECJ)
MA	Maternity Allowance
MAF	Medical Assessment Framework
MAT	Medical Appeal Tribunal
Maternity Allowance Regulations	Social Security (Maternity Allowance) Regulations 1987
Maternity Benefit Regulations	Social Security (Maternity Benefit) Regulations 1975
Medical Evidence Regulations	Social Security (Medical Evidence) Regulations 1976
MIG	Minimum Income Guarantee
Migration regulations	Employment and Support Allowance (Transitional Provisions, Housing Benefit and Council Tax Benefit) (Existing Awards) (No.2) Regulations 2010
MRI	Magnetic resonance imaging
MS	Medical Services
NACRO	National Association for the Care and Resettlement of Offenders
NCB	National Coal Board
NCIP	Non-Contributory Invalidity Pension
NDPD	Notes on the Diagnosis of Prescribed Diseases

Table of Abbreviations used in this Series

NHS	National Health Service
NI	National Insurance
N.I.	Northern Ireland Law Reports
NICA	Northern Ireland Court of Appeal
NICs	National Insurance Contributions
NICom	Northern Ireland Commissioner '
NINo	National Insurance Number
NIRS 2	National Insurance Recording System
N.L.J.	New Law Journal
Northern Ireland Contributions and Benefits Act	Social Security Contributions and Benefits (Northern Ireland) Act 1992
N.P.C.	New Property Cases
NUM	National Union of Mineworkers
OCD	Obsessive compulsive disorder
OGA	Agricultural Insurance Organisation
Ogus, Barendt and Wikeley	A. Ogus, E. Barendt and N. Wikeley, *The Law of Social Security* (4th edn, Butterworths, 1995)
O.J.	Official Journal
Old Cases Act	Industrial Injuries and Diseases (Old Cases) Act 1975
OPA	Overseas Pensions Act 1973
OPB	One Parent Benefit
O.P.L.R.	Occupational Pensions Law Reports
OPSSAT	Office of the President of Social Security Appeal Tribunals
Overlapping Benefits Regulations	Social Security (Overlapping Benefits) Regulations 1979
Overpayments Regulations	Social Security (Payments on account, Overpayments and Recovery) Regulations
P.	Probate, Divorce and Admiralty Law Reports
P. & C.R.	Property and Compensation Reports
PAYE	Pay As You Earn
PCA	Personal Capability Assessment
PD	Prescribed Diseases
P.D.	Practice Direction
Pens. L.R.	Pensions Law Reports
Persons Abroad Regulations	Social Security Benefit (Persons Abroad) Regulations 1975
Persons Residing Together Regulations	Social Security Benefit (Persons Residing Together) Regulations 1977
PIE	Period of Interruption of Employment
PILON	Pay In Lieu of Notice

PIW	Period of Incapacity for Work
P.I.W.R.	Personal Injury and Quantum Reports
P.L.R.	Estates Gazette Planning Law Reports
Polygamous Marriages Regulations	Social Security and Family Allowances (Polygamous Marriages) Regulations 1975
PPF	Pension Protection Fund
PPU	ECJ urgent preliminary ruling procedure
Present regulations	Employment and Support Allowance (Transitional Provisions, Housing Benefit and Council Tax Benefit) (Existing Awards) (No.2) Regulations 2010
Prescribed Diseases Regulations	Social Security (Industrial Injuries) (Prescribed Diseases) Regulations 1985
PSCS	DWP's Pension Service Computer System
PTA	Pure Tone Audiometry
P.T.S.R.	Public and Third Sector Law Reports
PVS	Private of Voluntary Sectors
pw	per week
Q.B.	Queens Bench Law Reports
QBD (NI)	Queen's Bench Division (Northern Ireland)
r.	rule
R	Reported Decision
RC	Rules of the Court of Session
REA	Reduced Earnings Allowance
Recoupment Regulations	Social Security (Recoupment) Regulations 1990
reg.	regulation
RIPA	Regulation of Investigatory Powers Act 2000
RMO	Regional Medical Officer
rr.	rules
RSI	Repetitive Strain Injury
R.T.R.	Road Traffic Reports
s.	section
S	Scottish Decision
SAP	Statutory Adoption Pay
SAYE	Save As You Earn
SB	Supplementary Benefit
SBAT	Supplementary Benefit Appeal Tribunal
SBC	Supplementary Benefits Commission
Sch.	Schedule
S.C.	Session Cases

S.C. (H.L.)	Session Cases (House of Lords)
S.C. (P.C.)	Session Cases (Privy Council)
S.C.C.R.	Scottish Criminal Case Reports
S.C.L.R.	Scottish Civil Law Reports
SDA	Severe Disablement Allowance
SDP	Severe Disability Premium
SEC	Social Entitlement Chamber
SERPS	State Earnings Related Pension Scheme
Severe Disablement Allowance Regulations	Social Security (Severe Disablement Regulations Allowance) Regulations 1984
SF	Social Fund
S.J.	Solicitors Journal
S.J.L.B.	Solicitors Journal Law Brief
S.L.T.	Scots Law Times
SMP	Statutory Maternity Pay
SMP (General) Regulations	Statutory Maternity Pay (General) Regulations
SMP (General) Regulations 1986	Statutory Maternity Pay (General) Regulations 1986
SP	Senior President
SPC	State Pension Credit
SPCA	State Pension Credit Act 2002
SPCA(NI)	State Pension Credit Act (Northern Ireland) 2002
SPC Regulations	State Pension Credit Regulations 2002
SPP	Statutory Paternity Pay
SPP and SAP (Administration) Regs 2002	Statutory Paternity Pay and Statutory Adoption Pay (Administration) Regulations 2002
SPP and SAP (General) Regulations 2002	Statutory Paternity Pay and Statutory Adoption Pay (General) Regulations 2002
SPP and SAP (National Health Service)	Statutory Paternity Pay and Statutory Adoption Pay (National Health Service Employees) Regulations 2002
SPP and SAP (Weekly Rates) Regulations	Statutory Paternity Pay and Statutory Adoption Pay (Weekly Rates) Regulations 2002
ss.	sections
SSA	Social Security Agency
SSA 1975	Social Security Act 1975
SSA 1978	Social Security Act 1978
SSA 1979	Social Security Act 1979
SSA 1981	Social Security Act 1981
SSA 1986	Social Security Act 1986

SSA 1989	Social Security Act 1989
SSA 1990	Social Security Act 1990
SSA 1992	Social Security Act 1992
SSA 1998	Social Security Act 1998
SS(A) Act	Social Security (Amendment) Act
SSAA 1992	Social Security Administration Act 1992★
SSAC	Social Security Advisory Committee
SSAT	Social Security Appeal Tribunal
SSCBA 1992	Social Security Contributions and Benefits Act 1992★
SSCB(NI) Act 1992	Social Security Contributions (Northern Ireland) Act 1992
SS(CP)A	Social Security (Consequential Provisions) Act 1992
SSHBA 1982	Social Security and Housing Benefits Act 1982
SSHD	Secretary of State for the Home Department
SS(MP) A 1977	Social Security (Miscellaneous Provisions) Act 1977
SS (No.2) A 1980	Social Security (No.2) Act 1980
SSP	Statutory Sick Pay
SSPA 1975	Social Security Pensions Act 1975
SSP (Gen.) Regulations	Statutory Sick Pay (General) Regulations 1982
SSP (General) Regulations 1982	Statutory Sick Pay (General) Regulations 1982
SSPA 1975	Social Security Pensions Act 1975
SSWP	Secretary of State for Work and Pensions
State Pension Credit Regulations	State Pension Credit Regulations 2002
S.T.C.	Simon's Tax Cases
S.T.C. (S.C.D.)	Simon's Tax Cases: Special Commissioners Decisions
S.T.I.	Simon's Tax Intelligence
STIB	Short-Term Incapacity Benefit
Strasbourg Court	European Court of Human Rights
T	Tribunal of Commissioners' Decision
Taxes Act	Income and Corporation Taxes Act 1988
T.C.	Tax Cases
TC	Tax Credits
TCA	Tax Credits Act
TCA 1999	Tax Credits Act 1999
TCA 2002	Tax Credits Act 2002

TC (Claims and Notifications) Regs 2002	Tax Credits (Claims and Notifications) Regulations 2002
TCGA	Taxation of Chargeable Gains Act 1992
TCTM	Tax Credits Technical Manual
TEC	Treaty Establishing the European Community
TEU	Treaty on European Union
TFEU	Treaty on the Functioning of the European Union
The Board	Commissioners for Revenue and Customs
TMA 1970	Taxes Management Act 1970
T.R.	Taxation Reports
Transfer of Functions Act	Social Security Contributions (Transfer of Functions etc.) Act 1999
Treaty	Rome Treaty
UB	Unemployment Benefit
UKAIT	UK Asylum and Immigration Tribunal
UKBA	UK Border Agency of the Home Office
UKFTT	United Kingdom First-tier Tribunal Tax Chamber
UKHL	United Kingdom House of Lords
U.K.H.R.R.	United Kingdom Human Rights Reports
UKSC	United Kingdom Supreme Court
UKUT	United Kingdom Upper Tribunal
Unemployment, Sickness and Invalidity Benefit Regs	Social Security (Unemployment, Sickness and Invalidity Benefit) Regulations 1983
URL	Uniform resource locator
USI Regs	Social Security (Unemployment, Sickness and Invalidity Benefit) Regulations 1983
UT	Upper Tribunal
VAMS	Veterans Agency Medical Service
VAT	Value Added Tax
VCM	Vinyl Chloride Monomer-Related
VERA 1992	Vehicle Excise and Registration Act 1992
VWF	Vibration White Finger
W	Welsh Decision
WAO	Wet Arbeidsongeschiktheid (Netherlands law of 18 February 1966 on invalidity insurance for employees)
WAZ	Wet Arbeidsongeschiktheid Zelfstandigen (Netherlands law of 24 April 1997 on invalidity insurance for self-employed persons)
WCA	Work Capability Assessment

Table of Abbreviations used in this Series

WCAt	First Element of Limited Work Capability Assessment
WFHRAt	Work Focused Health Related Assessment
WFTC	Working Families Tax Credit
WIA	Wet Werk en Inkomen naar Arbeidsvermogen (Netherlands law of 10 November 2005 on work and income according to labour capacity)
Widow's Benefit and Retirement Pensions Regs	Social Security (Widow's Benefit and Retirement Pensions) Regulations 1979
Wikeley, Annotations	N. Wikeley, "Annotations to Jobseekers Act 1995 (c.18)" in *Current Law Statutes Annotated* (1995)
Wikeley, Ogus and Barendt	Wikeley, Ogus and Barendt, *The Law of Social Security* (5th edn, Butterworths, 2002)
W.L.R.	Weekly Law Reports
Workmen's Compensation Acts	Workmen's Compensation Acts 1925 to 1945
WPS	War Pensions Scheme
WRA 2007	Welfare Reform Act
WRAAt	Second Element of Work Related Activity Assessment
WRPA 1999	Welfare Reform and Pensions Act 1999
WRP(NI)O 1999	Welfare Reform and Pensions (Northern Ireland) Order
WTC	Working Tax Credit
WTC (Entitlement and Maximum Rate) Regulations 2002	Working Tax Credit (Entitlement and Maximum Rate) Regulations 2002
W.T.L.R.	Wills & Trusts Law Reports

* Where the context makes it seem more appropriate, these could also be referred to as Contributions and Benefits Act 1992, Administration Act 1992.

TABLE OF CASES

TABLE OF COMMISSIONERS' DECISIONS 1948–2009

[Northern Ireland Commissioners' decisions from 2010 and all Upper Tribunal decisions will be found in the Table of Cases, above.]

TABLE OF EUROPEAN MATERIALS

TABLE OF STATUTES

TABLE OF STATUTORY INSTRUMENTS

1

PART I

NEW LEGISLATION

NEW STATUTES

Welfare Reform Act 2009

(2009 c.24)

An Act to amend the law relating to social security; to make provision enabling disabled people to be given greater control over the way in which certain public services are provided for them; to amend the law relating to child support; to make provision about the registration of births; and for connected purposes. [12th November 2009]

Conditions for contributory jobseeker's allowance

12.—(1) Section 2 of the Jobseekers Act 1995 (c. 18) (jobseeker's   1.002 allowance: the contribution-based conditions) is amended as follows.

(2)–(4)—*amendments made by these subsections have been taken into account in the Updating sections of this Supplement.*

(5)—*omitted as not yet in force.*

(6) In paragraph 45 of Schedule 1 to the National Insurance Contributions Act 2002 (c. 19) (which amended section 2(2)(b) of the Jobseekers Act 1995 (c. 18)), for "section 2(2)(b) and (3)" substitute "section 2(3)".

General Note

This section and the regulations made under it significantly tighten the con-   1.003 tribution conditions for CBJSA. They mean that the requisite level of earnings in the tax year relied on for the first contribution condition is now 26 times that year's lower earnings limit, rather than 25, and the conditions now only count earnings at that lower earnings limit so that new claimants will have to have worked for at least 26 weeks in one of the last two tax years (in effect each week's work at or above the LEL generates in essence one "contribution" (a virtual equivalent of the old regime of NI stamps) towards the target of 26 contributions, and has redolence with the earliest years of the National Insurance scheme operative from 1913, which worked on "flat-rate" contributions. Prior to these amendments, when the level was 25 times the LEL and the scheme looked also to earnings between the lower and upper earnings limits, a high earner could qualify on less than four weeks' work in the tax year and someone at the national minimum wage could qualify in about 12 weeks. The relevant regulations made

3

under subs.(2A) are the Social Security (Contribution Conditions for Job-seeker's Allowance and Employment and Support Allowance) Regulations 2010 (SI 2010/2446), and amendments effected by them to the JSA Regulations are taken into account in the update to p.934 of Volume II in Part III of the Supplement.

Subs. (6)

1.004   This initially strange provision means that the change effected in 2002 by inserting words into s.2(2)(b), whereby for contributions conditions purposes only earnings between the lower and upper earnings limit counted, remains operative by inserting (presumably from 2002?) that limit into s.2(3), the amendment being noted in the updates to pp.37–38 of Volume II in Part III of this Supplement.

Conditions for contributory employment and support allowance

1.005   **13.**—(1) Paragraph 1 of Schedule 1 to the Welfare Reform Act 2007 (c. 5) (employment and support allowance: conditions relating to national insurance) is amended as follows.

(2)–(4)—*amendments made by these subsections have been taken into account in the Updating sections of this Supplement.*
(5)—*omitted as not yet in force.*

General Note

1.006   The changes effected from November 1, 2010 by this section and the regulations made under it significantly tighten the contribution conditions for CESA by requiring a more recent and stronger connection with the world of work. It does so in that the first condition can from then only be satisfied in one of the last *two* (rather than three) tax years (April 6 to April 5) complete before the start of the relevant benefit year (early January) (as with JSA); and by raising the requisite level of earnings in the tax year relied on to 26 (rather than 25) times that year's lower earnings limit. Moreover, since the conditions now only count earnings at that lower earnings limit (ignoring earnings in excess of it) new claimants will have to have worked for at least 26 weeks in one of the last two tax years (in effect each week's work at or above the LEL generates in essence one "contribution" (a virtual equivalent of the old regime of NI stamps) towards the target of 26 contributions, and has redolence with the earliest years of the National Insurance scheme operative from 1913, which worked on "flat-rate" contributions. Prior to these amendments, when the level was 25 times the LEL and the scheme looked also to earnings between the lower and upper earnings limits, a high earner could qualify on less than four weeks' work in the tax year and someone at the national minimum wage could qualify in about 12 weeks. The relevant regulations made under subss.(3) and (3A) are the Social Security (Contribution Conditions for Jobseeker's Allowance and Employment and Support Allowance) Regulations 2010 (SI 2010/2446), and amendments effected by them to the ESA Regulations are taken into account in the updates to pp.1008–1010 of Volume I in Part II of the Supplement.

NEW REGULATIONS AND ORDERS

The Employment and Support Allowance (Transitional Provisions, Housing Benefit and Council Tax Benefit) (Existing Awards) (No.2) Regulations 2010

(SI 2010/1907) (as amended)

Coming into force in accordance with regulation 1(2) and (3)

ARRANGEMENT OF REGULATIONS

PART 1

GENERAL

PART 2

CONVERSION DECISIONS

PART 3

AFTER THE CONVERSION PHASE

PART 4

MISCELLANEOUS

SCHEDULES

The Secretary of State for Work and Pensions makes the following Regulations in exercise of the powers conferred by sections 123(1)(d) and (e), 135(1), 137(1) and 175(1), (3) and (4) of the Social Security Contributions and Benefits Act 1992, section 79(4) of the Social Security Act 1998, paragraphs 4(4) and (6), 20(1) and 23(1) of Schedule 7 to the Child Support, Pensions and Social Security Act 2000, sections 22, 24, 25(2), (3) and (5), 28(2) and 29 of, and paragraph 2 of Schedule 2 and paragraphs 1(1), 3(b), 7 and 8(1) of Schedule 4 to, the Welfare Reform Act 2007.

The Secretary of State has not referred these Regulations to the Social Security Advisory Committee as it appears to the Secretary of State that by reason of urgency it is inexpedient to do so.

The Secretary of State has not undertaken consultation with organisations appearing to the Secretary of State to be representative of the authorities concerned, as it appears to the Secretary of State that by reason of urgency it is inexpedient to do so.

GENERAL NOTE

Introduction

1.008   These Regulations establish the framework within which most current awards of incapacity benefit, income support on the basis of incapacity or disability, or severe disablement allowance will either be converted to awards of ESA or terminated.

Legislative history

The Regulations are in the same terms as the Employment and Support   **1.009**
Allowance (Transitional Provisions, Housing Benefit and Council Tax Benefit)
(Existing Awards) Regulations 2010 (SI 2010/875) ("the former Regulations").
However, on March 10, 2010, when the former Regulations were made, paras 7
and 8 of Sch.4 to the Welfare Reform Act 2007 ("the Act")—which were listed
in the preamble as being among the powers under which they were said to have
been made—had not been brought into force. To regularise matters:

- those paras were brought into force with effect on July 27, 2010 by the
  Welfare Reform Act 2007 (Commencement No.12) Order 2010 (SI
  2010/1905) ("the Commencement Order");
- the former Regulations were revoked by the Employment and Support
  Allowance (Transitional Provisions, Housing Benefit and Council Tax Benefit) (Existing Awards) (Revocation) Regulations 2010 (SI 2010/1906) with
  effect from August 27, 2010, before they came into force; and
- the present Regulations were made in the same terms as the former Regulations under powers which, as a result of the Commencement Order, the
  Secretary of State now possesses.

The Regulations have subsequently been amended by the Employment and
Support Allowance (Transitional Provisions, Housing Benefit and Council Tax
Benefit) (Existing Awards) (No.2) (Amendment) Regulations 2010 (SI
2010/2430) with effect from November 1, 2010.

Personal scope

By reg.3, the Regulations apply to any person who, on or after October 1,   **1.010**
2010, is entitled to an "existing award". That phrase is not defined in the
Regulations. However, by virtue of s.11 Interpretation Act 1978, the definition
in para.11 of Sch.4 to the Act applies. That provision defines "existing award" as
meaning an award of incapacity benefit, an award of severe disablement allowance and an award of income support made to a person who falls within certain
income support prescribed categories (specifically, disabled workers, certain
"eligible persons" (namely, those qualifying young persons who satisfy
reg.13(2)(b) or (bb) of the Income Support (General) Regulations 1987 (SI
1987/1967)), persons who are, or are treated as, incapable of work, certain
disabled students, deaf students and blind persons). However, under reg.4(5),
the conversion process does not apply to anyone who will reach pensionable age
before April 6, 2014.

It is possible for a person to have two existing awards (as where an award of
incapacity benefit or severe disablement allowance is topped up by income
support). However, for ease of exposition, this note is written as if there is only
one existing award in any case. Where there are two such awards, what is said
below applies to both of them.

The conversion process

The conversion of existing awards to awards of ESA is governed by Pt 2 of the   **1.011**
Regulations. Under reg.4 the Secretary of State may give notice to any person
who is entitled to an existing award informing him or her that, depending on the
satisfaction of certain conditions, that award is either to be converted to an award
of ESA or terminated. The issue of such a notice begins the "conversion
phase".

The decision maker then makes a "conversion decision" under reg.5, i.e. s/he decides whether the notified person ("P") satisfies the basic conditions of entitlement to ESA under s.1(3) of the Act (except, of course, the condition in s.1(3)(f) that s/he should not be entitled to income support). That process involves carrying out a work capability assessment. If P does satisfy those conditions then, by virtue of reg.7, the existing award qualifies for conversion. Otherwise, it does not.

The Secretary of State then notifies P of the conversion decision under reg.5(5).

Existing awards that qualify for conversion

1.012   Where the existing award is to be converted to an award of ESA, that notice must specify how much ESA is to be paid and the effective date (determined in accordance with reg.13) from which it will be paid (reg.5(3)). In those circumstances, the conversion phase ends immediately before that effective date. This means that P potentially becomes entitled to the work-related activity component or the support component under s.2 or s.4 of the Act as modified by paras 3 and 4 of Sch.1 to these Regulations.

The amount of the converted award of ESA is determined by reg.8 and may include a "transitional addition" calculated under regs 9 to 12. In broad terms, the transitional addition is calculated as the difference (if any) between the amount of the existing award (or awards) and the amount that would otherwise be payable by way of ESA. The effect should be that no claimant is worse off as a result of the conversion process. However, any transitional addition reduces, ultimately to nil, under regs 18–21, by the amount of any increases in ESA rates after the conversion decision (e.g. as a result of annual up-rating). The effect is that the combined amount of the basic ESA award (including the appropriate component) and the transitional addition will remain the same until the ESA award has increased to a level which exceeds that amount.

Where the existing award qualifies for conversion it takes effect as a single award (i.e. even if there were two existing awards before conversion) of ESA at the rate specified in the conversion decision (reg.14(1)). The exception is where P would continue to be entitled to income support other than on the basis of incapacity for work or disability. In such a case P can elect (before the effective date) to remain on income support (reg. 14(2A)) subject (in certain cases) to the loss of the disability premium (reg.14(2B)).

Existing awards that do not qualify for conversion

1.013   In cases where P does not satisfy the conditions of entitlement to ESA, and therefore the existing award does not qualify for conversion, that award comes to an end immediately before the effective date (reg.15(2)). The conversion phase ends on the same day (reg.5(6)(a)) but that circumstance has no significance in cases where the existing award is not converted to ESA. Again there is an exception for people who remain entitled to income support other than on the basis of incapacity for work or disability (reg.15(2A) and (2B)).

Revision and supersession during the conversion phase

1.014   Regulation 17 contains detailed rules for taking into account relevant changes in circumstances and other "relevant events" which occur before the effective date of the conversion decision. Effectively, the decision maker must treat the conversion decision as if it had not been made, and then revise or supersede the decision making for the existing award so as to reflect the change in circumstance. He must then decide whether to revise or supersede the conversion decision.

Other changes
The Regulations also make a number of consequential amendments and   **1.015**
modifications which are taken into account at the appropriate places in the noter-up.

PART 1

GENERAL

Citation and commencement

1.—(1) These Regulations may be cited as the Employment and   **1.016**
Support Allowance (Transitional Provisions, Housing Benefit and
Council Tax Benefit) (Existing Awards) (No. 2) Regulations 2010.

(2) Subject to paragraph (3), these Regulations come into force on 1st
October 2010.

(3) Regulations 24 (revocation of transitional claims provisions) and
25(2) (amendment of the 2008 Regulations) and [¹paragraphs 1A and 2]
of Schedule 4 (consequential amendments to the 2008 Regulations)
come into force on 31st January 2011.

AMENDMENT

1. Employment and Support Allowance (Transitional Provisions, Housing   **1.017**
Benefit and Council Tax Benefit) (Existing Awards) (No. 2) (Amendment)
Regulations 2010 (SI 2010/2430), reg.2 (November 1, 2010).

Interpretation

2.—(1) In these Regulations—   **1.018**
"the 2007 Act" means the Welfare Reform Act 2007;
"the 2008 Regulations" means the Employment and Support
    Allowance Regulations 2008;
"benefit week" has the same meaning as in the 2008 Regulations;
"contributory allowance" means an employment and support
    allowance to which a person is entitled by virtue of these
    Regulations which was based on an award of incapacity benefit
    or severe disablement allowance to which the person was
    entitled;
"conversion decision", in relation to a notified person, has the
    meaning given in regulation 5(2);
"effective date", in relation to a conversion decision, is to be con-
    strued in accordance with regulation 13;
"enactment" includes an enactment contained in subordinate legis-
    lation (within the meaning of the Interpretation Act 1978);
"income-related allowance" means an employment and support
    allowance to which a person is entitled by virtue of these

Regulations which was based on an award of income support to which the person was entitled;

"notified person" has the meaning given in regulation 4(2);

"pensionable age" has the meaning given by the rules in paragraph 1 of Schedule 4 to the Pensions Act 1995;

"relevant deduction", in relation to a person, includes such of the following deductions as fall to be made in relation to the person—

(a) any deduction made under any of the following provisions of the Social Security (Claims and Payments) Regulations 1987—

(i) regulation 34A (deductions of mortgage interest which shall be made from benefit and paid to qualified lenders),

(ii) regulation 34B (deductions of mortgage interest which may be made from benefits and paid to qualified lenders in other cases), or

(iii) regulation 35 (deductions which may be made from benefit and paid to third parties);

(b) any deduction made under the Community Charges (Deductions from Income Support) (No.2) Regulations 1990 (deductions which may be made from benefit for meeting sums due in respect of community charges);

(c) any deduction made under the Fines (Deductions from Income Support) Regulations 1992 (deductions which may be made from an offender's benefit);

(d) any deduction made under the Council Tax (Deductions from Income Support) Regulations 1993 (deductions which may be made from benefit for meeting sums due in respect of council tax);

(e) any deduction in respect of overpayment recovery or recovery of social fund loans made under any of the following provisions of the Administration Act—

(i) section 71 (overpayments-general),

(ii) section 74 (income support and other payments), or

(iii) section 78 (recovery of social fund awards).

(2) A requirement under these Regulations to give a notice (or to notify) is a requirement to give notice in writing; and for that purpose—

(a) a message sent by electronic communication shall be treated as a notice given in writing; and

(b) electronic communication has the meaning given in section 15(1) of the Electronic Communications Act 2000.

(3) For the purposes of these Regulations, the conversion phase, in relation to any person entitled to an existing award or awards, is the period which—

(a) begins in accordance with regulation 4(4); and

(b) ends in accordance with regulation 5(6).

(4) In these Regulations, any reference to Step 1, 2 or 3, in relation to any person, is to be construed in accordance with regulation 8.

Persons to whom these Regulations apply

[¹ **3.**—In these Regulations, regulations 4 to 22 apply to any person who, on or after 1st October 2010, is entitled to an existing award.]   1.019

AMENDMENT

1. Employment and Support Allowance (Transitional Provisions, Housing Benefit and Council Tax Benefit) (Existing Awards) (No.2) (Amendment) Regulations 2010 (SI 2010/2430), reg.3 (November 1, 2010).

PART 2

CONVERSION DECISIONS

The notice commencing the conversion phase

4.—(1) Subject to paragraph (5), the Secretary of State may at any time issue a notice to any person who is entitled to an existing award.   1.020

(2) Any person to whom such a notice is issued is referred to in these Regulations as a notified person.

(3) The notice must inform the notified person—

(a) that an existing award is to be converted into an award of an employment and support allowance if certain conditions are satisfied;

(b) that, if those conditions are not satisfied, the existing award will not be converted and will terminate by virtue of these Regulations;

(c) of the requirements that must be met in order to satisfy those conditions; and

(d) of such other matters as the Secretary of State considers appropriate.

(4) The issue of the notice to a notified person begins the conversion phase in relation to that person, with effect from the date of issue.

(5) No notice may be issued to any person—

(a) who reaches pensionable age at any time before 6th April 2014; or

(b) at any time when payment of the existing award to the person is subject to adjustment under regulation 4 of the Social Security (Transitional Payments) Regulations 2009 (adjustment of subsequent payments following an adjusting payment of benefit).

(6) Where a person is entitled to—

(a) an existing award of incapacity benefit or severe disablement allowance; and

(b) an existing award of income support,

the notice issued to the person under this regulation shall have effect in relation to both such awards.

Deciding whether an existing award qualifies for conversion

1.021 **5.**—(1) In relation to the existing award or awards to which a notified person ("P") is entitled, the Secretary of State must, except where paragraph (8)(a) applies, make a conversion decision in accordance with these Regulations.

(2) A conversion decision is—

(a) a decision that P's existing award or awards qualify for conversion into an award of an employment and support allowance in accordance with regulation 7 (qualifying for conversion); or

(b) a decision that P's existing award or awards do not qualify for conversion into an award of an employment and support allowance.

(3) A notice of a conversion decision under paragraph (2)(a) must specify the amount of an employment and support allowance to which P is entitled on the effective date (subject to any relevant deductions).

(4) The amount referred to in paragraph (3) is to be determined in accordance with regulation 8 (amount of an employment and support allowance on conversion).

(5) The Secretary of State must notify P of the Secretary of State's conversion decision.

(6) The conversion phase ends in relation to P—

(a) immediately before the effective date of the conversion decision notified to P; or

(b) if earlier, when P's entitlement to the award or awards to which the notice under regulation 4 (notice commencing the conversion phase) relates otherwise ceases to be subject to conversion (because entitlement to the award has terminated or for some other reason).

(7) The effective date of any conversion decision is to be determined in accordance with regulation 13 (effective date of a conversion decision).

(8) In the event that P's entitlement to an existing award ceases to be subject to conversion (for example, because P's entitlement to an award of income support has ceased to fall within paragraph (c) of the definition of "existing award" in paragraph 11 of Schedule 4 to the 2007 Act)—

(a) before a conversion decision is made, the Secretary of State must notify P that the conversion phase has ended without a conversion decision being made; or

(b) after the making of a conversion decision but before its effective date, the Secretary of State must notify P that the conversion decision shall not come into effect.

(9) On the giving of a notice under paragraph (8)(b), the conversion decision to which it relates shall lapse with immediate effect.

Application of certain enactments for purpose of making conversion decisions

6.—(1) The enactments listed in paragraph (2) apply, subject to the modifications specified in Schedule 1, for the purposes of—
    (a) enabling the Secretary of State to make in relation to any person a conversion decision under this Part; and
    (b) providing for the revision of such decisions at any time before the effective date.
    (2) The listed enactments are—
    (a) Part 1 of the 2007 Act;
    (b) the 2008 Regulations;
    (c) regulation 32(1) and (1A) of the Social Security (Claims and Payments) Regulations 1987 (information to be given);
    (d) Chapter 2 of Part 1 of the Social Security Act 1998 (social security decisions and appeals); and
    (e) the Social Security and Child Support (Decisions and Appeals) Regulations 1999.
    (3) In the application of the enactments listed in paragraph (2)(d) and (e), the conversion decision is to be treated as if it were a decision as to a person's entitlement to an employment and support allowance which had been made on a claim.

1.022

Qualifying for conversion

7.—[¹(1)] [¹Subject to paragraph (2), for the purposes of regulation 5(2)(a)] (deciding whether an existing award qualifies for conversion), an existing award or awards to which a notified person [¹("P")] is entitled qualify for conversion into an award of an employment and support allowance [¹ under these Regulations] only if [¹ P] satisfies the basic conditions set out in section 1(3)(a) to (d) and (f) of the 2007 Act.
    [¹(2) Where P is entitled to an award of an employment and support allowance under the 2007 Act and it has been determined in respect of that entitlement that P—
    (a) has limited capability for work, or
    (b) is to be treated as having limited capability for work, other than by virtue of regulation 30 of the 2008 Regulations,
in relation to the conversion of P's existing award, P is to be taken as having satisfied the condition set out in section 1(3)(a) of the 2007 Act (limited capability for work).]

1.023

Amendment

1. Employment and Support Allowance (Transitional Provisions, Housing Benefit and Council Tax Benefit) (Existing Awards) (No.2) (Amendment) Regulations 2010 (SI 2010/2430), reg.4 (November 1, 2010).

Amount of an employment and support allowance on conversion

1.024   **8.**—[¹(1)] For the purposes of regulation 5(3), the amount of an employment and support allowance to which a notified person is entitled shall be determined as follows.

Step 1

Determine in accordance with Part 1 of the 2007 Act and the 2008 Regulations the amount (if any) of an employment and support allowance to which the notified person would be entitled if, on a claim made by that person—
(a) it had been determined that the person was entitled to an award of an employment and support allowance; and
(b) the assessment phase had ended.

Step 2

Determine in accordance with regulations 9 to 12—
[¹(a)] whether the notified person is entitled to a transitional addition; and
[¹(b)] if so, the amount of the transitional addition.

Step 3

Aggregate the amounts (if any) which result from Steps 1 and 2.
[¹(2) In a case to which regulation 7(2) applies (cases where a person is already entitled to an award of an employment and support allowance), a determination that the person has, or does not have, limited capability for work-related activity made in respect of the person's current entitlement to an award of an employment and support allowance is to be treated as having been made for the purposes of Step 1.]

AMENDMENT

1.025   1. Employment and Support Allowance (Transitional Provisions, Housing Benefit and Council Tax Benefit) (Existing Awards) (No.2) (Amendment) Regulations 2010 (SI 2010/2430), reg.5 (November 1, 2010).

Determining entitlement to a transitional addition

1.026   **9.**—(1) In relation to any notified person whose existing award or awards qualify for conversion into an employment and support allowance—
(a) the person's entitlement (if any) to a transitional addition; and
(b) the amount of any such transitional addition,
are to be determined in accordance with regulation 10(2) (transitional addition: incapacity benefit or severe disablement allowance) or 11(2) (transitional addition: income support).

(2) The amount of transitional addition to which a notified person is entitled is subject to reduction in accordance with regulations 18 to 20.

(3) The entitlement of a notified person to any transitional addition terminates in accordance with regulation 21 (termination of transitional addition).

Transitional addition: incapacity benefit or severe disablement allowance

10.—(1) This regulation applies to any notified person who is entitled   1.027
to an existing award of incapacity benefit or severe disablement allowance (and for these purposes it is irrelevant whether the person is also entitled to any existing award of income support).

(2) In any case falling within paragraph (1)—

(a) the notified person shall be entitled to a transitional addition if Amount A exceeds Amount B; and

(b) the amount of transitional addition to which the notified person is entitled under this paragraph shall be equal to the amount of any such excess.

(3) Amount A is the amount of the weekly rate of the existing award applicable to the notified person.

(4) To calculate Amount B—

(a) take the amount prescribed under paragraph (2) of regulation 67 of the 2008 Regulations (prescribed amounts for purpose of calculating a contributory allowance) which is applicable to the notified person; and

(b) add the amount of the applicable component determined in accordance with regulation 12(5).

(5) In paragraph (3), the reference to the weekly rate of an existing award applicable to the notified person is to—

[¹(a) in the case of incapacity benefit, the weekly rate payable—

  (i) under section 30B(2), (6) or (7) (subject to any deduction made in accordance with section 46(3) of the Pension Schemes Act 1993) of the Contributions and Benefits Act (incapacity benefit: rate),

  (ii) under section 40(5) or 41(4) of that Act (long-term incapacity benefit for widows and for widowers),

  (iii) under section 80, 81 or 86A of that Act (incapacity benefit: beneficiary's dependent children; restrictions on increase—child not living with beneficiary etc; and increases for adult dependants),

  (iv) by virtue of regulation 11(4) of the Social Security (Incapacity Benefit) (Transitional) Regulations 1995 (former sickness benefit), or

  (v) by virtue of regulations 17(1) (transitional awards of long-term incapacity benefit) or 17A (awards of incapacity benefit in cases where periods of interruption of employment and periods of incapacity for work link) of those Regulations; or]

(b) in the case of severe disablement allowance, the weekly rate payable under [¹sections 68(7), 69(1) and 90] of the Contributions and Benefits Act (as they have effect by virtue of article 4

15

of the Welfare Reform and Pensions Act 1999 (Commencement No.9 and Transitional and Savings Provisions) Order 2000).

[¹(6) Subject to paragraph (7), in determining the weekly rate of incapacity benefit or severe disablement allowance for the purposes of paragraph (5) the following amounts shall be disregarded—

(a) any relevant deduction within the meaning of regulation 2(1) (interpretation); and

(b) any other deduction relating to the existing award which is made by virtue of the Contributions and Benefits Act, the Administration Act or any other Act which is amended by Schedule 3 to the 2007 Act, the Social Security (Incapacity for Work) Act 1994 or by virtue of regulations made under those Acts.

(7) Where any of the enactments referred to in paragraph (6)(b) provide for an additional amount of incapacity benefit or severe disablement allowance to be payable in prescribed circumstances (such as an increase for an adult dependant) but that additional amount is reduced or not payable in relation to P (such as where the dependant has earnings in excess of the standard amount of an increase), in determining the weekly rate of incapacity benefit or severe disablement allowance, only the reduced additional amount (if any) is to be taken into account.]

AMENDMENT

1. Employment and Support Allowance (Transitional Provisions, Housing Benefit and Council Tax Benefit) (Existing Awards) (No.2) (Amendment) Regulations 2010 (SI 2010/2430), reg.6 (November 1, 2010).

Transitional addition: income support

1.028   **11.**—(1) This regulation applies to any notified person who is entitled to an existing award of income support (and for these purposes it is irrelevant whether the person is also entitled to any existing award of incapacity benefit or severe disablement allowance).

(2) In any case falling within paragraph (1)—

(a) the notified person shall be entitled to a transitional addition if Amount C exceeds Amount D; and

(b) the amount of transitional addition to which the notified person is entitled under this paragraph shall be equal to the amount of any such excess.

(3) To calculate Amount C—

(a) take the notified person's weekly applicable amount under regulation 17 or 18 of, and Schedule 2 to, the Income Support (General) Regulations 1987 (applicable amounts);

(b) disregard any amount determined in accordance with (as the case may be) regulation 17(1)(e) or 18(1)(f) of, and Schedule 3 to, those Regulations (housing costs); and

(c) disregard any amount included in the person's applicable amount—

(i) under regulation 17(1)(b), (c) or (d) of those Regulations in respect of a child or young person who is a member of the notified person's family, or

16

(ii) under regulation 18(1)(b), (c), (d) or (e) of those Regulations in respect of a child or young person who is a member of the same household as the notified person,

as those provisions have effect by virtue of regulations 1 and 7 of the Social Security (Working Tax Credit and Child Tax Credit) (Consequential Amendment) Regulations 2003.

(4) To calculate Amount D—

(a) take the amount prescribed under regulation 67(1) or 68(1) of the 2008 Regulations (prescribed amounts for purpose of calculating an income-related allowance) which is applicable to the notified person;

(b) disregard any amount determined in accordance with (as the case may be) regulation 67(1)(c) or 68(1)(d) (housing costs) of the 2008 Regulations; and

(c) add the amount of the applicable component determined in accordance with regulation 12(5) of these Regulations.

Regulations 10 and 11: supplementary

12.—(1) This regulation has effect for the purposes of applying regulations 10 and 11 in relation to any notified person.   1.029

(2) Subject to paragraphs (3) and (4)—

(a) Amounts A and C are to be calculated in respect of the benefit week which ends immediately before the effective date of the notified person's conversion decision; and

(b) Amounts B and D are to be calculated in respect of the benefit week the first day of which is the effective date of the notified person's conversion decision.

(3) Where—

(a) by virtue of an order made under section 150 of the Administration Act (annual up-rating of benefits), there is an increase in—

(i) the weekly rate which, in accordance with regulation 10(3) (transitional addition: incapacity benefit or severe disablement allowance), is to be used to calculate Amount A, or

(ii) the applicable amount which, in accordance with regulation 11(3) (transitional addition: income support), is to be used to calculate Amount C; and

(b) that increase takes effect from any day in the benefit week referred to in paragraph (2)(b), the calculation of Amount A or C is to be made using the increased weekly rate or applicable amount (as the case may be).

(4) Where—

(a) there is a change of circumstances in relation to a notified person which, but for subparagraph (b), would have resulted in an increase or decrease of the weekly rate or applicable amount referred to in paragraph (3)(a)(i) or (ii); and

(b) that increase or decrease would have taken effect from any day in the benefit week referred to in paragraph (2)(b), the calculation of Amount A or C is to be made using the weekly rate or applicable amount (as the case may be) which would have been payable in respect of the existing award if it had not been subject to conversion under these Regulations.

(5) The "applicable component", in relation to the notified person, means—

    (a) the work-related activity component, if it has been determined in accordance with the enactments applied by regulation 6 (application of certain enactments for purpose of making conversion decisions) that the notified person does not have and is not to be treated as having limited capability for work-related activity; or

    (b) the support component, if it has been determined in accordance with those enactments that the notified person has or is to be treated as having limited capability for work-related activity.

The effective date of a conversion decision

1.030   **13.**—(1) For the purposes of determining the date on which a conversion decision takes effect in relation to any notified person—

    (a) take the date on which the person is notified of the conversion decision; and

    (b) unless paragraph (2) applies, determine the first complete fortnightly period in respect of which the person's existing benefit is payable after that date, and the effective date of the person's conversion decision is the first day of the benefit week immediately following the end of the fortnightly period referred to in sub-paragraph (b).

(2) Where existing benefit is payable to the notified person in respect of a period other than a fortnight—

    (a) determine the second complete benefit week in respect of which the person's existing benefit is payable after the date on which the person is notified of the conversion decision; and

    (b) the effective date of the person's conversion decision is the first day of the benefit week immediately following the end of that second complete benefit week.

(3) "Existing benefit", in relation to a notified person, means the benefit in respect of the person's existing award or awards.

Conversion decision that existing award qualifies for conversion

1.031   **14.**—(1) [¹Subject to paragraph (2A), paragraphs (2) to (6)] apply in any case where the conversion decision is a decision that a notified person's ("P") existing award or awards qualify for conversion into an employment and support allowance.

(2) On the effective date of the conversion decision—

    (a) P's existing award; or

    (b) both of P's existing awards (as the case may be),

are by virtue of this paragraph converted into, and shall have effect on and after that date as, a single award of an employment and support allowance of such amount as is specified in the conversion decision.

[¹(2A) Where P—

    (a) has an existing award of income support;

(b) would, on the effective date of P's conversion decision, remain entitled to income support (by virtue of another provision of the Income Support (General) Regulations 1987) were P not a person to whom regulation 6(4)(a) or 13(2)(b) or (bb) of, or paragraph 7(a) or (b), 10, 12 or 13 of Schedule 1B(c) to, those Regulations (persons incapable of work or disabled) applied; and

(c) notifies the Secretary of State before the effective date of P's conversion decision that P wishes to remain entitled to income support on that date, paragraph (2B) applies instead of paragraphs (2) and (4).

(2B) Where paragraph (2A) applies, any entitlement of P to one or both of—

(a) an existing award of incapacity benefit or severe disablement allowance; or

(b) a disability premium by virtue of paragraph 12(1)(b) of Schedule 2 to the Income Support (General) Regulations 1987 (additional condition for the higher pensioner and disability premiums),

shall terminate immediately before the effective date of P's conversion decision.]

[¹(3) In a case to which regulation 7(2) applies (cases where a person is already entitled to an award of an employment and support allowance), any entitlement of P to an award of an employment and support allowance by virtue of the 2007 Act shall terminate immediately before the effective date of P's conversion decision.

(4) Where, immediately before the effective date of the conversion decision, any relevant deduction was made from the existing award or awards, or from an award of an employment and support allowance which terminates in accordance with paragraph (3), an equivalent deduction shall be made from the award of an employment and support allowance to which P is entitled by virtue of these Regulations.

(5) Where, immediately before the effective date of the conversion decision, P is entitled to be credited with any earnings under regulation 8B(2)(a) of the Social Security (Credits) Regulations 1975 (credits for incapacity for work), P shall not be entitled to be so credited under that regulation on or after that date.

(6) Where—

(a) paragraph (2) applies,

(b) P is a member of a joint-claim couple, and

(c) immediately before the effective date of that conversion decision that couple was entitled to a disability premium by virtue of paragraph 20H(1)(b) or (d) of Schedule 1 to the Jobseeker's Allowance Regulations 1996 (additional conditions for higher pensioner and disability premium: severe disablement allowance or incapacity benefit), paragraph 20H(1)(ee) of that Schedule (limited capability for work) shall be treated as satisfied in relation to that couple on the effective date of that conversion decision.

(7) In this regulation—

(a) paragraphs (2) to (6) are subject to regulation 17 (changes of circumstances before the effective date); and

(b) "joint-claim couple" has the same meaning as in section 1(4) of
the Jobseekers Act 1995.]

AMENDMENT

1.032 1. Employment and Support Allowance (Transitional Provisions, Housing
Benefit and Council Tax Benefit) (Existing Awards) (No.2) (Amendment) Regulations 2010 (SI 2010/2430), reg.7 (November 1, 2010).

Conversion decision that existing award does not qualify for conversion

1.033 **15.**—(1) [¹Subject to paragraphs (2A) and (4), paragraphs (2), (3)
and (6) apply] in any case where the conversion decision is a decision
that a notified person's ("P") existing award or awards do not qualify for
conversion into an employment and support allowance.

(2) P's entitlement to one or both of—

(a) an existing award of incapacity benefit or severe disablement
allowance; or

(b) an existing award of income support (being an award made to a
person incapable of work or disabled),

shall terminate by virtue of this paragraph immediately before the effective date of P's conversion decision.

[¹(2A) Where P—

(a) has an existing award of income support, and

(b) would, on the effective date of P's conversion decision, remain
entitled to income support (by virtue of another provision of the
Income Support (General) Regulations 1987) were P not a person
to whom regulations 6(4)(a) or 13(2)(b) or (bb) of, or paragraph
7(a) or (b), 10, 12 or 13 of Schedule 1B to, those Regulations
(persons incapable of work or disabled) applied, P's existing
award of income support shall only terminate under paragraph
(2)(b) if P notifies the Secretary of State before the effective date
of P's conversion decision that P does not wish to remain entitled
to income support on that date.

(2B) Where paragraph (2A) applies, and P's existing award of income
support does not terminate under paragraph (2)(b), any entitlement of
P to a disability premium by virtue of paragraph 12(1)(b) of Schedule 2
to the Income Support (General) Regulations 1987 (additional condition for the higher pensioner and disability premiums) shall terminate
immediately before the effective date of P's conversion decision.]

(3) Where, immediately before [¹the effective date of P's conversion
decision], P is entitled to be credited with any earnings under regulation
8B(2)(a) of the Social Security (Credits) Regulations 1975 (credits for
incapacity for work), P shall not be entitled to be so credited under that
regulation on or after that date.

(4) Paragraph (5) applies where—

(a) a conversion decision within the meaning of regulation 5(2)(b)
("the earlier conversion decision") is made by virtue of either of

the following provisions of the 2008 Regulations (as they apply by virtue of regulation 6)—

    (i) regulation 22(1) (failure to provide information or evidence requested in relation to limited capability for work), or

    (ii) regulation 23(2) (failure to attend for a medical examination to determine whether the claimant has limited capability for work); and

(b) after P is notified of the earlier conversion decision, the Secretary of State is satisfied (or where the conversion decision is appealed to the First-tier Tribunal, that tribunal determines) that P had good cause for failing to—

    (i) provide the information requested, or

    (ii) attend for or submit to the medical examination for which P was called.

(5) Where this paragraph applies—

(a) the earlier conversion decision is treated as never having been made;

(b) any entitlement of P—

    (i) to an existing award which was terminated by virtue of paragraph (2), or

    (ii) to be credited with earnings which was terminated by virtue of paragraph (3),

shall be reinstated with effect from the effective date of the earlier conversion decision;

(c) the Secretary of State must make a conversion decision ("the new conversion decision") in accordance with regulation 5 (deciding whether an existing award qualifies for conversion) in relation to the existing award or awards to which P is entitled;

(d) the notice issued under regulation 4 (notice commencing the conversion phase) has effect in relation to that existing award or those existing awards; and

(e) with the exception of regulation 4 (notice commencing the conversion phase), the remaining provisions of this Part, including this regulation, apply to the new conversion decision.

[[1](6) Where—

(a) paragraph (2) applies; and

(b) P is a member of a joint-claim couple,

any entitlement of that couple to a disability premium by virtue of paragraph 20H(1)(b) or (d) of Schedule 1 to the Jobseeker's Allowance Regulations 1996 (additional conditions for higher pensioner and disability premium: severe disablement allowance or incapacity benefit) shall terminate immediately before the effective date of P's conversion decision.

(7) In this regulation—

(a) paragraphs (2), (2A), (3) and (6) are subject to regulation 17 (changes of circumstances before the effective date); and

(b) "joint-claim couple" has the same meaning as in section 1(4) of the Jobseekers Act 1995.]

AMENDMENT

1. Employment and Support Allowance (Transitional Provisions, Housing Benefit and Council Tax Benefit) (Existing Awards) (No.2) (Amendment) Regulations 2010 (SI 2010/2430), reg.8 (November 1, 2010).

PART 3

AFTER THE CONVERSION PHASE

Application of other enactments applying to employment and support allowances

1.034   **16.**—(1) The enactments listed in paragraph (2) apply, subject to the modifications specified in Schedule 2, for the purposes of—
  (a) providing for the revision or supersession of any person's conversion decision at any time on or after that decision's effective date; and
  (b) enabling any other matter to be determined in connection with any person's entitlement or continuing entitlement to an award of an employment and support allowance by virtue of these Regulations.
(2) The listed enactments are—
(a) Part 1 of the 2007 Act;
(b) Chapter 2 of Part 1 of the Social Security Act 1998 (social security decisions and appeals);
(c) any other Act which is amended by Schedule 3 to the 2007 Act;
(d) the Social Security (Recovery of Benefits) Act 1997; and
(e) the following regulations—
    (i) this Part of these Regulations,
    (ii) the 2008 Regulations, and
    (iii) the Regulations listed in Schedule 3 to these Regulations (being regulations consequentially amended by regulations made under Part 1 of the 2007 Act).
(3) In the application of those enactments, the conversion decision is to be treated as if it were a decision as to a person's entitlement to an employment and support allowance which had been made on a claim.

Changes of circumstances before the effective date

1.035   **17.**—Where, on or after the effective date of any person's conversion decision, the Secretary of State is notified of any change of circumstances or other relevant event which occurred before that date [¹and which would have been relevant to the existing award or awards], the Secretary of State—
  [¹(a) must treat any award—
        (i) converted by virtue of regulation 14(2) (conversion decision that existing award qualifies for conversion), or

(ii) terminated by virtue of regulation 14(2B)(a) (termination of an existing award of incapacity benefit or severe disablement allowance where entitlement to award of income support continues), regulation 14(3) (termination of award of an employment and support allowance where that entitlement already exists) or regulation 15(2) (termination of existing awards which do not qualify for conversion),

as if that award had not been converted or terminated;

(b) must treat any entitlement to be credited with earnings terminated by virtue of regulation 14(5) or 15(3) as if it had not been terminated;

(c) must treat any entitlement to a disability premium terminated by virtue of regulations 14(2B)(b), 15(2B) or 15(6) as if it had not been terminated;]

[¹(d)] must take account of the change of circumstances or other relevant event for the purposes of determining whether to revise or supersede a decision ("the earlier decision") relating to the award or awards in respect of which the conversion decision was made;

[¹(e)] in an appropriate case, must revise or supersede the earlier decision;

[¹(f)] if any earlier decision is revised or superseded, must determine whether to revise the conversion decision made in relation to P; and

[¹(g)] in an appropriate case, must revise that conversion decision.

AMENDMENT

1. Employment and Support Allowance (Transitional Provisions, Housing Benefit and Council Tax Benefit) (Existing Awards) (No.2) (Amendment) Regulations 2010 (SI 2010/2430), reg.9 (November 1, 2010).

Reducing the transitional addition: general rule

18.—(1) The amount of any transitional addition to which a person is entitled by virtue of these Regulations shall be reduced (but not below nil) by a sum equal to the aggregate amount of all relevant increases which occur on or after the effective date in the amount payable to the person by way of an employment and support allowance.   1.036

(2) For the purposes of paragraph (1), a relevant increase is—

(a) in relation to a person entitled to a contributory allowance, an increase in any amount applicable to the person under regulation 67(2)(a) or (3) of the 2008 Regulations; and

(b) in relation to a person entitled to an income-related allowance, an increase in any amount applicable to the person under regulation 67(1)(a) or (b) or (3) or 68(1)(a), (b) or (c) of the 2008 Regulations, which is not excluded by paragraph (3).

(3) In relation to any person, the excluded increases are—

(a) any increase applicable to the benefit week the first day of which is the effective date of the person's conversion decision; and

(b) any increase resulting from the reversal (on appeal or otherwise) of any decision made by the Secretary of State that a person who was previously entitled to the support component has become entitled to the work-related activity component.

Reducing the transitional addition: increases for dependent children

1.037   **19.**—(1) Paragraphs (2) and (3) apply to any person ("T") who—

[¹(a) on the day before the effective date of T's conversion decision, was entitled in connection with an existing award of incapacity benefit or severe disablement allowance to an increase under—

    (i) in the case of incapacity benefit, section 80 of the Contributions and Benefits Act (beneficiary's dependent children), or

    (ii) in the case of severe disablement allowance, section 90 of that Act (beneficiaries under sections 68 and 70), as those sections have effect by virtue of article 3 of the Tax Credits (Commencement No. 3 and Transitional Provisions and Savings) Order 2003; and]

(b) on and after the effective date, is entitled by virtue of these Regulations to an employment and support allowance which includes an amount by way of a transitional addition.

(2) The amount of the transitional addition shall be reduced in accordance with paragraph (3) on the termination, on or after the effective date, of T's entitlement to child benefit in respect of the child or qualifying young person—

(a) for whom; or

(b) for whose care by an adult dependant,

T was entitled to the increase referred to in paragraph (1)(a).

[¹(3) The amount of the transitional addition shall be reduced (but not below nil) by a sum equal to the amount of the increase referred to in paragraph (1)(a) payable to T on the day before the effective date, in respect of the child or qualifying young person in relation to whom child benefit terminated.]

AMENDMENT

1. Employment and Support Allowance (Transitional Provisions, Housing Benefit and Council Tax Benefit) (Existing Awards) (No.2) (Amendment) Regulations 2010 (SI 2010/2430), reg.10 (November 1, 2010).

Reducing the transitional addition: increases for adult dependants

1.038   **20.**—(1) Paragraphs (2) and (3) apply to any person ("T") who—

(a) on the day before the effective date of T's conversion decision, was entitled in connection with an existing award of incapacity benefit or severe disablement allowance to an increase under—

    (i) section 86A of the Contributions and Benefits Act (incapacity benefit: increases for adult dependants), or

(ii) section 90 of the Contributions and Benefits Act (adult dependants of beneficiaries in receipt of severe disablement allowance); and

(b) on and after the effective date, is entitled by virtue of these Regulations to an employment and support allowance which includes an amount by way of a transitional addition.

(2) The amount of the transitional addition shall be reduced in accordance with paragraph (3) on the occurrence, on or after the effective date, of any of the following events—

(a) the death of the adult dependant in respect of whom T was entitled to the increase referred to in paragraph (1)(a);

(b) the permanent separation of T and that adult dependant;

(c) the termination of the entitlement of either T or that adult dependant to child benefit; or

(d) the award to that adult dependant of a personal benefit (within the meaning of the Social Security (Overlapping Benefits) Regulations 1979) which is equal to or more than the amount which, on the day before the effective date, was the amount of the increase referred to in paragraph (1)(a) to which T was entitled.

[¹(3) The amount of the transitional addition shall be reduced (but not below nil) by a sum equal to the amount which, on the day before the effective date, was the amount of the increase referred to in paragraph (1)(a) payable to T.]

AMENDMENT

1. Employment and Support Allowance (Transitional Provisions, Housing Benefit and Council Tax Benefit) (Existing Awards) (No.2) (Amendment) Regulations 2010 (SI 2010/2430), reg.11 (November 1, 2010).

Termination of transitional addition

21.—(1) Any entitlement to a transitional addition which a person ("T") may have by virtue of these Regulations terminates on whichever is the earlier of— 1.039

(a) the reduction in accordance with regulations 18 to 20 (reducing the transitional addition: general rule and increases for dependent children and adult dependants) of the amount of the transitional addition to nil;

(b) subject to [¹paragraphs (2), (3) and (4)], the termination in accordance with the enactments applied by regulation 16 of T's entitlement to [¹an employment and support allowance (entitlement to which arises from sections 1(2)(a) or 1(2)(b) of the 2007 Act), or to a contributory allowance or to an income-related allowance]; and

(c) 5th April 2020.

(2) Nothing in paragraph (1)(b) prevents reinstatement of a person's entitlement to a transitional addition following the reversal on appeal of any determination which results in [¹a termination of the person's entitlement to which that provision refers].

[[1](3) Any termination by virtue of paragraph (1)(b) of T's entitlement to a transitional addition under regulation 10(2)(a) (transitional addition: incapacity benefit or severe disablement allowance) shall instead have effect as a suspension of that entitlement in Case 1.

(4) Any termination by virtue of paragraph (1)(b) of T's entitlement to a transitional addition under regulation 11(2)(a) (transitional addition: income support) shall instead have effect as a suspension of that entitlement in Case 1 or Case 2.

(5) Case 1 is where—

(a) on a subsequent claim made by T for an employment and support allowance, a period of limited capability for work is treated under regulation 145(1) or (2) of the 2008 Regulations (linking rules) as a continuation of an earlier period of limited capability for work;

(b) T's entitlement to an allowance which is referred to in paragraph (1)(b) ("T's old entitlement") was in respect of that earlier period; and

(c) in a case to which regulation 145(1) of the 2008 Regulations applies (12 week linking rule), it is determined, in respect of that subsequent claim, that T has, or is treated as having, limited capability for work, other than under regulation 30 of the 2008 Regulations.

(6) Case 2 is where—

(a) the reason for terminating T's entitlement to an employment and support allowance arising from section 1(2)(b) of the 2007 Act (financial position), or to an income-related allowance, as the case may be, was that the condition set out in paragraph 6(1)(f) of Schedule 1 to the 2007 Act (no entitlement to income-related allowance where other member of a couple engages in remunerative work) had ceased to be satisfied in T's case;

(b) the condition referred to in sub-paragraph (a) is subsequently satisfied;

(c) T again becomes entitled to an allowance which is referred to in sub-paragraph (a); and

(d) that entitlement commences before the end of the 12 week period which begins with the date of termination of T's old entitlement.

(7) In Cases 1 and 2, the amount of the transitional addition or additions, as the case may be, to which T becomes entitled from the commencement of T's subsequent entitlement to an allowance which is referred to in paragraph (1)(b) is to be determined by reference to the amount of the transitional addition or additions, as the case may be, to which T was entitled on the termination of T's old entitlement, subject to any subsequent adjustment of that amount that would have been made under this Part.]

AMENDMENT

1. Employment and Support Allowance (Transitional Provisions, Housing Benefit and Council Tax Benefit) (Existing Awards) (No.2) (Amendment) Regulations 2010 (SI 2010/2430), reg.12 (November 1, 2010).

PART 4

MISCELLANEOUS

Disapplication of certain enactments following conversion decision

22.—Where a conversion decision has been made in relation to any   1.040
person, the following enactments shall not apply to that person with
effect from the conversion decision's effective date—

    (a) sections 30A, [¹30C,] 40 or 41 of the Contributions and Benefits
        Act (incapacity benefit);

    (b) section 68 of the Contributions and Benefits Act (as it has effect
        by virtue of article 4 of the Welfare Reform and Pensions Act 1999
        (Commencement No. 9, and Transitional and Savings Provisions)
        Order 2000);

    (c) regulation 13(2)(b) or (bb) of, or paragraph 7(a) or (b), 10, 12 or
        13 of Schedule 1B to, the Income Support (General) Regulations
        1987 (prescribed category of persons for the purposes of entitle-
        ment on grounds of incapacity or disability);

    (d) the Income Support Transitional Regulations 1987; and

    (e) the Incapacity Benefit Transitional Regulations 1995.

AMENDMENT

1. Employment and Support Allowance (Transitional Provisions, Housing
Benefit and Council Tax Benefit) (Existing Awards) (No.2) (Amendment) Regulations 2010 (SI 2010/2430), reg.13 (November 1, 2010).

Treatment of claims until coming into force of regulation 24

23.—*amends sub-paras (a), (b) and (c) of reg.2(2) of the Employment*   1.041
and Support Allowance (Transitional Provisions) Regulations 2008 (claim for
existing award), and is covered in the Updating sections of this Supplement.

[¹Termination of entitlement to the disability premium for persons incapable of work: income support

23A.—(1)–(3) *amend para.12 of Sch.2 to the Income Support (General)*   1.042
Regulations 1987 (additional condition for the higher pensioner and disability
premiums), and are covered in the Updating sections of this Supplement.

    (4) Where a person—

    (a) is or becomes entitled to an award of income support, and

    (b) is a person to whom paragraph 7(a) or (b) of Schedule 1B to the
        Income Support (General) Regulations 1987 (persons incapable
        of work) applies, paragraphs 12(1)(b), 12(1A) and 12(5) of
        Schedule 2 to the Income Support (General) Regulations 1987
        continue to apply to that person as if paragraphs (2) and (3) of this
        regulation had no effect.]

AMENDMENT

1. Employment and Support Allowance (Transitional Provisions, Housing Benefit and Council Tax Benefit) (Existing Awards) (No.2) (Amendment) Regulations 2010 (SI 2010/2430), reg.14 (November 1, 2010).

Revocation of transitional claims provisions

1.043   **24.**—*amends reg.2(2) of the Employment and Support Allowance (Transitional Provisions) Regulations 2008, and is covered in the Forthcoming Changes section of this Supplement.*

Amendment of the 2008 Regulations

1.044   **25.**—*(1)—revokes reg.31 of the 2008 Regulations (claimant who claims jobseeker's allowance to be treated as not having limited capability for work), and is covered in the Updating sections of this Supplement.*

(2)—amends reg.144(2)(a) of the 2008 Regulations (which sets out exceptions from the requirement to serve a period of waiting days at the beginning of a period of limited capability for work) and is covered in the Forthcoming Changes section of this Supplement.

Consequential amendments

1.045   **26.**—Schedule 4 (which makes amendments consequential on these Regulations) has effect.

Amendments to legislation relating to Housing Benefit and Council Tax Benefit

1.046   **27.**—Schedule 5 (which makes amendments to legislation relating to Housing Benefit and Council Tax Benefit) has effect.

SCHEDULES

SCHEDULE 1   **Regulation 6(1)**

MODIFICATION OF ENACTMENTS: MAKING CONVERSION DECISIONS

PART 1

MODIFICATION OF PART 1 OF THE 2007 ACT

1.047   [¹1].—Any reference to a claimant is to be read as if it were a reference to a notified person.
[²2.—Section 1 is to be read as if—
(a) for subsection (2), there were substituted—
   "(2) Subject to the provisions of this Part, a notified person is entitled to an employment and support allowance if the person satisfies the basic conditions and—
      (a) is entitled to an existing award of incapacity benefit or severe disablement allowance;
      (b) is entitled to an existing award of income support and satisfies the conditions set out in Part 2 of Schedule 1, unless subsection (2)(c) applies; or
      (c) is entitled to an existing award of income support by virtue of—

> (i) regulation 13(2)(b) or (bb) of the Income Support (General) Regula-
> tions 1987 (circumstances in which persons in relevant education
> may be entitled to income support), or
> (ii) paragraph 10 (disabled students) or 12 (deaf students) of Schedule
> 1B to those Regulations,

and satisfies the conditions set out in Part 2 of Schedule 1, with the exception of
the condition in paragraph 6(1)(g).”; and

(b) subsection (3)(e) were omitted.]

[¹3].—Section 2 is to be read as if, in subsections (2)(a) and (3)(a), references to the
assessment phase were to the conversion phase.

[¹4].—Section 4 is to be read as if, in subsections (4)(a) and (5)(a), references to the
assessment phase were to the conversion phase.

[¹5].—Section 5 does not apply.

[¹6].—Schedule 1 to the 2007 Act is to be read as if—

(a) paragraphs 1 to 5 were omitted; and

(b) in paragraph 6, after sub-paragraph (1), there were inserted—

> “(1A) Paragraphs (1B) and (1C) apply in relation to any person (“P”) whose
> existing award of income support is subject to conversion under the Employment
> and Support Allowance (Transitional Provisions, Housing Benefit and Council
> Tax Benefit) (Existing Awards) (No. 2) Regulations 2010 (“the 2010 Regula-
> tions”).
>
> (1B) In determining for the purposes of paragraph (1)(a) whether P’s income
> exceeds the applicable amount, any amount to which P may become entitled by
> way of a transitional addition under Part 2 of the 2010 Regulations shall be
> disregarded.
>
> (1C) But where—
> (a) P’s existing award would qualify for conversion under Part 2 of the 2010
> Regulations but for the fact that the condition set out in paragraph (1)(a) is
> not satisfied in P’s case; and
> (b) P would otherwise be entitled to an amount of transitional addition under
> Part 2 of the 2010 Regulations as a result of carrying out Step 2, the
> condition set out in paragraph (1)(a) shall be treated as having been
> satisfied and the amount of an employment and support allowance which
> applies to P as a result of Step 1 shall be nil.”.

PART 2

MODIFICATION OF THE 2008 REGULATIONS

[¹7].—Any reference to a claimant is to be read as if it were a reference to the notified   **1.048**
person.

[¹8].—Part 2 (which makes provision about the assessment phase) does not apply.

[¹9].—Part 3 (which makes provision about contribution conditions which do not apply
by virtue of modifications contained in these Regulations) does not apply.

[¹10].—Regulation 30 (which provides for payment of the allowance pending determination of limited capability for work) does not apply.

[²10A.—In the case of a person who is entitled to an existing award of income support
and who is a person to whom paragraph (1) of regulation 6 of the Social Security (Habitual
Residence) Amendment Regulations 2004 applies, regulation 70 (special cases: supplemental—persons from abroad) is to be read as if—

(a) the word “or” at the end of paragraph (4)(k) were omitted; and

(b) at the end of paragraph (4)(jj) the word “or” and the following sub-paragraph were
added—

> “(l) a person who is entitled to an existing award of income support where that
> person is a person to whom paragraph (1) of regulation 6 of the Social Security
> (Habitual Residence) Amendment Regulations 2004 applies”.]

[¹11]. Regulation 75 (payments treated as not being payments to which section 3 of the
2007 Act applies) is to be read as if—

(a) the existing provisions were renumbered as paragraph (1);

(b) at the end of that paragraph there were added—

"(g) any pension payment or PPF periodic payment which is made to a notified person and which falls within paragraph (2)."; and

(c) after that paragraph there were added—

"(2) This paragraph applies to any pension payment or PPF periodic payment made to the notified person where, immediately before the effective date of the person's conversion decision, section 30DD(1) of the Contributions and Benefits Act (incapacity benefit: reduction for pension payments and PPF periodic payments)—

(a) did not apply to the notified person by virtue of regulation 26 of the Social Security (Incapacity Benefit) Regulations 1994 (persons whose benefit is not to be reduced under section 30DD(1)); or

(b) was not treated as applying to the notified person by virtue of—

(i) regulation 19(1)(c) or (2)(c) of those Regulations (persons formerly entitled to severe disablement allowance); or

(ii) article 3 of the Welfare Reform and Pensions Act 1999 (Commencement No.9, and Transitional and Savings Provisions) Order 2000 (transitional provision in relation to incapacity benefit).".

[¹12].—Regulation 144 (requirement to serve a period of waiting days at the beginning of a period of limited capability for work) does not apply.

PART 3

MODIFICATION OF OTHER SECONDARY LEGISLATION

Social Security (Claims and Payments) Regulations 1987

1.049 [¹13].—Regulation 32 of the Social Security (Claims and Payments) Regulations 1987 (information to be given and changes to be notified) is to be read as if it were modified so as to enable the Secretary of State to require from any person entitled to an existing award—

(a) under paragraph (1), information or evidence for determining whether [² . . .] an existing award should be converted into an award of an employment and support allowance; and

(b) under paragraph (1A), information or evidence in connection with payment of benefit in the event that an existing award is converted into an award of an employment and support allowance.

AMENDMENT

1. Employment and Support Allowance (Transitional Provisions, Housing Benefit and Council Tax Benefit) (Existing Awards) (No. 2) (Amendment) Regulations 2010 (SI 2010/2430), reg.15 (November 1, 2010).

2. Employment and Support Allowance (Transitional Provisions, Housing Benefit and Council Tax Benefit) (Existing Awards) (No. 2) (Amendment) Regulations 2010 (SI 2010/2430), reg.16 (November 1, 2010).

SCHEDULE 2   **Regulation 16(1)**

MODIFICATION OF ENACTMENTS: AFTER THE CONVERSION PHASE

PART 1

MODIFICATION OF PART 1 OF THE 2007 ACT

1.050 [¹1].—Any reference to a claimant is to be read as if it were a reference to a person in relation to whom a conversion decision has been made under these Regulations.

[¹2].—Section 1 (employment and support allowance) is to be read as if—

[²(a) for subsection (2), there were substituted—

"(2) Subject to the provisions of this Part, a person is entitled to an employment and support allowance if the person satisfies the basic conditions and—

30

(a) in accordance with Part 2 of the Employment and Support Allowance (Transitional Provisions, Housing Benefit and Council Tax Benefit) (Existing Awards) (No. 2) Regulations 2010, the effect of the conversion decision that was made in relation to the person was to convert the person's existing award or awards into a single award of an employment and support allowance;

(b) that conversion decision has come into effect; and

(c) where—

    (i) the effect of that conversion decision is that the person is entitled to an income-related allowance, or

    (ii) the effect of that conversion decision is that the person is entitled to a contributory allowance and the person subsequently becomes entitled to an income-related allowance,

the person also satisfies the conditions set out in Part 2 of Schedule 1 (conditions relating to financial position), except for the condition in paragraph 6(1)(g) in the case of a person who, before that conversion decision was made, had been entitled to an existing award of income support by virtue of regulation 13(2)(b) or (bb) of the Income Support (General) Regulations 1987 (circumstances in which persons in relevant education may be entitled to income support), or paragraph 10 (disabled students) or 12 (deaf students) of Schedule 1B to those Regulations.";
and]

(b) for subsection (7), there were substituted—

"(7) In this Part—

"contributory allowance" means an employment and support allowance to which a person is entitled by virtue of the Employment and Support Allowance (Transitional Provisions, Housing Benefit and Council Tax Benefit) (Existing Awards) (No. 2) Regulations 2010 which was based on an award of incapacity benefit or severe disablement allowance to which the person was entitled; and

"income-related allowance" means an employment and support allowance to which a person is entitled by virtue of the Employment and Support Allowance (Transitional Provisions, Housing Benefit and Council Tax Benefit) (Existing Awards) (No. 2) Regulations 2010 which was based on an award of income support to which the person was entitled.".

[¹3].—Section 2 (amount of contributory allowance) is to be read as if—

(a) in subsection (1)(a), after the words "such amount" there were inserted ", or the aggregate of such amounts,"; and

(b) except for the purposes of applying regulation 147A of the 2008 Regulations (claimants appealing a decision), in subsections (2)(a) and (3)(a), references to the assessment phase were to the conversion phase.

[¹4].—Section 4 (amount of income-related allowance), except for the purposes of applying regulation 147A of the 2008 Regulations as modified by paragraph 15 of this Schedule, is to be read as if, in subsections (4)(a) and (5)(a), references to the assessment phase were to the conversion phase.

[²4A.—Schedule 1 to the 2007 Act (employment and support allowance: additional conditions) is to be read as if, in paragraph 6, after sub-paragraph (1), there were inserted—

"(1A) Paragraphs (1B) and (1C) apply where any person ("P") is entitled by virtue of the Employment and Support Allowance (Transitional Provisions, Housing Benefit and Council Tax Benefit) (Existing Awards) (No. 2) Regulations 2010 ("the 2010 Regulations") to an employment and support allowance which is attributable to an income-related allowance.

(1B) In determining for the purposes of paragraph 6(1)(a) whether P's income exceeds the applicable amount, the amount of any transitional addition to which P is entitled under the 2010 Regulations shall be disregarded.

(1C) Where—

(a) P ceases to satisfy the condition set out in sub-paragraph (1)(a); but

(b) otherwise remains entitled to an amount by way of a transitional addition under the 2010 Regulations, the condition set out in sub-paragraph (1)(a) shall be treated as satisfied in P's case and the amount of income-related allowance to which P is entitled shall be the amount of the transitional addition."]

PART 2

MODIFICATION OF OTHER PRIMARY LEGISLATION

Social Security Act 1998

1.051   [¹5].—Schedule 3 to the Social Security Act 1998 (decisions against which an appeal lies) is to be read as if, after paragraph 8D, there were inserted—
"*Conversion of certain existing awards into awards of an employment and support allowance*
        8E.—A conversion decision within the meaning of the Employment and Support Allowance (Transitional Provisions, Housing Benefit and Council Tax Benefit) (Existing Awards) (No. 2) Regulations 2010."

Social Security Contributions and Benefits Act 1992

1.052   [¹6].—Section 44B of the Social Security Contributions and Benefits Act 1992 (deemed earnings factors: 2010–11 onwards) is to be read as if, after subsection (5), there were inserted—
"(5A) In determining whether Condition C is satisfied in relation to any pensioner, the following entitlements of the pensioner to an earnings factor credit may be aggregated if the weeks to which they relate comprise a continuous period—
        (a) any entitlement arising by virtue of—
                (i) section 44C(3)(c) below (eligibility for earnings factor enhancement in respect of a week in which severe disablement allowance was payable), or
                (ii) section 44C(3)(d) below (eligibility for earnings factor enhancement in respect of a week in which long-term incapacity benefit was, or would have been, payable); and
        (b) where an award of severe disablement allowance or long-term incapacity benefit was converted into an award of an employment and support allowance by virtue of the Employment and Support Allowance (Transitional Provisions, Housing Benefit and Council Tax Benefit) (Existing Awards) (No. 2) Regulations 2010, any entitlement arising by virtue of regulation 5A(2)(ba) of the Additional Pension and Social Security Pensions (Home Responsibilities) (Amendment) Regulations 2001 (earnings factor credits eligibility for pensioners to whom employment and support allowance was payable).".

[²"*Income Tax (Earnings and Pensions) Act 2003*

1.053   **6A.**—The Income Tax (Earnings and Pensions) Act 2003 is to be read as if—
        (a) in section 660(1) (taxable benefits: UK benefits), in Table A—
                (i) in the first column, after the entry for "Contributory employment and support allowance", there were inserted a new entry "Contributory employment and support allowance (including any transitional addition to which a person is entitled in connection with that award)",
                (ii) in the second column, corresponding to the entry inserted by sub-paragraph (i), there were inserted "WRA 2007",
                (iii) in the third column, corresponding to the entry inserted by sub-paragraph (i), there were inserted "Section 1(2) (as modified and applied by the Employment and Support Allowance (Transitional Provisions, Housing Benefit and Council Tax Benefit) (Existing Awards) (No. 2) Regulations 2010 ("the 2010 Regulations"))", and
                (iv) under the text inserted in the second and third columns by sub-paragraphs (ii) and (iii), there were inserted "Any provision made for Northern Ireland which corresponds to section 1(2) of WRA 2007 (as modified and applied by any provision made for Northern Ireland which corresponds to those contained in the 2010 Regulations)";
        (b) in section 661(1) (taxable social security income), after "contributory employment and support allowance" there were inserted "contributory employment and support

allowance (including any transitional addition to which a person is entitled in connection with that award),"; and

(c) in section 677(1) (UK social security benefits wholly exempt from tax), in Table B—

    (i) in the first column, after the entry for "Income-related employment and support allowance", there were inserted a new entry "Income-related employment and support allowance (including any transitional addition to which a person is entitled in connection with that award)",

    (ii) in the second column, corresponding to the entry inserted by sub-paragraph (i), there were inserted "WRA 2007",

    (iii) in the third column, corresponding to the entry inserted by sub-paragraph (i), there were inserted "Section 1(2) (as modified and applied by the Employment and Support Allowance (Transitional Provisions, Housing Benefit and Council Tax Benefit) (Existing Awards) (No. 2) Regulations 2010 ("the 2010 Regulations"))", and

    (iv) under the text inserted in the second and third columns by sub-paragraphs (ii) and (iii), there were inserted "Any provision made for Northern Ireland which corresponds to section 1(2) of WRA 2007 (as modified and applied by any provision made for Northern Ireland which corresponds to those contained in the 2010 Regulations)".]

PART 3

MODIFICATION OF THE 2008 REGULATIONS

[¹**7**].—Any reference to a claimant is to be read as if it were a reference to a person in relation to whom a conversion decision has been made under these Regulations.   **1.054**

[¹**8**].—Part 2 (which makes provision about the assessment phase) does not apply, except for the purposes of applying regulation 147A of the 2008 Regulations.

[¹**9**].—Part 3 (which makes provision about contribution conditions which do not apply by virtue of modifications contained in these Regulations) does not apply.

[¹**10**].—In its application to a person who has made and is pursuing an appeal against a conversion decision which embodies a determination that the person does not have limited capability for work, regulation 30 (which provides for payment of the allowance pending determination of limited capability for work) is to be read as if, after paragraph (3), before "decision" there were inserted "conversion".

[¹**11**].—Regulation 45 (exempt work) is to be read as if, for the definition of "specified work" in paragraph (10), there were substituted—

""specified work" means—

    (a) work done in accordance with paragraph (4); [²or]

    (b) work done in accordance with regulation 17(4)(a) of the Social Security (Incapacity for Work) (General) Regulations 1995; [² . . .].

[¹**12**].—Regulation 67 (prescribed amounts) is to be read as if—

(a) in paragraph (1), after sub-paragraph (c) there were added—

    "(d) the amount of any transitional addition to which the person is entitled under regulation 11 of the Employment and Support Allowance (Transitional Provisions, Housing Benefit and Council Tax Benefit) (Existing Awards) (No. 2) Regulations 2010.";

(b) in paragraph (2), for the words from "is the amount" to the end, there were substituted "are such of the following amounts as may apply in the person's case—

    "(a) the amount determined in accordance with paragraph 1(1) of Schedule 4; and

    (b) the amount of any transitional addition to which the person is entitled under regulation 10 of the Employment and Support Allowance (Transitional Provisions) (Existing Awards) Regulations 2010.".

[¹**13**].—Regulation 68 (polygamous marriages) is to be read as if, in paragraph (1), after sub-paragraph (d) there were added—

"(e) the amount of any transitional addition to which the person is entitled under regulation 11 of the Employment and Support Allowance (Transitional Provisions, Housing Benefit and Council Tax Benefit) (Existing Awards) (No. 2) Regulations 2010.".

[¹14].—Regulation 75 (payments treated as not being payments to which section 3 of the 2007 Act applies) is to be read subject to the same modifications as are specified in paragraph 38 of Schedule 1 to these Regulations.

[¹15].—In its application to a person who has made and is pursuing an appeal against a conversion decision which embodies a determination that the person does not have limited capability for work, Regulation 147A (claimants appealing a decision) is to be read as if there were substituted—

"Claimants appealing a decision

147A.—(1) This regulation applies where a person has made and is pursuing an appeal against a conversion decision which embodies a determination that the person does not have limited capability for work.

[²(1A) A person to whom this regulation applies who has made and is pursuing an appeal against a conversion decision in respect of an existing award of incapacity benefit or severe disablement allowance shall be treated as having satisfied the conditions in Part 1 of Schedule 1 to the Act (contributory allowance: conditions relating to national insurance).]

(2) Subject to paragraph (3), where this regulation applies, a determination of limited capability for work by the Secretary of State under regulation 19 shall not be made until the appeal is determined by the First-tier Tribunal.

(3) Paragraph (2) does not apply where either—

(a) the claimant suffers from some specific disease or bodily or mental disablement from which the claimant was not suffering when entitlement began; or

(b) a disease or bodily or mental disablement from which the claimant was suffering at that date has significantly worsened.

(4) Where this regulation applies and the Secretary of State makes a determination—

(a) in a case to which paragraph (3) applies (including where the determination is not the first such determination) that the claimant does not have, or by virtue of regulation 22 or 23 is to be treated as not having, limited capability for work; or

(b) subsequent to a determination that the claimant is to be treated as having limited capability for work by virtue of a provision of these Regulations other than regulation 30, that the claimant is no longer to be so treated,

this regulation and regulation 30 apply as if that determination had not been made.

(5) Where this regulation applies and—

(a) the claimant is entitled to an employment and support allowance by virtue of being treated as having limited capability for work in accordance with regulation 30;

(b) neither of the circumstances in paragraph (3) applies or, subsequent to the application of either of those circumstances, the claimant has been determined not to have limited capability for work; and

(c) the claimant's appeal is dismissed, withdrawn or struck out,

the claimant is to be treated as not having limited capability for work from the first day of the benefit week following the date on which the Secretary of State was notified by the First-tier Tribunal that the appeal is dismissed, withdrawn or struck out.

(6) Where a claimant's appeal is successful, any entitlement to which this regulation applies shall terminate on the first day of the benefit week following the date on which the Secretary of State was notified by the First-tier Tribunal of that decision.".

[¹16].—Schedule 5 (prescribed amounts in special case) is to be read as if any reference to the amount—

(a) applicable to a person under regulation 67(1)(a); or

(b) to which a person is entitled under regulation 67(1)(a),

included the amount of any transitional addition to which the person is entitled under regulation 67(1)(d) (see modification made by paragraph 52(a) of this Schedule).

PART 4

MODIFICATION OF OTHER SECONDARY LEGISLATION

Social Security (Claims and Payments) Regulations 1987

[¹17].—The Social Security (Claims and Payments) Regulations 1987 are to be read **1.055** subject to the modifications set out in paragraphs [²18 to 22] of this Schedule.

[¹18].—Regulation 3 (claims not required for entitlement to benefits in certain cases) is to be read as if—

(a) after the words "was made" in paragraph (j)(ii), there were inserted—
   "[² . . .]
   [²(k) the beneficiary—
      (i) has made and is pursuing an appeal against a conversion decision made by virtue of the Employment and Support Allowance (Transitional Provisions, Housing Benefit and Council Tax Benefit) (Existing Awards) (No. 2) Regulations 2010 which embodies a determination that the beneficiary does not have limited capability for work; or
      (ii) was entitled to an employment and support allowance by virtue of the Employment and Support Allowance (Transitional Provisions, Housing Benefit and Council Tax Benefit) (Existing Awards) (No. 2) Regulations 2010 and has made and is pursuing an appeal against a later decision which embodies a determination that the beneficiary does not have limited capability for work;"; and

(b) after paragraph [²(k)], there were added—
   "[²(l)] in the case of an employment and support allowance where the beneficiary is entitled to an existing award which is subject to conversion under the Employment and Support Allowance (Transitional Provisions, Housing Benefit and Council Tax Benefit) (Existing Awards) (No. 2) Regulations 2010.".

[¹19].—In regulation 26C (employment and support allowance) any reference to an employment and support allowance includes any transitional addition to which the beneficiary is entitled under the Employment and Support Allowance (Transitional Provisions, Housing Benefit and Council Tax Benefit) (Existing Awards) (No. 2) Regulations 2010.

[¹20].—Regulation 32(1B) (information to be given and changes to be notified) is to be read as if—

(a) the word "or" at the end of sub-paragraph (a) were omitted; and

(b) after that sub-paragraph, there were inserted—
   "(ab) the amount of any transitional addition to which the beneficiary is entitled under the Employment and Support Allowance (Transitional Provisions, Housing Benefit and Council Tax Benefit) (Existing Awards) (No. 2) Regulations 2010; or".

[¹21].—Schedule 9 (deductions from benefit and direct payments to third parties) is to be read as if—

(a) in paragraph 1 (interpretation)—
   (i) in sub-paragraph (3), after the words ""employment and support allowance" means", there were inserted "(subject to sub-paragraph (4))", and
   (ii) after sub-paragraph (3), there were added—
      "(4) In the application of sub-paragraph (3) to a beneficiary whose award of an employment and support allowance is by virtue of the Employment and Support Allowance (Transitional Provisions, Housing Benefit and Council Tax Benefit) (Existing Awards) (No. 2) Regulations 2010 ("the 2010 Regulations"), any reference to an employment and support allowance includes any transitional addition to which the beneficiary is entitled under those Regulations.
      (5) Where a specified benefit awarded to a beneficiary is subject to conversion under the 2010 Regulations and—
         (a) immediately before the effective date of the conversion decision made in relation to the beneficiary, any deduction is being made in accordance with this Schedule from sums payable to the beneficiary by way of the specified benefit; and

35

(b) with effect from that date, the award of specified benefit is converted into an award of an employment and support allowance under the 2010 Regulations, any deduction falling within paragraph (a) shall have effect as a deduction from the employment and support allowance to which the beneficiary is entitled.".

(b) in paragraph 8—

(i) in sub-paragraph (4), for paragraph (a)(iv), there were substituted—

"(iv) in the case of an employment and support allowance, the applicable amount for the family as is awarded under the provisions specified in sub-paragraph (5); or", and

(ii) after sub-paragraph (4) there were added—

"(5) The specified provisions are—

(a) where the person is entitled to an employment and support allowance by virtue of the Employment and Support Allowance (Transitional Provisions, Housing Benefit and Council Tax Benefit) (Existing Awards) (No. 2) Regulations 2010 ("the 2010 Regulations")—

(i) paragraph (1)(a), (b) and (d) of regulation 67 (prescribed amounts); or

(ii) paragraph (1)(a), (b), (c) and (e) of regulation 68 (polygamous marriages), of the Employment and Support Allowance Regulations (as modified by paragraphs [²12 and 13] of Schedule 2 to the 2010 Regulations); and

(b) in any other case, paragraph (1)(a) and (b) of regulation 67 or paragraph (1)(a) to (c) of regulation 68 of the Employment and Support Allowance Regulations.".

[¹**22**].—Schedule 9B (deductions from benefit in respect of child support maintenance and payment to persons with care) is to be read as if—

(a) in paragraph (1) (interpretation), the existing provision becomes sub-paragraph (1); and

(b) there were added—

"(2) In the application of this Schedule to a beneficiary whose award of an employment and support allowance is by virtue of the Employment and Support Allowance (Transitional Provisions, Housing Benefit and Council Tax Benefit) (Existing Awards) (No. 2) Regulations 2010 ("the 2010 Regulations"), any reference to an employment and support allowance includes any transitional addition to which the beneficiary is entitled under those Regulations.

(3) Where a specified benefit awarded to a beneficiary is subject to conversion under the 2010 Regulations and—

(a) immediately before the effective date of the conversion decision made in relation to the beneficiary, any deduction is being made in accordance with this Schedule from sums payable to the beneficiary by way of the specified benefit; and

(b) with effect from that date, the award of specified benefit is converted into an award of an employment and support allowance under the 2010 Regulations,

any deduction falling within paragraph (a) shall have effect as a deduction from the employment and support allowance to which the beneficiary is entitled.".

[²*Community Charges (Deductions from Income Support) (Scotland) Regulations 1989*

1.056   **22A**.—Regulation 1 of the Community Charges (Deductions from Income Support) (Scotland) Regulations 1989 (citation, commencement and interpretation) is to be read as if, after paragraph (2), there were inserted—

"(2A) In the application of these Regulations to a debtor whose entitlement to an employment and support allowance is by virtue of the Employment and Support Allowance (Transitional Provisions, Housing Benefit and Council Tax Benefit) (Existing Awards) (No. 2) Regulations 2010 ("the 2010 Regulations"), any reference to an employment and support allowance includes any transitional addition to which the debtor is entitled under those Regulations.

(2B) Where a debtor's award of income support is subject to conversion under the 2010 Regulations and—

(a) immediately before the effective date of the conversion decision made in relation to the debtor, any deduction is being made under these Regulations from sums payable to the debtor by way of income support; and

(b) with effect from that date, the award of income support is converted into an award of an employment and support allowance under the 2010 Regulations,

any deduction falling within sub-paragraph (a) shall have effect as a deduction from the employment and support allowance to which the debtor is entitled."]

Community Charges (Deductions from Income Support) (No. 2) Regulations 1990

[¹23].—Regulation 1 of the Community Charges (Deductions from Income Support) (No. 2) Regulations 1990 (citation, commencement and interpretation) is to be read as if, after paragraph (2), there were inserted—
    "(2A) In the application of these Regulations to a debtor whose entitlement to an employment and support allowance is by virtue of the Employment and Support Allowance (Transitional Provisions, Housing Benefit and Council Tax Benefit) (Existing Awards) (No. 2) Regulations 2010 ("the 2010 Regulations"), any reference to an employment and support allowance includes any transitional addition to which the debtor is entitled under those Regulations.
    (2B) Where a debtor's award of income support is subject to conversion under the 2010 Regulations and—

(a) immediately before the effective date of the conversion decision made in relation to the debtor, any deduction is being made under these Regulations from sums payable to the debtor by way of income support; and

(b) with effect from that date, the award of income support is converted into an award of an employment and support allowance under the 2010 Regulations,

any deduction falling within sub-paragraph (a) shall have effect as a deduction from the employment and support allowance to which the debtor is entitled.".

1.057

Fines (Deductions from Income Support) Regulations 1992

[¹24].—Regulation 1 of the Fines (Deductions from Income Support) Regulations 1992 (citation, commencement and interpretation) is to be read as if, after paragraph (2), there were inserted—
    "(2A) In the application of these Regulations to an offender whose entitlement to an employment and support allowance is by virtue of the Employment and Support Allowance (Transitional Provisions, Housing Benefit and Council Tax Benefit) (Existing Awards) (No. 2) Regulations 2010 ("the 2010 Regulations"), any reference to an employment and support allowance includes any transitional addition to which the offender is entitled under those Regulations.
    (2B) Where an offender's award of income support is subject to conversion under the 2010 Regulations and—

(a) immediately before the effective date of the conversion decision made in relation to the offender, any deduction is being made under these Regulations from sums payable to the offender by way of income support; and

(b) with effect from that date, the award of income support is converted into an award of an employment and support allowance under the 2010 Regulations,

any deduction falling within sub-paragraph (a) shall have effect as a deduction from the employment and support allowance to which the offender is entitled.".

1.058

Council Tax (Deductions from Income Support) Regulations 1993

[¹25].—Regulation 1 of the Council Tax (Deductions from Income Support) Regulations 1993 (citation, commencement and interpretation) is to be read as if, after paragraph (2), there were inserted—
    "(2A) In the application of these Regulations to a debtor whose entitlement to an employment and support allowance is by virtue of the Employment and Support Allowance (Transitional Provisions, Housing Benefit and Council Tax Benefit) (Existing Awards) (No. 2) Regulations 2010 ("the 2010 Regulations"), any reference to an employment and support allowance includes any transitional addition to which the debtor is entitled under those Regulations.
    (2B) Where a debtor's award of income support is subject to conversion under the 2010 Regulations and—

1.059

(a) immediately before the effective date of the conversion decision made in relation to the debtor, any deduction is being made under these Regulations from sums payable to the debtor by way of income support; and

(b) on that date, the award of income support is converted into an award of an employment and support allowance under the 2010 Regulations,

any deduction falling within sub-paragraph (a) shall have effect as a deduction from the employment and support allowance to which the debtor is entitled.".

[²Social Security and Child Support (Decisions and Appeals) Regulations 1999

1.060   **25A.**—(1) Regulation 3 of the Social Security and Child Support (Decisions and Appeals) Regulations 1999 (revision of decisions) is to be read as if—

(a) in the case of a revision of a decision to award jobseeker's allowance made following the reinstatement of an existing award in accordance with regulation 15(5) of the Employment and Support Allowance (Transitional Provisions, Housing Benefit and Council Tax Benefit) (Existing Awards) (No. 2) Regulations 2010 ("the 2010 Regulations"), the words "within one month of the date of notification of the original decision" in paragraph (1)(a) were omitted;

(b) in the case of a conversion decision where there has been a change of circumstances to which regulation 12(4) of the 2010 Regulations (calculation of transitional addition) applies, paragraph (9)(a) were omitted; and

(c) in paragraph (9)(a), for "in the case of an advance award under regulation 13, 13A or 13C of the Claims and Payments Regulations" there were substituted, "in the cases of an advance award under regulation 13, 13A or 13C of the Claims and Payments Regulations or a conversion decision within the meaning of regulation 5(2)(a) of the 2010 Regulations".

(2) Regulation 6(2)(a)(i) of those Regulations (supersession of decisions) is to be read as if for "in the case of an advance award under regulation 13, 13A or 13C of the Claims and Payments Regulations or regulation 146 of the Employment and Support Allowance Regulations" there were substituted "in the cases of an advance award under regulation 13, 13A or 13C of the Claims and Payments Regulations or regulation 146 of the Employment and Support Allowance Regulations or a conversion decision within the meaning of regulation 5(2)(a) of the 2010 Regulations".]

Additional Pension and Social Security Pensions (Home Responsibilities) (Amendment) Regulations 2001

1.061   [¹**26**].—Regulation 5A of the Additional Pension and Social Security Pensions (Home Responsibilities) (Amendment) Regulations 2001 (earnings factor credits eligibility for pensioners to whom employment and support allowance was payable) is to be read as if—

(a) the word "or" at the end of paragraph (2)(b) were omitted; and

(b) after that paragraph (2)(b), there were inserted—

"(ba) that allowance was an employment and support allowance to which the pensioner was entitled by virtue of the Employment and Support Allowance (Transitional Provisions, Housing Benefit and Council Tax Benefit) (Existing Awards) (No. 2) Regulations 2010 and either—

(i) long-term incapacity benefit or severe disablement allowance was payable to the pensioner immediately before its conversion into an employment and support allowance in accordance with those Regulations; or

(ii) the condition in sub-paragraph (b) was satisfied; or".

AMENDMENT

1. Employment and Support Allowance (Transitional Provisions, Housing Benefit and Council Tax Benefit) (Existing Awards) (No.2) (Amendment) Regulations 2010 (SI 2010/2430), reg.15 (November 1, 2010).

2. Employment and Support Allowance (Transitional Provisions, Housing Benefit and Council Tax Benefit) (Existing Awards) (No.2) (Amendment) Regulations 2010 (SI 2010/2430), reg.17 (November 1, 2010).

SCHEDULE 3   **Regulation 16(2)(e)(iii)**

LIST OF REGULATIONS THAT APPLY AFTER THE CONVERSION PHASE

The regulations referred to in regulation 16(2)(e)(iii) are—   **1.062**

The Social Security (Benefit) (Married Women and Widows Special Provisions) Regulations 1974

The Social Security (Benefit) (Members of the Forces) Regulations 1975

The Social Security (Airmen's Benefits) Regulations 1975

The Social Security (Mariners' Benefits) Regulations 1975

The Social Security (Credits) Regulations 1975

The Social Security (Medical Evidence) Regulations 1976

The Social Security (Overlapping Benefits) Regulations 1979

The Statutory Sick Pay (General) Regulations 1982

The Statutory Maternity Pay (General) Regulations 1986

The Income Support (General) Regulations 1987

The Social Security (Claims and Payments) Regulations 1987

The Social Fund (Recovery by Deductions from Benefits) Regulations 1988

The Social Security (Payments on account, Overpayments and Recovery) Regulations 1988

The Social Fund Cold Weather Payments (General) Regulations 1988

The Community Charges (Deductions from Income Support) (No.2) Regulations 1990

The Child Support (Maintenance Assessment Procedure) Regulations 1992

The Child Support (Maintenance Assessments and Special Cases) Regulations 1992

The Fines (Deductions from Income Support) Regulations 1992

The Council Tax (Deductions from Income Support) Regulations 1993

The Jobseeker's Allowance Regulations 1996

The Social Security Benefits (Maintenance Payments and Consequential Amendments) Regulations 1996

[¹The Employment Protection (Recoupment of Jobseeker's Allowance and Income Support) Regulations 1996]

The Child Support Departure Direction and Consequential Amendments Regulations 1996

The Social Security and Child Support (Decisions and Appeals) Regulations 1999

The Social Security (Immigration and Asylum) Consequential Amendments Regulations 2000

The Social Fund Winter Fuel Payment Regulations 2000

The Child Support (Maintenance Calculations and Special Cases) Regulations 2000

The Child Support (Variations) Regulations 2000

The Child Support (Maintenance Calculation Procedure) Regulations 2000

The Social Security (Crediting and Treatment of Contributions, and National Insurance Numbers) Regulations 2001

The Children (Leaving Care) Social Security Benefits Regulations 2001

The Social Security (Loss of Benefit) Regulations 2001

The State Pension Credit Regulations 2002

The Social Security (Jobcentre Plus Interviews for Partners) Regulations 2003

The Age-Related Payments Regulations 2005

The Social Fund Maternity and Funeral Expenses (General) Regulations 2005

AMENDMENT

1. Employment and Support Allowance (Transitional Provisions, Housing Benefit and Council Tax Benefit) (Existing Awards) (No.2) (Amendment) Regulations 2010 (SI 2010/2430), reg.18 (November 1, 2010).

SCHEDULE 4   **Regulation 26**

CONSEQUENTIAL AMENDMENTS

The Social Security (Claims and Payments) Regulations 1987

1.063   [¹1].—*Amends para. 8(4) of Sch. 9 to the Social Security (Claims and Payments) Regulations 1987 (deductions from benefit and direct payments to third parties), and is covered in the Updating sections of this Supplement.*

[² *The Jobseeker's Allowance Regulations 1996*

1.064   **1A.**—(1) In regulation 55(4) of the Jobseeker's Allowance Regulations 1996 (short periods of sickness), for the words after "allowance", where it appears for the first time, to the end of that paragraph, substitute "or 8 weeks of the person's entitlement to statutory sick pay.".

(2) In regulation 55A(1) of those Regulations (periods of sickness and persons receiving treatment outside Great Britain), omit "incapacity benefit," and ", severe disablement allowance or income support".

(3) In paragraph 20H of Schedule 1 to those Regulations (additional conditions for higher pensioner and disability premium) omit sub-paragraph (2).]

The Employment and Support Allowance (Transitional Provisions) Regulations [³2008]

1.065   [¹2].—In regulation 2(3) of the Employment and Support Allowance (Transitional Provisions) Regulations 2008 (claim for existing award), omit the words "severe disablement allowance,".

AMENDMENT

1. Employment and Support Allowance (Transitional Provisions, Housing Benefit and Council Tax Benefit) (Existing Awards) (No.2) (Amendment) Regulations 2010 (SI 2010/2430), reg.15 (November 1, 2010).

2. Employment and Support Allowance (Transitional Provisions, Housing Benefit and Council Tax Benefit) (Existing Awards) (No.2) (Amendment) Regulations 2010 (SI 2010/2430), reg.19 (January 31, 2011).

3. Employment and Support Allowance (Transitional Provisions, Housing Benefit and Council Tax Benefit) (Existing Awards) (No.2) (Amendment) Regulations 2010 (SI 2010/2430), reg.19 (November 1, 2010).

SCHEDULE 5   **Regulation 27**

Amendments to legislation relating to Housing Benefit and Council Tax Benefit

1.066   *Omitted as not within the subject matter of these books.*

(SI 2010/1988)

The Vaccine Damage Payments (Specified Disease) (Revocation and Savings) Order 2010

(SI 2010/1988)

In force September 1, 2010

ARRANGEMENT OF ORDER

The Secretary of State for Work and Pensions makes the following Order in exercise of the power conferred by sections 1(2)(i) and 2(2) of the Vaccine Damage Payments Act 1979.

Citation, commencement and interpretation

1.—This Order may be cited as the Vaccine Damage Payments (Speci-   1.068
fied Disease) (Revocation and Savings) Order 2010 and comes into force
on 1st September 2010.

2.—The "2009 Order" means the Vaccine Damage Payments (Specified Disease) Order 2009.

Revocation

3.—Subject to article (4), the 2009 Order is revoked.   1.069

Savings

4.—The 2009 Order shall continue to apply to any vaccination admin-   1.070
istered prior to the date this Order comes into force.

PART II

UPDATING MATERIAL
VOLUME I

NON MEANS TESTED BENEFITS AND EMPLOYMENT AND SUPPORT ALLOWANCE

Commentary by

David Bonner

Ian Hooker

Richard Poynter

Robin White

Nick Wikeley

Penny Wood

p.4, *annotation to the Vaccine Damage Act 1979, s.1 (payments to persons severely disabled by vaccination)*

With effect from September 1, 2010, influenza caused by the pan- **2.001**
demic influenza A (H1N1) 2009 virus ("swine flu") was removed from
the list of diseases to which the Act applies by the Vaccine Damage
Payments (Specified Disease) (Revocation and Savings) Order 2010 (SI
2010/1988) (see the "New Legislation" section of this Supplement).
Article 4 of the Order ensures, however, that protection under the Act
remains applicable to anyone who received the vaccination prior to
September 1, 2010.

p.62, *annotation to the Social Security Contributions and Benefits Act
1992, s.30E (incapacity benefit: reduction for councillor's allowance)*

The prescribed amount is £95 from October 1, 2010 (£93 for the 12 **2.002**
months prior to that). See further update to p.795.

p.73, *annotation to the Social Security Contributions and Benefits Act
1992, s.39*

With effect from January 1, 2011 the amount prescribed for the **2.003**
purposes of subs.(2A) of this section will be £97.65. See the Rate of
Bereavement Benefits Regulations 2010 (SI 2010/2818), reg.2.

p.76, *annotation to the Social Security Contributions and Benefits Act
1992, s.39C*

With effect from January 1, 2011, the amount prescribed for the **2.004**
purposes of subs.(1A) of this section is £97.65. See the Rate of Bereavement Benefits Regulations 2010 (SI 2010/2818), reg.3.

p.77, *annotation to the Social Security Contributions and Benefits Act
1992, s.39C (meaning of "spouse")*

A further attempt to claim bereavement benefits by the survivor of a **2.005**
long-standing common law marriage has been rejected by Judge Levenson in *ES v SSWP (MA)* [2010] UKUT 200 (AAC). An argument
was made that earlier cases had turned, directly or indirectly, upon the
meaning given to the words "marriage" and "husband", which had been
the terminology used in relation to the benefits existing previously only
for widows. Bereavement benefits, on the other hand, were available for
a "spouse" whose partner had died, and earlier cases had not focused on
the change in terminology. Judge Levenson held that as a matter of
interpreting the new entitlements the word "spouse" still required a valid
marriage subsisting at the time of the partner's death. He also held that
as a matter of human rights law, the difference of treatment, though
discriminatory, was justified as a proportionate measure protecting a
valid preference for the institution of marriage in our society.

p.100, *annotation to Social Security Contributions and Benefits Act 1992, s.44 (pensionable age—gender reassignment)*

2.006   The decision of Judge Jupp in the case reported at [2009] UKUT 49 (AAC) has been reversed by the Court of Appeal in *Timbrell v Secretary of State for Work and Pensions* [2010] EWCA Civ 701. The court held that where the claimant had changed her gender to that of female, and claimed her pension before the Gender Recognition Act 2004 became law, she was entitled to be paid a pension from the age of 60 notwithstanding that she would not have satisfied the requirements to change her gender under that Act because she would not have made an application under the GRA. The claimant would have declined to make an application because the effect of a certificate issued under the Act would have been to dissolve her marriage, and the claimant had no intention of ending her marriage either then, or now. The court held that she was entitled to assert her right under Directive 79/7 because the United Kingdom did not, at that time, have any effective means by which she could do so. This meant that the court effectively followed the decision in *Richards v Secretary of State for Work and Pensions* (C-423/04) [2006] E.C.R. I-3585 ECJ. Furthermore, counsel made a concession to the court that the Secretary of State would not argue that her right to the pension would cease from a date when the GRA had come into force. Note, however, that for someone claiming after that date, no entitlement will arise because the United Kingdom has not been held to remain in breach of the Directive.

p.103, *modification of the Social Security Contributions and Benefits Act 1992, s.44B*

2.007   Note that for the purpose of making "conversion decisions" under the "Migration Regulations" from October 1, 2010, s.44B is to be read as if there were inserted after subs.(5) a new subs.(5A) as set out in Sch.1, para.6 of those Regulations: see the Employment and Support Allowance (Transitional Provisions, Housing Benefit and Council Tax Benefit) (Existing Awards) (No.2) Regulations 2010 (SI 2010/1907) (as amended) set out in the "New Legislation" section of this Supplement.

p.126, *annotation to the Social Security Contributions and Benefits Act 1992, s.64 (attendance allowance—conditions as to age)*

2.008   The lack of an equivalent lowest rate of benefit in Attendance Allowance was attacked by the claimant in *CS v SSWP* [2009] UKUT 257 (AAC). He was aged 71 and excluded from making a claim for DLA. He argued that the absence of benefit at the lowest rate was discrimination on the ground of age contrary to the Human Rights Act 1998. Judge S.M. Lane rejected that argument (though she accepted that his right to a social security benefit was within art.1 of Protocol 1 and that the difference in treatment was discrimination on the ground of age). She held that this discrimination was justified. It was rational and proportionate, she said, to distinguish those who were affected by disability at a younger age and whose earning capacity was thus reduced; retirement pension was there to make provision, at least in part, for those over retiring age. (cf. *NT v SSWP* [2009] UKUT 37 (AAC); *R (DLA) 1/09*, in relation to the mobility component of DLA.)

p.148, *annotation to the Social Security Contributions and Benefits Act 1992, s. 72 (requires attention and the effect of aids and appliances)*

The question of whether a claimant "requires" attention will also be   2.009
affected by whether some aid or device might assist the claimant so as to eliminate the need for attention. This matter was considered by Judge Ward in the case of *SF v SSWP* [2010] UKUT 78 (AAC). There, the claim had been refused by the First-tier Tribunal on the ground that the claimant's need for assistance in bathing could be obviated by the provision of a bath-board, or by the fitting of a bath with showering facilities. Judge Ward followed an earlier decision in *CDLA/304/07* in holding that it must be found to be reasonable for the claimant to obtain such devices. He remitted the case to a new tribunal for further findings to be made as to the availability of such measures and consideration of the timing as well as the cost with which they might be accomplished within the six-month qualifying period of that claim. In the instant case it was argued that major alterations might not have been reasonable because the claimant was moving house at that time.

p.179, *annotation to the Social Security Contributions and Benefits Act 1992, s. 73 (lower rate mobility component)*

In *SSWP v PA* [2010] UKUT 401 (AAC) Judge Mark upheld a   2.010
decision in favour of a claimant for lower rate mobility component who suffered severely from Crohn's Disease, which made him unexpectedly and urgently incontinent. The judge held, that on the evidence before the tribunal and before the Upper Tribunal, that the claimant had shown a sufficient need for supervision in assisting him to find a public toilet and assisting him in cleaning himself.

p.194, *Social Security Contributions and Benefits Act 1992, s. 82*

Section 82 should have been omitted with effect from April 6, 2010.   2.011
Increases of Maternity Allowance for adult dependants were abolished from that date by s.15 of the Welfare Reform Act 2009. There is a saving provided by s.15(2)(a) in respect of a claim made before April 6, 2010 and ending after that date.

p.195, *Social Security Contributions and Benefits Act 1992, s.83, s.84, and s.85*

These sections of the act were all abolished by s.4 of the Pensions Act   2.012
2007 with effect from April 6, 2010. It should be noted, however, that there is a saving in respect of each increase provided by subss.(5) to (8) of s.4. In the case of a claimant who is entitled to an increase by virtue

of a claim made before that date, entitlement will continue until April 6, 2020, or until their entitlement otherwise ceases, whichever is the earlier.

p.198, *Social Security Contributions and Benefits Act 1992, s.90*

2.013 Section 90 should have been omitted with effect from April 6, 2010. Increases of Carer's Allowance for adult dependants were abolished from that date by section 15 of the Welfare Reform Act 2009. There is a saving provided by s.15(2)(b) and s.15(3) in respect of a claimant who has made a claim before that date and was then entitled to an increase in Carer's Allowance for an adult dependant (or would have been but for the effect of fluctuating earnings—see s.92). In such a case the claimant will remain entitled to the increase until April 6, 2020, or until their entitlement otherwise ceases, whichever is the earlier.

pp.211 and 214, *annotation to the Social Security Contributions and Benefits Act 1992, s.94(1) (by accident)*

2.014 *SSWP v Scullion* is now also reported as [2010] AACR 29.

pp.234–236, *annotation to the Social Security Contributions and Benefits Act 1992, s.103 (disablement pension: loss of faculty must be the result of the relevant accident)*

2.015 Where medical experts differ on whether there is loss of faculty or whether it was the result of the relevant industrial accident(s), the First-tier Tribunal must give sufficient reasons for preferring the view of one expert and rejecting that of the other(s). See Judge Wikeley in *DB v SSWP (II)* [2010] UKUT 144 (AAC) at paras 40–51, citing statements by different three-judge panels of the Upper Tribunal in *Hampshire CC v JP* [2009] UKUT 239 (AAC) (now reported as [2010] AACR 15); and *BB v South London & Maudsley NHS Trust and Ministry of Justice* [2009] UKUT 157 (AAC). The relevant factors for a tribunal to consider are set out in Judge Edward Jacob's *Tribunal Practice and Procedure* (London: Legal Action Group, 2009), at paras 11.119–11.129. They relate to "the expert(s), the area of expertise and the evidence" (para.44). As regards the experts, matters to consider are each expert's qualifications, expertise and experience on the issue material to the appeal. On expertise, the tribunal must "bear in mind the limits to which the doctors' areas of expertise can actually provide answers to the issue in the appeal" (para.46). On the expert evidence itself, it is a question of examining the "factual basis and soundness of the experts respective reasoned opinions" (para.47). This may be difficult where, as in this case, there was a clash between the "majority view" of the "medical establishment" and the "minority view" provided by one of the experts. As Judge Wikeley noted, experience in hindsight of changes in medical opinion indicates that the fact that an expert is in the minority does not mean that his or her opinion is thereby necessarily wrong. Lacking hindsight, the tribunal, drawing on the expertise of its medical members in full compliance with the rules of natural justice and fairness, "will have to form its own best judgment today on the soundness of the science and reasons underpinning [the minority expert's evidence] in this appeal" (para.50).

p.262, *Social Security Contributions and Benefits Act, s.150A*

This is actually s.150A of the Administration Act, and has erroneously been included in Volume I. It should be deleted. **2.016**

pp.339–340, *annotation to the Social Security Contributions and Benefits Act 1992, Sch.7, Pt V Retirement Allowance*

Note that there is a fuller exposition of *SSWP v NH (II)* [2010] UKUT 84 (AAC) in the update to pp.1389–1390, below. **2.017**

pp.387–425, *modification of Pt I of the Welfare Reform Act 2007 (Employment and Support Allowance)*

Note that for the purpose of making "conversion decisions" under the "Migration Regulations", from October 1, 2010, any reference to "a claimant" is to be read as referring to a "notified person" under those Regulations. See reg.6(1) and Sch.1, para.1 to those Regulations: the Employment and Support Allowance (Transitional Provisions, Housing Benefit and Council Tax Benefit) (Existing Awards) (No.2) Regulations 2010 (SI 2010/1907) (as amended) set out in the "New Legislation" section of this Supplement. **2.018**

After a conversion decision has been made, references to "a claimant" are to be read as references to someone in respect of which a conversion decision has been made: see reg.16(1) and Sch.2, para.1 to those Regulations.

p.388, *modification of the Welfare Reform Act 2007, s.1(2)*

Note that for the purpose of making "conversion decisions" under the "Migration Regulations", from November 1, 2010, subs.(2) is to be read as if there were substituted the text set out in Sch.1, para.2 to those Regulations: see the Employment and Support Allowance (Transitional Provisions, Housing Benefit and Council Tax Benefit) (Existing Awards) (No.2) Regulations 2010 (SI 2010/1907) (as amended) set out in the "New Legislation" section of this Supplement. **2.019**

After a conversion decision has been made, subs.(2) is to be read as modified by reg.16(1) and Sch.2, para.(2)(a) to those Regulations.

From October 1 to November 1, 2010 the modifications were worded differently. In respect of making conversion decisions, Sch.1, para.28 to the unamended "Migration Regulations" (SI 2010/1907) read:

"Section 1 is to be read as if—
    (a) for subsection (2), there were substituted—
        "(2) Subject to the provisions of this Part, a notified person is entitled to an employment and support allowance if the person satisfies the basic conditions and—

      (a) is entitled to an existing award of incapacity benefit or severe disablement allowance;

      (b) is entitled to an existing award of income support and satisfies the conditions set out in Part 2 of Schedule 1, unless subsection (2)(c) applies; or

      (c) is entitled to an existing award of income support by virtue of paragraph 10 (disabled students) or 12 (deaf students) of Schedule 1B to the Income Support (General) Regulations 1987 and satisfies the conditions set out in Part 2 of Schedule 1, with the exception of the condition in paragraph 6(1)(g).”; and

   (b) subsection (3)(e) were omitted.”

As regards application to a person in relation to whom a conversion decision had been made, Sch.2, para.42(a) to the unamended “Migration Regulations” (SI 2010/1907) read:

   “Section 1 (employment and support allowance) is to be read as if—

      (a) for subsection (2), there were substituted—

         “(2) Subject to the provisions of this Part, a person is entitled to an employment and support allowance if the person satisfies the basic conditions and—

            (a) in accordance with Part 2 of the Employment and Support Allowance (Transitional Provisions, Housing Benefit and Council Tax Benefit) (Existing Awards) (No. 2) Regulations 2010, the effect of the conversion decision that was made in relation to the person was to convert the person's existing award or awards into a single award of an employment and support allowance; and

            (b) that conversion decision has come into effect.”

p.388, *modification of the Welfare Reform Act 2007, s.1(7)*

2.020   From October 1, 2010, after a “conversion decision” has been made under the “Migration Regulations”, subs.(7) is to read as if there were substituted the text contained in Sch.2, para.2(2)(b) to those Regulations: see the Employment and Support Allowance (Transitional Provisions, Housing Benefit and Council Tax Benefit) (Existing Awards) (No.2) Regulations 2010 (SI 2010/1907) (as amended) set out in the “New Legislation” section of this Supplement.

p.393, *modification of the Welfare Reform Act 2007, s.2*

2.021   Note that for the purpose of making “conversion decisions” under the “Migration Regulations”, from October 1, 2010, references to the “assessment period” in subs.(2)(a) and (3)(a) are to read as ones to the “conversion phase” under those Regulations: see reg.6(1) and Sch.1, para.3 to those Regulations: see the Employment and Support Allowance (Transitional Provisions, Housing Benefit and Council Tax Benefit)

(Existing Awards) (No.2) Regulations 2010 (SI 2010/1907) (as amended) set out in the "New Legislation" section of this Supplement.

After a conversion decision has been made, as regards persons in relation to whom a conversion decision has been made under those Regulations, subs.(2) and (3) are to be read subject to the modifications set out in Sch.2, para.3 to those Regulations.

p.428, *amendments to the Welfare Reform Act 2007, Sch.1, para.1 (conditions relating to national insurance)*

With effect from November 1, 2010, s.13(1)–(3) of the Welfare Reform Act 2009 amended para.1(1) to read:

2.022

"**1.**—(1) The first condition is that—
  (a) the claimant has actually paid Class 1 or Class 2 contributions in respect of one of the last [two] complete tax years ("the base tax year") before the beginning of the relevant benefit year,
  (b) those contributions must have been paid before the relevant benefit week, and
  [(c) the claimant's earnings determined in accordance with sub-paragraph (2) must be not less than the base tax year's lower earnings limit multiplied by 26.]"

See further the General Note to the amending provisions in the "New Legislation" section of this Supplement.

With effect from October 1 (for purposes of making regulations) and November 1, 2010 (for all other purposes), s.13(1), (4) of the Welfare Reform Act 2009 substituted new paras 1(2), (3) to read:

"[(2) The earnings referred to in sub-paragraph (1)(c) are the aggregate of—
  (a) the claimant's relevant earnings for the base tax year upon which primary Class 1 contributions have been paid or treated as paid, and
  (b) the claimant's earnings factors derived from Class 2 contributions.

(3) Regulations may make provision for the purposes of sub-paragraph (2)(a) for determining the claimant's relevant earnings for the base tax year.

(3A) Regulations under sub-paragraph (3) may, in particular, make provision—
  (a) for making that determination by reference to the amount of a person's earnings for periods comprised in the base tax year;
  (b) for determining the amount of a person's earnings for any such period by—
    (i) first determining the amount of the earnings for the period in accordance with regulations made for the purposes of section 3(2) of the Contributions and Benefits Act, and
    (ii) then disregarding so much of the amount found in accordance with sub-paragraph (i) as exceeded the base tax

year's lower earnings limit (or the prescribed equivalent).]"

pp.428–429, *modification of the Welfare Reform Act 2007, Sch.1, paras 1–5 (conditions relating to national insurance)*

2.023   Note that for the purpose of making "conversion decisions" under the "Migration Regulations", from October 1, 2010, Sch.1 is to be read as if paras 1–5 were omitted. See reg.6(1) and Sch.1, para.6(a) to those Regulations: the Employment and Support Allowance (Transitional Provisions, Housing Benefit and Council Tax Benefit) (Existing Awards) (No.2) Regulations 2010 (SI 2010/1907) (as amended) set out in the "New Legislation" section of this Supplement.

pp.430–431, *annotation to the Welfare Reform Act 2007, Sch.1, paras (1)–(3)*

2.024   The changes effected from November 1, 2010 by s.13 of the Welfare Reform Act 2009 (see update to p.428, above) significantly tighten the contribution conditions for CESA by requiring a more recent and stronger connection with the world of work. They do so in that the first condition can from then only be satisfied in one of the last *two* (rather than three) tax years (April 6 to April 5) complete before the start of the relevant benefit year (early January) (as with JSA); and by raising the requisite level of earnings in the tax year relied on to 26 (rather than 25) times that year's lower earnings limit. Moreover, the conditions now only count earnings at that lower earnings limit (ignoring earnings in excess of it) so that new claimants will have to have worked for at least 26 weeks in one of the last two tax years. Prior to these amendments, when the level was 25 times the LEL and the scheme looked also to earnings between the lower and upper earnings limits, a high earner could qualify on less than four weeks' work in the tax year, and someone at the national minimum wage could qualify in about 12 weeks.

The regulations made under subss.(3) and (3A) are the Social Security (Contribution Conditions for Jobseeker's Allowance and Employment and Support Allowance) Regulations 2010 (SI 2010/2446), and amendments effected by them to the ESA Regulations are taken into account in the updates to pp.1008–1010 in this Part of the Supplement.

p.432, *modification of the Welfare Reform Act 2007, Sch.1, para.6*

2.025   Note that for the purpose of making "conversion decisions" under the "Migration Regulations" (or revising such decisions before their effective date (see reg.13 of those Regulations for "effective date")), from October 1, 2010, para.6 is to be read as if after sub-para.(1) there were inserted paras (1A) to (1C) as set out in Sch.1, para.6(b) to those Regulations: see reg.6 of and Sch.1, para.6(b) to the Employment and Support Allowance (Transitional Provisions, Housing Benefit and Council Tax Benefit) (Existing Awards) (No.2) Regulations 2010 (SI 2010/1907) (as amended) set out in the "New Legislation" section of this Supplement.

After a conversion decision has been made, for the purpose of revising or superseding a conversion decision on or after its effective date (or deciding any other matter in connection with a person's entitlement to ESA under the Migration Regulations), from November 1, 2010, para.6 is to be read as if after sub-para.(1) there were inserted paras (1A) to (1C) as set out in Sch.2, para.4A to those Regulations: see reg.16 of and Sch.2, para.4A to the Employment and Support Allowance (Transitional Provisions, Housing Benefit and Council Tax Benefit) (Existing Awards) (No.2) Regulations 2010 (SI 2010/1907) (as amended) set out in the "New Legislation" section of this Supplement.

pp.444–445, *entry into force of Welfare Reform Act 2007, Sch.4, paras (7) and (8)*

Both provisions were brought into force on July 27, 2010 by art.2 of   **2.026** the Welfare Reform Act 2007 (Commencement No.12) Order 2010 (SI 2010/1905). They enabled the making of the "Migration Regulations"—the Employment and Support Allowance (Transitional Provisions, Housing Benefit and Council Tax Benefit) (Existing Awards) (No.2) Regulations 2010 (SI 2010/1907) (as amended) (see the "New Legislation" section of this Supplement). These enable the conversion of existing awards of incapacity benefit, income support for those incapable of work and severe disablement allowance (termed globally "incapacity benefits") into awards of employment and support allowance ("transitional allowances", so that there will be no loss of money for successful transferees), in other words, the gradual migration of existing recipients of such benefits to ESA, provided, of course, that they meet the more stringent ESA test of limited capability for work. The Explanatory Note to the original "Migration Regulations" (SI 2010/875) (revoked and re-made in the same terms because paras 7 and 8 of this Schedule had not been brought into force when the original regulations were made), which was attached to the Explanatory Note for the No.2 Regulations (SI 2010/1907), identifies the policy intent, timetable for and effects of, the migration process:

> "The policy intent is, with few exceptions, for existing incapacity benefits customers to go through the migration process between October 2010 and the end of March 2014. This will determine if they qualify for Employment and Support Allowance and will eventually enable the other incapacity benefit schemes to be wholly wound down.
>
> Migration to the Employment and Support Allowance regime, (to which the Government committed in the December 2008 White Paper), will align and simplify the benefit system, by ensuring that, over time, all customers with a health condition or disability in similar circumstances will be treated equally, receiving support to get into to work and the same level of financial help.
>
> Some current incapacity benefits customers will be found fit for work and disallowed benefit on grounds of incapacity. They may claim

Jobseeker's Allowance or remain on Income Support if they qualify on grounds other than incapacity." paras 7.2–7.4 (footnotes omitted).

The exceptions mentioned include those who reach state pension age during migration and those over pension age in receipt of SDA. The migration of existing "national insurance credits only" claimants will take place when the main migration has been completed.

p.530, *annotation to the Social Security Benefit (Computation of Earnings) Regulations 1996, reg.8*

2.027   *CG/0607/2008* has been considered and distinguished in *KJ v SSWP (CA)* [2010] UKUT 218 (AAC). The case concerned a full-time employee who reduced his hours in order to be able to care for his sick mother and to enable him to claim carer's allowance. For the month of March 2008, the employee was paid the pro rata equivalent of his full-time salary for two days and the reduced amount for the remaining days in the month, but he also received a tax rebate. The question which arose was how this monthly pay should be used for the purpose of determining his earnings in relation to his claim for carer's allowance. The Upper Tribunal judge concluded that this was not a case in which earnings fluctuated such that the more flexible provisions in reg.8(3) applied; that paragraph contemplated a situation in which the amount "has changed more than once". There was no basis for separating out the March salary into two payments: one attributable to the first two days of the month and so attributable to only one week. The "normal" calculation in converting the monthly pay into weekly earnings applied.

p.532, *correction to the Social Security Benefit (Computation of Earnings) Regulations 1996, reg.9*

2.028   Regulation 9 should read as follows:

"Earnings of employed earners

9.—(1) Subject to paragraphs (2) and (3), "earnings", in the case of employment as an employed earner, means any remuneration or profit derived from that employment and includes—
   (a) any bonus or commission;
   (b) any payment in lieu of remuneration except any periodic sum paid to a claimant on account of the termination of his employment by reason of redundancy;
   (c) any payment in lieu of notice;
   (d) any holiday pay except any payable more than four weeks after the termination or interruption of employment;
   (e) any payment by way of a retainer;
   (f) any payment made by the claimant's employer in respect of expenses not wholly, exclusively and necessarily incurred in the performance of the duties of the employment, including any payment made by the claimant's employer in respect of—

     (i) travelling expenses incurred by the claimant between his home and place of employment;

     (ii) expenses incurred by the claimant under arrangements made for the care of a member of his family owing to the claimant's absence from home;

(g) any award of compensation made under section 112(4) or 117(3)(a) of the Employment Rights Act 1996 (remedies and compensation);

(h) any such sum as is referred to in section 112(3) of the Contributions and Benefits Act (certain sums to be earnings for social security purposes);

(i) where—

     (i) a payment of compensation is made in respect of employment which is not part-time employment and that payment is not less than the maximum weekly amount, the amount of the compensation less the deductible remainder, where that is applicable;

     (ii) a payment of compensation is made in respect of employment which is part-time employment, the amount of the compensation;

[¹(j) any remuneration paid by or on behalf of an employer to the claimant in respect of a period throughout which the claimant is—

     (i) on maternity leave;

     (ii) on paternity leave;

     (iii) on adoption leave; or

     (iv) absent from work because he is ill.]

(2) For the purposes of paragraph (1)(i)(i) the "deductible remainder"—

(a) applies in cases where dividing the amount of the compensation by the maximum weekly amount produces a whole number plus a fraction; and

(b) is equal to the difference between—

     (i) the amount of the compensation; and

     (ii) the product of the maximum weekly amount multiplied by the whole number.

[²(3) "Earnings" shall not include any payment in respect of expenses—

(a) wholly, exclusively and necessarily incurred in the performance of the duties of the employment; or

(b) arising out of the claimant's participation in a service user group.]

(4) In this regulation—

[¹"adoption leave" means a period of absence from work on ordinary or additional adoption leave under section 75A or 75B of the Employment Rights Act 1996;]

"compensation" means any payment made in respect of or on the termination of employment in a case where a person has not received or received only part of a payment in lieu of notice due or which would have been due to him had he not waived his right to receive it, other than—

(a) any payment specified in paragraph (1)(a) to (h);

(b) any payment specified in paragraph (3);

(c) any redundancy payment within the meaning of section 135 of the Employment Rights Act 1996;

(d) any refund of contributions to which that person was entitled under an occupational pension scheme;

(e) any compensation payable by virtue of section 173 or section 178(3) or (4) of the Education Reform Act 1988;

[²"enactment" includes an enactment comprised in, or an instrument made under, an Act of the Scottish Parliament;]

[¹"maternity leave" means a period during which a woman is absent from work because she is pregnant or has given birth to a child, and at the end of which she has a right to return to work either under the terms of her contract of employment or under Part 8 of the Employment Rights Act 1996;]

"maximum weekly amount" means the maximum weekly amount which, on the date on which the payment of compensation is made, is specified in section 227(1) of the Employment Rights Act 1996;

"part-time employment" has the same meaning as in regulation 6(8) (calculation of earnings of employed earners);

[¹"paternity leave" means a period of absence from work on leave under section 80A or 80B of the Employment Rights Act 1996.]

[²"public authority" includes any person certain of whose functions are functions of a public nature;]

[²"service user group" means a group of individuals that is consulted by or on behalf of—

(a) a Health Board, Special Health Board or the Agency in consequence of a function under section 2B of the National Health Service (Scotland) Act 1978,

(b) a landlord authority in consequence of a function under section 105 of the Housing Act 1985,

(c) a public authority in consequence of a function under section 49A of the Disability Discrimination Act 1995,

(d) a best value authority in consequence of a function under section 3 of the Local Government Act 1999,

(e) a local authority landlord or registered social landlord in consequence of a function under section 53 of the Housing (Scotland) Act 2001,

(f) a relevant English body or a relevant Welsh body in consequence of a function under section 242 of the National Health Service Act 2006,

(g) a Local Health Board in consequence of a function under section 183 of the National Health Service (Wales) Act 2006,

  (h) the Commission or the Office of the Health Professions Adjudicator in consequence of a function under sections 4, 5, or 108 of the Health and Social Care Act 2008,

  (i) the regulator or a [3private registered provider of social housing] in consequence of a function under sections 98, 193 or 196 of the Housing and Regeneration Act 2008, or

  (j) a public or local authority in Great Britain in consequence of a function conferred under any other enactment,

for the purposes of monitoring and advising on a policy of that body or authority which affects or may affect persons in the group, or of monitoring or advising on services provided by that body or authority which are used (or may potentially be used) by those persons.]"

AMENDMENTS

1. The Social Security Benefit (Computation of Earnings) (Amendment) Regulations 2002 (SI 2002/2823), reg.2 (April 1, 2003).

2. The Social Security Benefit (Computation of Earnings) (Amendment) Regulations 2009 (SI 2009/2678), reg.2 (October 26, 2009).

3. The Housing and Regeneration Act 2008 (Consequential Provisions) (No.2) Order 2010 (SI 2010/671), art.4 and Sch.1, (April 1, 2010).

p.536, *correction to the Social Security Benefit (Computation of Earnings) Regulations 1996, reg.11*

Regulation 11 should read as follows: 2.029

"Calculation of earnings of self-employed earners

11.—(1) Except where paragraph (2) applies, where a claimant's earnings consist of earnings from employment as a self-employed earner the weekly amount of his earnings shall be determined by reference to his average weekly earnings from that employment—

  (a) over a period of one year; or

  (b) where the claimant has recently become engaged in that employment or there has been a change which is likely to affect the normal pattern of business, over such other period as may, in any particular case, enable the weekly amount of his earnings to be determined more accurately.

(2) Where the claimant's earnings consist of [¹any items to which paragraph (2A) applies] those earnings shall be taken into account over a period equal to such number of weeks as is equal to the number (less any fraction of the whole number) calculated in accordance with the formula—

$$\frac{S}{T + U}$$

where—
S is the earnings

T is the relevant earnings limit plus one penny; and

U is the total of the sums which would fall to be disregarded or deducted as appropriate under regulation 13(2) or (3) (calculation of net profit of self-employed earners).

[¹(2A) This paragraph applies to—

(a) royalties or other sums paid as a consideration for the use of, or the right to use, any copyright, design, patent or trade mark; or

(b) any payment in respect of any—

    (i) book registered under the Public Lending Right Scheme 1982, or

    (ii) work made under any international public lending right scheme that is analogous to the Public Lending Right Scheme 1982,

where the claimant is the first owner of the copyright, design, patent or trade mark, or any original contributor to the book or work concerned.]

(3) The period mentioned in paragraph (2) shall begin on the date on which the payment is treated as paid under regulation 7 (date on which earnings are treated as paid)."

AMENDMENTS

1. The Social Security Benefit (Computation of Earnings) (Amendment) Regulations 2009 (SI 2009/2678), reg.2 (October 26, 2009).

p.650, *amendment to the Social Security (Disability Living Allowance) Regulations 1991, reg.9*

2.030   With effect from May 5, 2010, art.4 and Sch.3 of the Local Education Authorities and Children's Services Authorities (Integration of Functions) (Local and Subordinate Legislation) Order 2010 (SI 2010/1172) amends reg.9(3)(b) by substituting for "local education authorities" the words "local authorities".

p.657, *amendment to the Social Security (Disability Living Allowance) Regulations, 1991, reg.12*

2.031   This regulation was amended by reg.2 of the Social Security (Disability Living Allowance) (Amendment) Regulations 2010 (SI 2010/1651) by the insertion after para.(1) of para.(1A) as follows:

"(1A)

(a) For the purposes of section 73(1AB)(a) of the Act (mobility component for the severely visually impaired) a person is to be taken to satisfy the condition that he has a severe visual impairment if—

    (i) he has visual acuity, with appropriate corrective lenses if necessary, of less than 3/60; or

    (ii) he has visual acuity of 3/60 or more, but less than 6/60, with appropriate corrective lenses if necessary, a complete loss of peripheral visual field and a central visual field of no more than 10° in total.

(b) For the purposes of section 73(1AB)(b), the conditions are that he has been certified as severely sight impaired or blind by a consultant ophthalmologist.

(c) In this paragraph—

　(i) references to visual acuity are to be read as references to the combined visual acuity of both eyes in cases where a person has both eyes;

　(ii) references to measurements of visual acuity are references to visual acuity measured on the Snellen Scale;

　(iii) references to visual field are to be read as references to the combined visual field of both eyes in cases where a person has both eyes.".

This amendment has effect from November 15, 2010, for the purposes only of enabling decisions as to entitlement to be taken. Entitlement to receive benefit will commence from April 11, 2011.

Note that for the purposes of determining entitlement to benefit under this provision an optometrist or an orthoptist who is registered with their appropriate professional Council is a health care professional for the purposes of s.39 of the Social Security Act 1998.

p.662, *annotation to the Social Security (Disability Living Allowance) Regulations 1991, reg.12 (unable to walk—use of crutches)*

R(M) 2/89 was approved by the Court of Appeal in *Sandu v Secretary*　2.032
of State for Work and Pensions [2010] EWCA Civ 962. The Court of Appeal also approved of the reasoning in *CDLA/97/2001*, which, like *Sandu*, was a case of a claimant with two legs, but only one of which could be used to bear any weight. In *CDLA/97/2001* the claim succeeded because the commissioner accepted that a person who could carry his weight only upon one leg could not be said to be walking any more than might a person who had only one leg, and this was so even though the claimant might make progress with crutches by moving alternate legs. The test was whether the claimant did, or could, rest any weight upon alternate legs. In the *Sandu* case the court declined an invitation to attempt any further or better definition of walking, though the matter was remitted to another tribunal for further findings of fact.

p.674, *annotation to the Social Security (Disability Living Allowance) Regulations 1991, reg.12(6), (disruptive and unpredictable behaviour)*

The sort of evidence necessary to satisfy the elements of para.(6) has　2.033
been considered again by Judge Mark in the case of an autistic child in *CM v SSWP* [2010] UKUT 318 (AAC). He accepts the approach adopted by Judge Levenson, but goes on to put the matter to be considered by a new tribunal thus:

"I fully accept that one must not confuse the requirements of 12(6)(b) with those of 12(6)(c). There must be a regular need actually to intervene and physically restrain the claimant to prevent him causing physical injury to himself or another, or damage to property, to satisfy 12(6)(b). There be unpredictable disruptive behaviour requiring another person to be present and watching over him whenever he is awake to satisfy 12(6)(c). The issues for the tribunal to address in this case for the purpose of 12(6)(b) are that of regularity, physical restraint and physical injury or damage to property. The issues for the tribunal to address for the purpose of 12(6)(c) are unpredictability of disruptive behaviour giving rise to the need for a person to be present and watching over him whenever he is awake. Interventions may be regular if they are frequent in one context but infrequent, or even rare, in another context provided that looked at overall there is a regular requirement to intervene and physically restrain the claimant.

If, however, the structured environment is such that there is no real risk of unpredictable violence or not such a risk as to make it reasonable for somebody to be present and watching over him whenever he is awake, then he cannot be said to need another person to be present and watching over him because of his unpredictable disruptive behaviour. If, in practice, he is regularly left alone in his room for lengthy periods while awake, or is not watched over at school because of his unpredictable disruptive behaviour, then that would suggest that his behaviour is not unpredictable, or at least is not unpredictable to such an extent as to require another person to be present and watching over him whenever he is awake" (paras 9, 10).

p.690, *annotation to Social Security (Invalid Care Allowance) Regulations 1976, reg.5 (meaning of "full-time education")*

2.034   The meaning of "full-time education" has been thoroughly explored by the Court of Appeal in *Secretary of State for Work and Pensions v Deane* [2010] EWCA Civ 699, when considering the appeal from the decision of Judge Mesher in [2009] UKUT 46 (AAC). The court began by holding that the definition of full-time education in reg.5 is not an exhaustive one. (This approach had been suggested by Judge Mesher, but was one not open to him, he felt, by reason of earlier precedents in the Court of Appeal.) In this case, however, the court held that they were not bound by those earlier decisions. In the case of *Wright-Turner* [2002] CARC 3567 (CA of NI), because the point appeared to have been conceded, and in any case did not then form a part of the narrower basis of that decision; and *Flemming* [2002] EWCA Civ 641 because, even if it had been accepted, it did not form a part of the decision. The court in the present case contrasted the wording of regs 4 and 8, in both of which the regulation expressly defines what is, and what is not, to be regarded as a part of that definition, with the wording of reg.5 that refers only to what is to be regarded as "full-time education". What this means is that the definition of full-time education by reference to attending a course for 21 or more hours per week is only a partial definition; there may be also be courses of a lesser period which are full-time education. This would have been enough to dispose of the case, because in the view of all the judges who have been involved in these cases, a normal three-year undergraduate degree course (which is what the claimant had been enrolled on) should be full-time education for the purposes of a claim to Carer's Allowance. However, they went on to hold, as well, that the proper approach to the assessment of hours of attendance was by reference to the expectation of the educational establishment rather than the actual hours worked by the student.

This should resolve most difficulties in relation to university courses, though the court did accept that there may still be difficult cases in relation to colleges and in cases where exemptions from course requirements have been made.

p.795, *amendment to the Social Security (Incapacity Benefit) Regulations 1994, reg.8 (amount of disregard from councillor's allowance)*

With effect from October 1, 2010, reg.3 of the Social Security (Miscellaneous Amendments) (No.4) Regulations 2010 (SI 2010/2126) increased the limit from £93 to £95.   2.035

p.816, *amendment to the Social Security (Incapacity Benefit—Increases for Dependants) Regulations 1994, reg.9 (increase of incapacity benefit for adult dependants and persons having the care of children or qualifying young persons)*

With effect from June 28, 2010, reg.5 of the Social Security (Miscellaneous Amendments) (No.3) Regulations 2010 (SI 2010/840) amended paras (1)(a) and (b) by replacing "is aged at least 60" with "has reached the qualifying age referred to in section 1(6) of the State Pension Credit Act 2002".   2.036

p.824, *amendment to the Social Security (Incapacity for Work) (General) Regulations 1995, reg.2(1): definition of "medical evidence"*

With effect from June 28, 2010, reg.6(2) of the Social Security (Miscellaneous Amendments) (No.3) Regulations 2010 (SI 2010/840) amended the definition of "medical evidence" by substituting for "doctor" in both places where it occurs, the term "health care professional".   2.037

p.850, *amendment to the Social Security (Incapacity for Work) (General) Regulations 1995: insertion of new reg.16A*

With effect from June 28, 2010, reg.6(3) of the Social Security (Miscellaneous Amendments) (No.3) Regulations 2010 (SI 2010/840) inserted before reg.17 a new reg.16A as follows: 2.038

"Persons to be treated as capable of work at the end of the period covered by medical evidence

16A. Where the Secretary of State is satisfied that it is appropriate in the circumstances of the case then a person may be treated as being capable of work if—
(a) the person has supplied medical evidence in accordance with regulation 28(2)(a);

(b) the period for which medical evidence was supplied has ended;

(c) the Secretary of State has requested further medical evidence; and

(d) the person has not, before whichever is the later of either the end of the period of six weeks beginning with the date of the Secretary of State's request or the end of six weeks beginning with the day after the end of the period for which medical evidence was supplied—

(i) supplied further medical evidence, or

(ii) otherwise made contact with the Secretary of State to indicate a wish to have the question of incapacity for work determined."

pp.850–851, *amendments to the Social Security (Incapacity for Work) (General) Regulations 1995, reg.17 (exempt work)*

2.039   With effect from June 28, 2010, reg.6(4)(a) of the Social Security (Miscellaneous Amendments) (No.3) Regulations 2010 (SI 2010/840) amended para.(3)(b) to read:

"(b) is supervised by a person employed by a public or local authority or [by a] voluntary organisation [or community interest company] engaged in the provision or procurement of work for persons who have disabilities."

From the same date, reg.6(4)(b) of those amending Regulations substituted a new para.(4)(a) as follows:

"(a) is done during a period of specified work, provided that—

(i) the person has not previously done specified work,

(ii) since the beginning of the last period of specified work, the person has ceased to be entitled to a relevant benefit for a continuous period exceeding 8 weeks, or

(iii) not less than 52 weeks have elapsed since the last period of specified work; or".

From the same date, reg.6(4)(c) of those amending Regulations added after para.(8) a new para.(9) as follows:

"(9) For the purposes of this regulation, a period of specified work begins on the first day on which any specified work is undertaken and continues for a period of 52 weeks, whether or not any further specified work is undertaken during that period."

With effect from October 1, 2010, reg.4 of the Social Security (Miscellaneous Amendments) (No.4) Regulations 2010 (SI 2010/2126) increased the earnings limit in paras (3) and (4) from £93 to £95.

p.853, *annotation to the Social Security (Incapacity for Work) (General) Regulations 1995, reg.17 (the current categories of exempt work)*

2.040   Note that the earnings limit of £93 was raised to £95 from October 1, 2010. See the update to pp.850–851.

pp.865–869, *annotation to the Social Security (Incapacity for Work) (General) Regulations 1995, reg.24: "dealing with the evidence, in particular with differing medical opinions and reports"*

In *PC v SSWP (ESA)* [2010] UKUT 340 (AAC), Judge Mark   2.041
thought that *CIB/908/2003* "is plainly and obviously correct" (para.15).

In *JM v SSWP (IB)* [2010] UKUT 386 (AAC), Judge Lane noted that although a tribunal had the power to exclude otherwise admissible evidence if its admission would be "unfair" (see r.15(2) of the Tribunal Procedure (First-tier Tribunal) (Social Entitlement Chamber) Rules 2008), it would be extremely unusual to do so in the case of a the report of a PCA examination criticised by the claimant as inadequate:

"Approached from both the general principle of civil evidence that relevant evidence is admissible (unless obtained in breach of legal privilege) and from the overriding objective, it is difficult to see how a PCA report could be excluded as unfair except in the most unusual of circumstances. The report is patently relevant to the proceedings. It goes to the central issue of the claimant continuing incapacity for work. The evidence is obtained lawfully and a claimant must participate in the examination if he wishes payment of benefit to continue. Re-examining a claimant at a later date will not necessarily give the tribunal an accurate view of the appellant's condition at the relevant date (the date of the Secretary of State's original decision). The tribunal has the expertise to judge the value of the report. In the instant appeal, the report also agreed in its main respects with the appellant's own assessment.

At the end of the day, the justification offered by the appellant amounts to little more than a sense of humiliation from a standard test that he did not understand. This is plainly not enough to raise an issue of exclusion of the report as a whole, let alone of the hearing test, which accepted the appellant's impairment." (paras 18, 19).

But where, as usual, the report is admitted, questions raised about the adequacy of the report and the examination are relevant to the *weight* that the tribunal should accord to the report (para.20).

p.881, *annotation to the Social Security (Incapacity for Work) (General) Regulations 1995, reg.27*

Charlton v Secretary of State for Work and Pensions [2009] EWCA Civ   2.042
42 is reported as *R(IB)2/09.*

p.883, *annotation to the Social Security (Incapacity for Work) (General) Regulations 1995, reg.27, paras (2)(a) and (c): "medical evidence"*

Note that from June 28, 2010, medical evidence can come from any   2.043
"health care professional" as defined in reg.2. See further update to p.824, above.

p.887, *annotation to the Social Security (Incapacity for Work) (General) Regulations 1995, reg.28*

2.044   In *PC v SSWP (ESA)* [2010] UKUT 340 (AAC), Judge Mark thought that *CIB/908/2003* "is plainly and obviously correct" (para.15).

pp.910–911, *annotation to the Social Security (Incapacity for Work) (General) Regulations 1995, Sch. "[C] Making and recording decisions"*

2.045   Where a tribunal has heard oral evidence from a claimant on the effect of his or her condition, it must ensure that, when considering the report of the HCP, it makes clear what it makes of the claimant's evidence, whether that agrees or disagrees with findings in the HCP report (*YD v SSWP (IB)* [2010] UKUT 290 (AAC), para.12). In that case, Judge Turnbull also said that where the claimant has given oral evidence, a tribunal will not necessarily then have to deal with each of the mental health descriptors at issue, "although it may often be desirable to do so" (para.13).

pp.981–1287, *modification of the Employment and Support Allowance Regulations 2008*

2.046   Note that for the purpose of making "conversion decisions" under the "Migration Regulations", from October 1, 2010, any reference in the ESA Regulations to a "claimant" is to be read as referring to a "notified person" under those "Migration Regulations". See reg.6(1) of and Sch.1, para.7 to those Regulations: the Employment and Support Allowance (Transitional Provisions, Housing Benefit and Council Tax Benefit) (Existing Awards) (No.2) Regulations 2010 (SI 2010/1907) (as amended) set out in the "New Legislation" section of this Supplement.

p.995, *amendment to the Employment and Support Allowance Regulations 2008, reg.2(1) (Interpretation: definition of "independent hospital")*

2.047   With effect from September 1, 2010, arts 2 and 25 of the Health and Social Care Act 2008 (Miscellaneous Consequential Amendments) Order 2010 (SI 2010/1881) amended reg.2(1) by substituting the following for the definition of "independent hospital":

   ""independent hospital"—
   > (a) in England, means a hospital as defined by section 275 of the National Health Service Act 2006 that is not a health service hospital as defined by that section;
   > (b) in Wales, has the meaning assigned to it by section 2 of the Care Standards Act 2000; and
   > (c) in Scotland, means an independent healthcare service as defined in section 2(5)(a) and (b) of the Regulation of Care (Scotland) Act 2001;"

p.997, *amendment to the Employment and Support Allowance Regulations 2008, reg.2(1) (Interpretation: definition of "medical examination centre")*

With effect from June 29, 2010, reg.9(1) and (2) of the Social Security 2.048 (Miscellaneous Amendments) (No.3) Regulations 2010 (SI 2010/840) amended reg.2(1) by revoking the definition of "medical examination ccntre".

p.998, *amendment to the Employment and Support Allowance Regulations 2008, reg.2(1) (Interpretation: definition of "period of limited capability for work")*

With effect from June 29, 2010, reg.9(1) and (2) of the Social Security 2.049 (Miscellaneous Amendments) (No.3) Regulations 2010 (SI 2010/840) amended the definition of "period of limited capability for work" to read as follows:

> ""period of limited capability for work" means [except in paragraph (5), a period throughout which a person has, or is treated as having, limited capability for work, and does not include a period which is outside the prescribed time for claiming as specified in regulation 19 of the Social Security (Claims and Payments) Regulations 1987];"

p.1001, *amendment to the Employment and Support Allowance Regulations 2008, reg.2(1) (Interpretation: definition of "training allowance")*

With effect from September 1, 2010, arts 28(1) and (2) of the Appren- 2.050 ticeships, Skills, Children and Learning Act 2009 (Consequential Amendments to Subordinate Legislation) (England) Order 2010 (SI 2010/1941) amended the definition of "training allowance" in reg.2(1) by substituting the words:

> "Young People's Learning Agency for England, the Chief Executive of Skills Funding"

for the words, "Learning and Skills Council for England".

p.1003, *amendment to the Employment and Support Allowance Regulations 2008, reg.2 (Interpretation: definition of "period of limited capability for work")*

With effect from June 29, 2010, reg.9(1) and (2) of the Social Security 2.051 (Miscellaneous Amendments) (No.3) Regulations 2010 (SI 2010/840) amended reg.2 by inserting a new paragraph (5) as follows:

> "(5) For the purposes of paragraph 4 of Schedule 1 to the Act (condition relating to youth) "period of limited capability for work" means a period throughout which a person has, or is treated as having, limited capability for work."

pp.1004–1017, *modification of the Employment and Support Allowance Regulations 2008, Pt 2 (the Assessment Phase) and Pt 3 (conditions of entitlement—contributory allowance)*

2.052   Note that for the purpose of making "conversion decisions" under the "Migration Regulations" from October 1, 2010, Pts 2 and 3 do not apply. See reg.6(1) of and Sch.1, paras 8 and 9 to those Regulations: the Employment and Support Allowance (Transitional Provisions, Housing Benefit and Council Tax Benefit) (Existing Awards) (No.2) Regulations 2010 (SI 2010/1907) (as amended) set out in the "New Legislation" section of this Supplement.

p.1004, *amendment to the Employment and Support Allowance Regulations 2008, reg.4(1) (end of the assessment phase)*

2.053   With effect from June 28, 2010, reg.9(3) of the Social Security (Miscellaneous Amendments) (No.3) Regulations 2010 (SI 2010/840) amended para.(1) by substituting "regulation 5" for "regulations 5 and 6".

pp.1005–1006, *amendments to the Employment and Support Allowance Regulations 2008, reg.5 (the assessment phase—previous claimants)*

2.054   With effect from June 28, 2010, reg.9(4)(a) of the Social Security (Miscellaneous Amendments) (No.3) Regulations 2010 (SI 2010/840) amended para.(1)(b) by replacing "regulation 6" with "and (4)".
         From the same date, reg.9(4)(b)–(g) amended para.(2) to read:

"(2) The circumstances are that—
    (a)
        (i) the claimant's current period of limited capability for work is to be treated as a continuation of an earlier period of limited capability for work under regulation 145(1) or (2);
        (ii) the claimant was entitled to an employment and support allowance in the earlier period of limited capability for work; [. . .]
        (iii) the assessment phase had not ended in the previous period for which the claimant was entitled to an employment and support allowance; [and]
        [(iv) the period for which the claimant was previously entitled was no more than 13 weeks; or]
    (b)
        (i) paragraph (3) or (5) of regulation 145 applies to the claimant; [. . .]
        (ii) the assessment phase had not ended in the previous period for which the claimant was entitled to an employment and support allowance; [and]
        (iii) the period for which the claimant was previously entitled was no more than 13 weeks."

From the same date, reg.9(4)(h) inserted after para.(3) a new para.(4) as follows:

"(4) Where a person has made and is pursuing an appeal against a decision of the Secretary of State that embodies a determination that the claimant does not have limited capability for work—
  (a) paragraph (3) does not apply; and
  (b) paragraph (1) does not apply to any period of limited capability for work to which regulation 147A(2) applies until a determination of limited capability for work has been made following the determination of the appeal by the First-tier Tribunal."

p.1006, *amendment to the Employment and Support Allowance Regulations 2008: omission of reg.6 (the assessment phase—claimants appealing against a decision)*

With effect from June 28, 2010, reg.9(5) of the Social Security (Miscellaneous Amendments) (No.3) Regulations 2010 (SI 2010/840) provided that reg.6 was to be omitted.   2.055

p.1007, *amendments to the Employment and Support Allowance Regulations 2008, reg.7 (circumstances where the condition that the assessment phase has ended before entitlement to the support component or the work-related activity component arises does not apply)*

With effect from June 28, 2010, reg.9(6)(a) of the Social Security (Miscellaneous Amendments) (No.3) Regulations 2010 (SI 2010/840) amended para.(1)(b)(iii) by adding after "allowance" the phrase "or that period was more than 13 weeks".   2.056
From the same date, reg.9(6)(b) amended para.(2) to read:

"(2) Paragraph (1)(b) does not apply to [any period of limited capability for work to which regulation 147A(2) applies until the determination of limited capability for work has been made following the determination of the appeal by the First-tier Tribunal]."

p.1008, *amendment to the Employment and Support Allowance Regulations 2008: insertion of new reg.7A*

With effect from November 1, 2010, reg.3(1) of the Social Security (Contribution Conditions for Jobseeker's Allowance and Employment and Support Allowance) Regulations 2010 (SI 2010/2446) inserted a new reg.7A at the beginning of Pt 3 (after the heading "CONDITIONS OF ENTITLEMENT—CONTRIBUTORY ALLOWANCE") to read: 2.057

"Conditions relating to national insurance and relevant earnings

7A.—(1) A claimant's relevant earnings for the purposes of paragraph 1(2)(a) of Schedule 1 to the Act (employment and support allowance: conditions relating to national insurance) are the total amount of the claimant's earnings at the lower earnings limit for the base tax year.

(2) For the purposes of paragraph (1), earnings which exceed the lower earnings limit are to be disregarded."

As noted in the General Note to that section in the "New Legislation" section of this Supplement and the updates to pp.428 and 430–431 above, the changes effected by s.13 of the Welfare Reform Act 2009 and this regulation made in consequence significantly tighten the contribution conditions for CESA. Together they mean that the requisite level of "relevant earnings" in the tax year relied on for the first contribution condition is now 26 times that year's lower earnings limit, rather than 25. This new regulation defines "relevant earnings" to cover only earnings at that lower earnings limit, so that new claimants will have to have worked for at least 26 weeks in one of the last two tax years (April 6 to April 5) complete before the start of the benefit year (beginning in early January) which includes the first day of claim in the relevant period of limited capability for work

p.1008, *amendment to the Employment and Support Allowance Regulations 2008, reg.8(1)(b) (relaxation of the first contribution condition)*

2.058   With effect from November 1, 2010, reg.3(2) of the the Social Security (Contribution Conditions for Jobseeker's Allowance and Employment and Support Allowance) Regulations 2010 (SI 2010/2446) substituted a new para.(1)(b) to read:

"(b) the claimant has—
   (i) earnings at the lower earnings limit in that tax year on which primary Class 1 contributions have been paid or treated as paid which in total, and disregarding any earnings which exceed the lower earnings limit for that year, are not less than that limit multiplied by 26; or
   (ii) earnings factors in that tax year derived from Class 2 contributions multiplied by 26."

pp.1009–1010, *annotation to the Employment and Support Allowance Regulations 2008, reg.8(1)(b) (relaxation of the first contribution condition)*

2.059   As noted in the General Note to that section in the "New Legislation" section of this Supplement and in the updates to pp.428 and 430–431 above, the changes effected by s.13 of the Welfare Reform Act 2009 and regulations made in consequence significantly tighten the contribution conditions for CESA, so that the requisite level of "relevant earnings" in the tax year, or the earnings factor from Class 2 contributions, relied on for the first contribution condition is now 26 times that year's lower earnings limit, rather than 25. New reg.7A (see the first update to p.1008, above) defines "relevant earnings" to cover only earnings at that lower earnings limit, so that new claimants will have to have worked for at least 26 weeks in one of the last two tax years (April 6 to April 5) complete before the start of the benefit year (beginning in early January) which includes the first day of claim in the relevant period of limited capability for work. Regulation 8 affords the claimants covered by it the concession that the first contribution condition can be met in any year rather than one of the two (previously three) tax years complete before the start of the benefit year which includes the first day of claim in the relevant period of limited capability for work. The amendment to para.(1)(b) (see second update to p.1008, above) achieves parity in terms of the requisite level of "relevant earnings" on which Class 1 contributions have been paid, or the earnings factor from Class 2 contributions made (each weekly one generating an earnings factor equivalent to that year's LEL), or a combination of the two, at 26 times the lower earnings limit for the tax year relied on.

p.1016, *amendment to the Employment and Support Allowance Regulations 2008: substitution of reg.13 (modification of the relevant benefit year)*

With effect from June 28, 2010, reg.9(7) of the Social Security (Miscellaneous Amendments) (No.3) Regulations 2010 (SI 2010/840) substituted reg.13 to read as follows: **2.060**

"Modification of the relevant benefit year

13.—(1) Where paragraph (2) applies, sub-paragraph (1)(f) of paragraph 3 of Schedule 1 to the Act has effect as if "relevant benefit year" is any benefit year which includes all or part of the period of limited capability for work which includes the relevant benefit week.

(2) This paragraph applies where a claimant has made a claim to employment and support allowance but does not satisfy—
(a) the first contribution condition;
(b) the second contribution condition; or
(c) both contribution conditions,
but would satisfy those conditions if the modified definition of "relevant benefit year" provided in paragraph (1) applied."

The previous version of reg.13 allowed for the modification of the normal rules around establishing the benefit year and relevant tax years for the purpose of meeting the contributory requirements of ESA. This is to help those who fail the contribution conditions when first making a claim, who may have paid significant contributions immediately before falling ill, and so would be able to re-claim and be successful in a later benefit year. But it only did so if was a break in the period of limited capability for work, by providing that the linking rules in reg.145 were to be disregarded. This was not likely often to occur. The substituted version removes the requirement for a break in the period of limited capability for work, and allows decision-makers and tribunals to look to any benefit year in which there occurs all or part of the period of limited capability for work of which the relevant week of claim is part.

p.1017, *amendment to the Employment and Support Allowance Regulations 2008, reg.14 (Meaning of education)*

2.061   With effect from September 1, 2010, art.28(3)(a) of the Apprentice-ships, Skills, Children and Learning Act 2009 (Consequential Amendments to Subordinate Legislation) (England) Order 2010 (SI 2010/1941) substituted the following heads for head (i) in reg.14(2)(a):

"(i) the Young People's Learning Agency for England;
(ia) the Chief Executive of Skills Funding;".

From the same date, art.28(3)(b) of the same Order substituted the words "Young People's Learning Agency for England, the Chief Executive of Skills Funding" for the words "Learning and Skills Council for England" in reg.14(2)(c) (except para.(2)(c)(i)).

From the same date, art.28(3)(c) of the same Order substituted the following head for head (i) in reg.14(2)(c):

"(i) in the case of a course funded by the Young People's Learning Agency for England or the Chief Executive of Skills Funding, in the student's learning agreement signed on behalf of the establishment which is funded by either of those bodies for the delivery of that course;".

p.1039, *modification of the Employment and Support Allowance Regulations 2008, reg.30*

2.062   Note that for the purpose of making "conversion decisions" under the "Migration Regulations", from October 1, 2010, reg.30 does not apply. See reg.6(1) of and Sch.1, para.10 to those Regulations: the Employment and Support Allowance (Transitional Provisions, Housing Benefit and Council Tax Benefit) (Existing Awards) (No.2) Regulations 2010 (SI 2010/1907) (as amended) set out in the "New Legislation" section of this Supplement.

p.1039, *amendment to the Employment and Support Allowance Regulations 2008, reg.30(2)*

2.063   With effect from June 28, 2010, reg.9(8) of the Social Security (Miscellaneous Amendments) (No.3) Regulations 2010 (SI 2010/840) amended para.(2) by adding "; or" at the end of para.(2)(b) and inserting a new para.(2)(c) to read:

"(c) that it has not, within the 6 months preceding the date of claim, been determined, in relation to the claimant's entitlement to any benefit, allowance or advantage, which is dependent upon the claimant being incapable of work, that the claimant is capable of work, or is to be treated as capable of work under regulation 7 or 8 of the Social Security (Incapacity for Work) (General) Regulations 1995 ("the 1995 Regulations"), unless—

(i) the claimant is suffering from some specific disease or bodily or mental disablement from which the claimant was not suffering at the time of that determination,

(ii) a disease or bodily or mental disablement from which the claimant was suffering at the time of that determination has significantly worsened, or

(iii) in the case of a claimant who was treated as capable of work under regulation 7 of the 1995 Regulations (failure to provide information), the claimant has since provided the information requested by the Secretary of State under that regulation."

This amendment prevents a claim for ESA, and consequential payment of the assessment phase rate of that benefit, where there has been a recent disallowance of IB, IS or SDA following a personal capability assessment, unless there is clear evidence of deterioration in a person's medical condition or where a new condition applies (para.(2)(c)(i), (ii)). An ESA payment can also be made where the disallowance related to the failure to provide a personal capability assessment questionnaire, but that has since been provided (para.(2)(c)(iii)). The amendment applies where the disallowance occurred in the six months before the ESA claim. It is the same as the policy that applies where ESA is claimed following a disallowance of benefit as a result of a work capability assessment or failure to supply requisite information (para.(2)(b)). It also reflects the policy that applied to Incapacity Benefit (IFW Regulations, reg.28).

p.1041, *revocation of the Employment and Support Allowance Regulations 2008, reg.31 (claimant who claims jobseeker's allowance to be treated as not having limited capability for work)*

Regulation 31 was revoked with effect from October 1, 2010 by reg.25(1) of the Employment and Support Allowance (Transitional Provisions, Housing Benefit and Council Tax Benefit) (Existing Awards) (No.2) Regulations 2010 (SI 2010/1907).   2.064

p.1042, *amendment to the Employment and Support Allowance Regulations 2008: insertion of new reg.32A*

With effect from June 28, 2010, reg.9(9) of the Social Security (Miscellaneous Amendments) (No.3) Regulations 2010 (SI 2010/840) inserted a new reg.32A reading as follows: 2.065

"Claimants to be treated as not having limited capability for work at the end of the period covered by medical evidence

32A. Where the Secretary of State is satisfied that it is appropriate in the circumstances of the case then a claimant may be treated as not having limited capability for work if—

(a) the claimant has supplied medical evidence in accordance with regulation 30(2)(a);

(b) the period for which medical evidence was supplied has ended;

(c) the Secretary of State has requested further medical evidence; and

(d) the claimant has not, before whichever is the later of either the end of the period of 6 weeks beginning with the date of the Secretary of State's request or the end of 6 weeks beginning with the day after the end of the period for which medical evidence was supplied—

(i) supplied further medical evidence, or

(ii) otherwise made contact with the Secretary of State to indicate that they wish to have the question of limited capability for work determined."

p.1058, *amendment to the Employment and Support Allowance Regulations 2008, reg.45 (exempt work)*

2.066　　With effect from June 28, 2010, reg.9(10)(a) of the Social Security (Miscellaneous Amendments) (No.3) Regulations 2010 (SI 2010/840) amended para.(3)(b) to read:

"(b) is supervised by a person employed by a public or local authority or [a] voluntary organisation [or community interest company] engaged in the provision or procurement of work for persons who have disabilities."

From the same date, reg.9(10)(b) of those Regulations substituted a new para.(4)(a) reading as follows:

"(a) is done during a period of specified work, provided that—

(i) the claimant has not previously done specified work,

(ii) since the beginning of the last period of specified work, the claimant has ceased to be entitled to a relevant benefit for a continuous period exceeding 12 weeks, or

(iii) not less than 52 weeks have elapsed since the last period of specified work; or".

Regulation 9(10)(c) also added from the same date a new para.(4)(c):

"(c) for the purposes of this regulation, a period of specified work begins on the first day on which any specified work is undertaken and continues for a period of 52 weeks, whether or not any further specified work is undertaken during that period."

With effect from October 1, 2010, reg.5(2) of the Social Security (Miscellaneous Amendments) (No.4) Regulations 2010 (SI 2010/2126) increased the earnings limit in paras (3) and (4) from £93 to £95.

p.1061, *annotation to the Employment and Support Allowance Regulations 2008, reg.45 (the current categories of exempt work)*

2.067　　Note that the earnings limit of £93 was raised to £95 from October 1, 2010. See the update to p.1058.

pp.1062–1067, *Employment and Support Allowance Regulations 2008, Pt 8 (Conditionality) Chapter 1 (work-focused health-related assessment)*

Note that on June 24, 2010, in a letter to the JCP customer repre-   **2.068** sentative group, the DWP announced the suspension of the work-focused health-related assessment for a period of two years from July 19, 2010. It noted that ongoing external evaluation had shown mixed results for the assessment. Its two-year suspension affords an opportunity for DWP reconsideration of the assessment's purpose and delivery, as well as freeing up capacity to deal with the demands of re-assessing existing incapacity benefits customers as part of the process of migration to ESA or—for those who fail the limited capability for work assessment—denial of ESA, cancellation of the existing award of an incapacity benefit and effective transfer either to JSA or (if qualifying in another category than "incapable of work") to IS. See further the Migration Regulations and the General Note to them in the "New Legislation" section of this Supplement.

p.1064, *amendment to the Employment and Support Allowance Regulations 2008, reg.49 (notification of assessment)*

With effect from June 28, 2010, reg.9(11) of the Social Security   **2.069** (Miscellaneous Amendments) (No.3) Regulations 2010 (SI 2010/840) added a new para.(3) to reg.49:

"(3) A claimant may be required to take part in a work-focused health-related assessment either by attendance in person or by telephone."

p.1065, *amendment to the Employment and Support Regulations 2008: omission of reg.50 (determination of the place of the work-focused health-related assessment)*

With effect from June 28, 2010, reg.9(12) of the Social Security   **2.070** (Miscellaneous Amendments) (No.3) Regulations 2010 (SI 2010/840) stipulated that reg.50 was to be omitted.

p.1067, *amendment to the Employment and Support Regulations 2008, reg.53 (failure to take part in a work-focused health-related assessment)*

With effect from June 28, 2010, reg.9(13) of the Social Security   **2.071** (Miscellaneous Amendments) (No.3) Regulations 2010 (SI 2010/840) amended para.(3) to read:

"(3) In determining whether a claimant has shown good cause for the failure to participate in a work-focused health-related assessment, the Secretary of State must take the following matters into account—
  (a) whether the claimant was outside Great Britain at the time of the notification;

[(b) that the physical or mental health or condition of the claimant made it impracticable for the claimant to take part in a work-focused health-related assessment;]

(c) the nature of any disability which the claimant has; [. . .]

[(ca) that the claimant had caring responsibilities in relation to a child and childcare was not reasonably available or was unsuitable due to the particular needs of the claimant or the child; and]

(d) any other matter which the Secretary of State considers appropriate."

p.1072, *amendment to the Employment and Support Regulations 2008, reg.61 (failure to take part in a work-focused interview)*

2.072   With effect from June 28, 2010, reg.9(14) of the Social Security (Miscellaneous Amendments) (No.3) Regulations 2010 (SI 2010/840) substituted para.(3)(i) to read:

"(i) that the physical or mental health or condition of the claimant made it impracticable for the claimant to attend at the time and place fixed for the interview;".

From the same date, it inserted after para.(3)(j) a new sub-para.(ja) to read:

"(ja) that the claimant had caring responsibilities in relation to a child and child care was not reasonably available or was unsuitable due to the particular needs of the claimant or the child; and".

p.1077, *modification of the Employment and Support Allowance Regulations 2008, reg.67 (Prescribed amounts)*

2.073   Note that for the purpose of making "conversion decisions" under the "Migration Regulations", from October 1, 2010, reg.67 is modified. See reg.16(1) of and Sch.2, para.12 to those Regulations: the Employment and Support Allowance (Transitional Provisions, Housing Benefit and Council Tax Benefit) (Existing Awards) (No.2) Regulations 2010 (SI 2010/1907) (as amended) set out in the "New Legislation" section of this Supplement.

p.1079, *modification of the Employment and Support Allowance Regulations 2008, reg.68 (Polygamous marriages)*

2.074   Note that for the purpose of making "conversion decisions" under the "Migration Regulations", from October 1, 2010, reg.68 is modified. See reg.16(1) of and Sch.2, para.13 to those Regulations: the Employment and Support Allowance (Transitional Provisions, Housing Benefit and Council Tax Benefit) (Existing Awards) (No.2) Regulations 2010 (SI 2010/1907) (as amended) set out in the "New Legislation" section of this Supplement.

p.1086, *modification of the Employment and Support Allowance Regulations 2008, reg.75 (Payments not to be treated as payments to which section 3 applies)*

Note that for the purpose of making "conversion decisions" under the 2.075 "Migration Regulations", from October 1, 2010, reg.75 is modified. See reg.16(1) of and Sch.2, para.14 to those Regulations: the Employment and Support Allowance (Transitional Provisions, Housing Benefit and Council Tax Benefit) (Existing Awards) (No.2) Regulations 2010 (SI 2010/1907) (as amended) set out in the "New Legislation" section of this Supplement.

pp.1086–1087, *amendment to the Employment and Support Allowance Regulations 2008, reg.76*

With effect from October 1, 2010, reg.5(3) of the Social Security 2.076 (Miscellaneous Amendments) (No.4) Regulations 2010 (SI 2010/2126) increased the limit from £93 to £95. The annotation should be amended accordingly.

p.1114, *amendment to the Employment and Support Allowance Regulations 2008, reg.106 (Notional income—deprivation and income on application)*

With effect from November 1, 2010, reg.11(2) of the Social Security 2.077 (Miscellaneous Amendments) (No.5) Regulations 2010 (SI 2010/2429) inserted the following new sub-paragraph after sub-para.(ga) in reg.106(2):

"(gb) any sum to which regulation 137(4A) (treatment of student loans) applies;".

p.1115, *annotation to the Employment and Support Allowance Regulations 2008, reg.106*

See the note to reg.137, update to p.1148, below. 2.078

p.1137, *amendment to the Employment and Support Allowance Regulations 2008, reg.131(1) (Interpretation), definition of "access funds"*

With effect from September 1, 2010, art.28(4)(a) of the Apprentice- 2.079 ships, Skills, Children and Learning Act 2009 (Consequential Amendments to Subordinate Legislation) (England) Order 2010 (SI 2010/1941) substituted the words "Young People's Learning Agency for England under sections 61 and 62 of the Apprenticeships, Skills, Children and Learning Act 2009 or the Chief Executive of Skills Funding under sections 100 and 101 of that Act" for the words "Learning and Skills Council for England under sections 5, 6 and 9 of the Learning and Skills Act 2000" in para.(d) of the definition of "access funds".

p.1138, *amendment to the Employment and Support Allowance Regulations 2008, reg.131(1) (Interpretation), definition of "education authority"*

2.080 With effect from May 5, 2010, art.5 of and para.81 of Sch.3 to the Local Education Authorities and Children's Services Authorities (Integration of Functions) (Local and Subordinate Legislation) Order 2010 (SI 2010/1172) substituted the words "a local authority as defined in section 579 of the Education Act 1996 (interpretation)" for the words "a local education authority as defined in section 212 of the Education Act 2002 (interpretation)" in the definition of "education authority" in reg.131(1).

p.1138, *amendment to the Employment and Support Allowance Regulations 2008, reg.131(1) (Interpretation), definition of "full-time course of advanced education"*

2.081 With effect from September 1, 2010, art.28(4)(b)(i) of the Apprenticeships, Skills, Children and Learning Act 2009 (Consequential Amendments to Subordinate Legislation) (England) Order 2010 (SI 2010/1941) substituted the words "Young People's Learning Agency for England, the Chief Executive of Skills Funding" for the words "Learning and Skills Council for England" in paras (a) and (b) (except para.(b)(i)) in the definition of "full-time course of advanced education".

From the same date, art.28(4)(b)(ii) of the same Order substituted the following sub-paragraph for sub-para.(i) in para.(b):

"(i) in the case of a course funded by the Young People's Learning Agency for England or the Chief Executive of Skills Funding, in the student's learning agreement signed on behalf of the establishment which is funded by either of those bodies for the delivery of that course; or".

p.1139, *amendment to the Employment and Support Allowance Regulations 2008, reg.131(1) (Interpretation), definition of "full-time course of study"*

2.082 With effect from September 1, 2010, art.28(4)(c)(i) of the Apprenticeships, Skills, Children and Learning Act 2009 (Consequential Amendments to Subordinate Legislation) (England) Order 2010 (SI 2010/1941) substituted the words "Young People's Learning Agency for England, the Chief Executive of Skills Funding" for the words "Learning and Skills Council for England" in paras (a) and (b) (except para.(b)(i)) in the definition of "full-time course of study".

From the same date, art.28(4)(c)(ii) of the same Order substituted the following sub-paragraph for sub-para.(i) in para.(b):

"(i) in the case of a course funded by the Young People's Learning Agency for England or the Chief Executive of Skills Funding, in the student's learning agreement signed on behalf of the establishment which is funded by either of those bodies for the delivery of that course; or".

p.1148, *amendment to the Employment and Support Allowance Regulations 2008, reg.137 (Treatment of student loans)*

With effect from November 1, 2010, reg.11(3)(a) of the Social Secu-   2.083
rity (Miscellaneous Amendments) (No.5) Regulations 2010 (SI
2010/2429) inserted the words "subject to paragraph (4A)" before the
words "the student" in reg.137(4)(b).

From the same date, reg.11(3)(b) of the same amending regulations
inserted the following new paragraph after para.(4):

> "(4A) A student is not to be treated as possessing any part of a student
> loan which has not been paid to that student in respect of an academic
> year where the educational institution at which the student was attend-
> ing a course has confirmed in writing that the student has suspended
> attendance at the course due to a health condition or disability that
> renders the student incapable of continuing that course.".

p.1148, *annotation to the Employment and Support Allowance Regulations 2008, reg.137*

The effect of the new reg.137(4A) is that a student whose university/   2.084
college has confirmed in writing that he or she "has suspended attendance at the course due to a health condition or disability that renders
[him or her] incapable of continuing that course" will not be treated as
possessing any part of a student loan that has not been paid to him or
her. Nor will it count as notional income (see the new reg.106(2)(gb),
above).

pp.1151–1152, *modification of the Employment and Support Allowance Regulations 2008, reg.144 (waiting days)*

Note that for the purpose of making "conversion decisions" under the   2.085
"Migration Regulations", from October 1, 2010, reg.144 does not apply.
See reg.6(1) of and Sch.1, para.10 to those Regulations: the Employment and Support Allowance (Transitional Provisions, Housing Benefit
and Council Tax Benefit) (Existing Awards) (No.2) Regulations 2010
(SI 2010/1907) (as amended) set out in the "New Legislation" section of
this Supplement.

p.1155, *amendment to the Employment and Support Allowance Regulations 2008, reg.147A (Claimants appealing a decision)*

With effect from June 28, 2010, reg.9(15) of the Social Security   2.086
(Miscellaneous Amendments) (No.3) Regulations 2010 (SI 2010/840)
inserted the following new regulation after reg.147:

"Claimants appealing a decision

147A.—(1) This regulation applies where a claimant has made and
is pursuing an appeal against a decision of the Secretary of State that

embodies a determination that the claimant does not have limited capability for work.

(2) Subject to paragraph (3), where this regulation applies, a determination of limited capability for work by the Secretary of State under regulation 19 shall not be made until the appeal is determined by the First-tier Tribunal.

(3) Paragraph (2) does not apply where either—

(a) the claimant suffers from some specific disease or bodily or mental disablement from which the claimant was not suffering when entitlement began; or

(b) a disease or bodily or mental disablement from which the claimant was suffering at that date has significantly worsened.

(4) Where this regulation applies and the Secretary of State makes a determination—

(a) in a case to which paragraph (3) applies (including where the determination is not the first such determination) that the claimant does not have or, by virtue of regulation 22 or 23, is to be treated as not having limited capability for work; or

(b) subsequent to a determination that the claimant is to be treated as having limited capability for work by virtue of a provision of these Regulations other than regulation 30, that the claimant is no longer to be so treated,

this regulation and regulation 30 apply as if that determination had not been made.

(5) Where this regulation applies and—

(a) the claimant is entitled to an employment and support allowance by virtue of being treated as having limited capability for work in accordance with regulation 30;

(b) neither of the circumstances in paragraph (3) applies, or, subsequent to the application of either of those circumstances, the claimant has been determined not to have limited capability for work; and

(c) the claimant's appeal is dismissed, withdrawn or struck out,

the claimant is to be treated as not having limited capability for work with effect from the beginning of the first day of the benefit week following the date on which the Secretary of State was notified by the First-tier Tribunal that the appeal is dismissed, withdrawn or struck out.

(6) Where a claimant's appeal is successful, subject to paragraph (7), any finding of fact or other determination embodied in or necessary to the decision of the First-tier Tribunal or on which the First-tier Tribunal's decision is based shall be conclusive for the purposes of the decision of the Secretary of State, in relation to an award made in a case to which this regulation applies, as to whether the claimant has limited capability for work or limited capability for work-related activity.

(7) Paragraph (6) does not apply where, due to a change of circumstances after entitlement to which this regulation applies began, the Secretary of State is satisfied that it is no longer appropriate to rely on such finding or determination."

p.1155, *modification of the Employment and Support Allowance Regulations 2008, reg.147A*

Note that from October 1, 2010, where a person has made and is   2.087
pursuing an appeal against a "conversion decision" under the "Migration Regulations", that embodies a determination that the person does
not have limited capability for work, reg.147A is to be read as if there
were substituted the text set out in Sch.2, para.15 to those Regulations:
see reg.16 of and Sch.2, para.15 to the Employment and Support
Allowance (Transitional Provisions, Housing Benefit and Council Tax
Benefit) (Existing Awards) (No.2) Regulations 2010 (SI 2010/1907) (as
amended) set out in the "New Legislation" section of this Supplement.
  From October 1 to October 31, 2010, the modification of reg.147A
made by reg.16 and Sch.2, para.15 did not include para.(1A).

p.1155, *annotation to the Employment and Support Allowance Regulations 2008, reg.147A*

Before June 28, 2010, reg.6 provided that where a claimant appealed   2.088
against a decision that he or she did not have limited capability for work
the assessment phase ended only when the appeal was determined by a
tribunal. In addition, reg.3(j) of the Social Security (Claims and Payments) Regulations 1987 (see Vol.III in this series) provided that a claim
was not required where a claimant had made and was pursuing an appeal
against such a decision. The intention was that once the claimant had
appealed, he or she would continue to be paid ESA at the assessment
rate pending the tribunal's decision on his or her appeal without the
claimant being required to make a further claim to ESA. This procedure,
however, raised a number of issues, for example, whether this prevented
retrospective payment of the relevant component in the case of a successful appeal. This is because under s.2(2)(a) and (3)(a) and s.4(4)(a) and
(5)(a) of the Welfare Reform Act 2007 one of the conditions of entitlement to the work-related activity/support component is that the assessment period has ended. It seems that in practice the DWP was paying the
appropriate component from the beginning of the 14th week after the
claimant's entitlement to ESA began if the appeal succeeded, under the
authority of ss.2(4)(b) and 4(6)(b) (see the advice given in paras 44644
and 44647 of Vol.8 of the *Decision Makers Guide*).
  With effect from June 28, 2010, however, reg.6 has been revoked and
replaced by reg.147A. Regulation 3(j) of the Claims and Payments
Regulations has also been amended (see below).
  Regulation 147A applies where a claimant has made and is pursuing
an appeal against a decision that he or she does not have limited capability for work (para.(1)). Paragraph (2) provides that the Secretary of
State will not make a determination of limited capability for work until
the appeal is decided by a tribunal. See also reg.30(3), which provides
that the condition in reg.30(2)(b)—that it has not been determined in

the previous six months that the claimant does not have limited capability for work or is to be treated as not having limited capability for work under regs 22 or 23—does not apply where the claimant is appealing against a decision that he or she does not have limited capability for work. Thus, provided that the claimant has submitted medical evidence in accordance with reg.30(2)(a), and so can be treated as having limited capability for work under reg.30(1) (and satisfies the other conditions of entitlement to ESA), the effect of reg.147A(2) is to allow an award of ESA (at the assessment rate) to be made. The claimant does not have to make a further claim for ESA because reg.3(j) of the Claims and Payments Regulations does not require a claim to be made where the claimant is appealing against a decision that he or she does not have limited capability for work. According to para.37 of DMG Memo 33/10 the award under reg.147A will normally begin on the day after the last day of entitlement under the award that is the subject of the appeal or the day the medical evidence begins, if later.

Paragraph (2) does not apply, however, if the claimant's condition significantly worsens or he or she develops a new condition. This exception is necessary because without it the Secretary of State would not be able to decide that the claimant has limited capability for work on the basis of the new/worsened condition pending the determination of the appeal. Note, however, that in the case of a new/worsened condition, if the Secretary of State determines that the claimant does not have, or is to be treated under reg.22 (failure to return the limited capability for work questionnaire) or reg.23 (failure to attend a medical examination) as not having, limited capability for work, or having determined that the claimant is to be treated as having limited capability for work (other than under reg.30) subsequently determines that he or she is no longer to be so treated, reg.147A and reg.30 will apply as if that determination had not been made (para.(4)).

Note that para.(2) only applies until the appeal is determined by a tribunal. It would not therefore seem to apply while a claimant pursues an appeal to the Upper Tribunal. As it is likely, however, that six months will have passed since the Secretary of State's decision on the claimant's original claim, reg.30(2)(b) will not prevent him or her being treated as having limited capability for work on a subsequent claim for ESA. Note that reg.30(2)(b) has not been amended following the introduction of reg.147A, so a decision under reg.147A is not a "treated as" decision within six months of which the claimant cannot be treated as having limited capability for work.

Under para.(5), where reg.147A applies and the claimant is receiving ESA under reg.30, and the claimant's appeal (in relation to his or her original/earlier claim) is then dismissed, withdrawn or struck out, the claimant will be treated as not having limited capability for work from the first day of the benefit week following the date on which the Secretary of State was notified by the tribunal of its decision. The purpose of this provision is to provide a mechanism to bring the decision awarding ESA pending the determination of the appeal to an end. Such a mechanism is needed because the tribunal's decision concerned the original decision that the claimant did not have limited capability for work and does not affect the decision to award ESA pending the outcome of the appeal. However, para.(5) will not apply if the claimant's condition has significantly worsened or he or she has developed a new condition (unless in such a case the Secretary of State has subsequently decided that the claimant does not have limited capability for work).

If the claimant's appeal is successful, subject to any change of circumstances that has occurred since the claimant was awarded ESA pending the determination of his or her appeal, any finding of fact or determination by the tribunal will be conclusive for the purposes of the Secretary of State's decision as to whether the claimant has limited capability for work or limited capability for work-related activity (paras (6) and (7)).

The result should therefore be that the claimant will be paid arrears of ESA, including the relevant component, from the beginning of the 14th week of his or her entitlement to ESA. It seems, however, that the DWP was not doing this where the claimant had claimed and been awarded JSA while the appeal was pending. This was apparently because of reg.31. Regulation 31 provided that a claimant who had claimed JSA and had a reasonable prospect of obtaining employment was to be treated as not having limited capability for work for the period of the JSA claim, even though it had been determined that he or she had (or was to treated under regs 20, 25, 26 or 29 as having) limited capability for work. The DWP stated that reg.31 would be revoked, and indeed this has happened (see reg.25(1) of the Employment and Support Allowance (Transitional Provisions, Housing Benefit and Council Tax Benefit) (Existing Awards) (No.2) Regulations 2010 (SI 2010/1907) which revokes reg.31 with effect from October 1, 2010). For an argument as to why full payment of arrears of ESA was possible even before the revocation of reg.31 (based on reg.3(5A) of the Decisions and Appeals Regulations) see *CPAG's Welfare Rights Bulletin 218 (October 2010)*.

In addition, note that reg.3(j) of the Claims and Payments Regulations was amended with effect from June 28, 2010, so that it now provides that a claim for ESA is not required where the claimant's appeal "relates to a decision to terminate or not to award a benefit *for which a claim was made*" (emphasis added). In other words, reg.3(j) does not apply where the appeal relates to a decision where a claim was not made because it was not required (under reg.3(j)). Without this amendment it would seem possible for ESA to remain in payment indefinitely on the basis of continuous appeals, supported by a medical certificate, each time a pending appeal award comes to an end.

See also the amendments to regs 5 and 7 in connection with the changes made by reg.147A.

Note the modified form of reg.147A where the claimant is appealing against a "conversion decision" under the "Migration Regulations" (see above).

p.1155, *amendment to the Employment and Support Regulations 2008, reg.148 (work or training beneficiaries)*

With effect from November 1, 2010, reg.21(2) of the Employment and Support Allowance (Transitional Provisions, Housing Benefit and 2.089

Council Tax Benefit) (Existing Awards) (No.2) Regulations 2010 (SI 2010/1907) amended para.(1) to read:

"(1) Subject to paragraph (2), a claimant is a "work or training beneficiary" on any day in a linking term where the claimant—
[(a) had limited capability for work—
　　(i) for more than 13 weeks in the most recent past period of limited capability for work; or
　　(ii) for 13 weeks or less in the most recent past period of limited capability for work where the claimant became entitled to an award of an employment and support allowance by virtue of a conversion decision which took effect from the commencement of the most recent past period of limited capability for work;]
(b) ceased to be entitled to an allowance or advantage at the end of that most recent past period of limited capability for work; and
[(c) became engaged in work or training within one month of so ceasing to be entitled.]"

From that same date, reg.21(3) of those amending regulations inserted into para.(3) after the definition of "allowance and advantage" a new definition reading:

""conversion decision" has the meaning given in regulation 5(2)(a) of the Employment and Support Allowance (Transitional Provisions, Housing Benefit and Council Tax Benefit) (Existing Awards) (No. 2) Regulations 2010;"

p.1156, *amendment to the Employment and Support Allowance Regulations 2008, reg.149 (linking rules—limited capability for work)*

2.090　　With effect from November 1, 2010, reg.22 of the Employment and Support Allowance (Transitional Provisions, Housing Benefit and Council Tax Benefit) (Existing Awards) (No.2) Regulations 2010 (SI 2010/1907) amended reg.149 to read:

"[(1) Where the circumstances in paragraph (2) apply, a work or training beneficiary is to be treated as having limited capability for work from the first day within the linking term in respect of which that beneficiary claims an employment and support allowance.]
(2) The circumstances are that—
(a) the work or training beneficiary provides evidence of limited capability for work in accordance with the Medical Evidence Regulations (which prescribe the form of the doctor's statement or other evidence required in each case); and
(b) [it had been determined that the work or training beneficiary had limited capability for work in the most recent past period of limited capability for work or where that determination was embodied in a conversion decision]—
　　(i) the claimant having been assessed in accordance with a limited capability for work assessment; or

82

(ii) as a result of the claimant being treated as having limited capability for work in accordance with regulation 20, 25, 26, 29 or 33(2) (persons to be treated as having limited capability for work)."

Note, however, that reg.22(4) of the amending Regulations provides that these changes:

"apply only in relation to the following cases—
(a) a claim for an employment and support allowance made on or after 1st November 2010, whether or not the claim is in respect of a period commencing before that date; and
(b) a claim for an advance award under regulation 13 of the Social Security (Claims and Payments) Regulations 1987—
    (i) made before 1st November 2010, and
    (ii) in respect of a period beginning on or after that date."

p.1157, *substitution of the Employment and Support Allowance Regulations 2008, reg.150 (linking rules—limited capability for work-related activity)*

With effect from November 1, 2010, reg.23(2) of the Employment and Support Allowance (Transitional Provisions, Housing Benefit and Council Tax Benefit) (Existing Awards) (No.2) Regulations 2010 (SI 2010/1907) substituted a new reg.150, reading as follows:

"Linking rules—limited capability for work-related activity

150. Where a work or training beneficiary was a member of the support group when the most recent past period of limited capability for work came to an end, that work or training beneficiary is to be treated as having limited capability for work-related activity from the first day within the linking term in respect of which that beneficiary claims an employment and support allowance."

Note, however, that reg.23(3) of the amending Regulations provides that this substitution will:

"apply only in relation to the following cases—
(a) a claim for an employment and support allowance made on or after 1st November 2010, whether or not the claim is in respect of a period commencing before that date; and
(b) a claim for an advance award under regulation 13 of the Social Security (Claims and Payments) Regulations 1987—
    (i) made before 1st November 2010, and
    (ii) in respect of a period beginning on or after that date."

p.1159, *amendment to the Employment and Support Allowance Regulations 2008, reg.154 (absence in order to receive NHS treatment)*

With effect from June 29, 2010, reg.9(1) and (16) of the Social Security (Miscellaneous Amendments) (No.3) Regulations 2010 (SI 2010/840) amended reg.154 by deleting paragraph (c) and the word "and" immediately preceding it.

2.091

2.092

p.1159, *amendment to the Employment and Support Allowance Regulations 2008, reg.155 (absence of member of family of member of Her Majesty's forces)*

2.093 With effect from June 29, 2010, reg.9(1) and (17) of the Social Security (Miscellaneous Amendments) (No.3) Regulations 2010 (SI 2010/840) amended reg.155 by deleting para.(b) and the word "and" immediately preceding it.

p.1163, *amendment to the Employment and Support Allowance Regulations 2008, reg.157(3)(a) (disqualification for misconduct etc.)*

2.094 With effect from April 1, 2010, reg.12(2) of the Social Security (Loss of Benefit) (Amendment) Regulations 2010 (SI 2010/1160), amended para.(3)(a) by inserting in the penultimate line ", or 6B" between "section" and "7".

pp.1188–1189, *annotation to the Employment and Support Regulations 2008, Sch.2: [A] Approaching the interpretation of the Schedule as a whole: Evidence and attention to detail*

2.095 Note that cases considered in the updates to pp.865–869, 887 and 910–911 are applicable equally here.

pp.1191–1192, *annotation to the Employment and Support Allowance Regulations 2008, Sch.2: "making and recording decisions"*

2.096 Where a tribunal has heard oral evidence from a claimant on the effect of his or her condition, it must ensure that, when considering the report of the HCP, it makes clear what it makes of the claimant's evidence, whether that agrees or disagrees with findings in the HCP report (*YD v SSWP (IB)* [2010] UKUT 290 (AAC), para.12). In that case, Judge Turnbull also said that where the claimant has given oral evidence, a tribunal will not necessarily then have to deal with each of the mental health descriptors at issue, "although it may often be desirable to do so" (para.13).

p.1193, *annotation to the Employment and Support Allowance Regulations 2008, Sch.2: Activity 6: manual dexterity: descriptors (e) "cannot physically use a conventional keyboard or mouse" and (f) "cannot do up/undo small buttons, such as shirt or blouse buttons"*

2.097 In *DW v SSWP (ESA)* [2010] UKUT 245 (AAC), Judge May considered a case where a claimant sometimes could physically use a keyboard using one hand, but was unable to do so using two, thus preventing him using "a shift key to form capital letters or for example the sign '@'" (para.3). Judge May thought that the proper approach to descriptor (e) was to follow a similar approach to that set out by the House of Lords in *Moyna* (reported as *R(DLA) 7/03*). He cited paras 18 and 19 in the Opinion of Lord Hoffman. The tribunal should "take a broad view and exercise a reasonable judgment as to whether the claimant satisfies the descriptor. There are no absolutes by which 'can' and 'cannot' can be defined" (para.5). The same approach was applicable to descriptor (f).

In *GS v SSWP (ESA)* [2010] UKUT 244 (AAC), Judge Jacobs considered that his functional and linguistic analysis of the PCA in *R(IB) 2/03*, para.7, was also the correct approach to the both the limited capability for work (Sch.2) and the limited capability for work-related activity (Sch.3) assessments for ESA. Both the claimant's representative and that of the SSWP agreed. In the case, the claimant had only one hand. Much of the focus at the tribunal concerned the claimant's ability to do up most of his shirt buttons with his one hand and his inability to deal with those on the cuff of that hand and also tight collar buttons. Judge Jacobs thought that:

> "the tribunal was wrong to consider the practicalities of dressing, the type of shirt and so on. Even the Secretary of State's representative, having submitted that a functional analysis was appropriate, was tempted into this type of speculation. It is important to appreciate the context. The ultimate purpose of the descriptors is to test a person's capability for work. They test the claimant's manual dexterity for work-related purposes. They do not test the claimant's ability to self-care. The reference to shirts and blouses is for the purpose of illustration. They are not words of definition or limitation.

> The proper approach to the interpretation and application of descriptor 6(f) is this. The descriptor tests the claimant's anatomical functions that would be involved in fastening or unfastening buttons. They include pinch grip, co-ordination of finger movements, and flexibility of the finger joints. The reference to small buttons identifies the size and shape of the object to which those functions are applied. The First-tier Tribunal should focus on the claimant's functional ability to perform the particular aspect of the activity covered by a descriptor. By doing that, it will avoid the myriad questions that otherwise appear to arise on descriptors. Is the ability to use a tap tested with wet or dry hands? What sort of surface is the £1 coin resting on? How smooth or thick are the pages of the book? And so on and so on" (paras 13, 14).

p.1197, new *annotation to the Employment and Support Allowance Regulations 2008, Sch.2: Activity 15 "execution of tasks"*

In *LF v SSWP* [2010] UKUT 352 (AAC), Judge Lane approved   **2.098** Judge Jacob's approach to the limited capability for work assessment in *GS v SSWP* (see update to p.1193, above):

> "Each of the various activities of the mental health assessment concerns a discrete aspect of mental functioning. The initiation of personal action is treated separately from the ability to complete tasks. I have accordingly come to the conclusion that the motivation to get started with an activity is not material to activity 15." (para.10).

pp.1197–1198, *annotation to the Employment and Support Allowance Regulations 2008, Sch.2: Activity 19: "coping with social situations"*

In *LF v SSWP* [2010] UKUT 352 (AAC), Judge Lane, with some   **2.099** caveats, agreed with Judge Williams' views set out in *JE v SSWP (ESA)* [2010] UKUT 50 (AAC). Judge Lane considered that:

"it is a matter of fact and degree whether a claimant can be said to be precluded from normal activities by overwhelming anxiety or fear. 'Precluded' and 'overwhelming' are strong words. In this context precluded means being prevented from doing something. It is not satisfied by a preference not to do something. 'Overwhelming' certainly indicates an overpowering feeling, or something approaching it. The descriptors refer to 'normal *activities*'. Whether the plural includes the singular in this context is a matter for full argument in a case in which the issue specifically arises." (para.21).

In *AP v SSWP (ESA)* [2010] UKUT 266 (AAC), Judge Parker stressed that "the guidance given to health care professionals [set out in the annotation] is in no sense prescriptive" (para.10). The starting point for all descriptors is ESA Regulations reg.19(2), against which background a tribunal, deploying its expertise, must apply them. Considering the role of the phrase "overwhelming fear or anxiety", she stated:

"The primary condition is thus that there is a specific disease or bodily or mental disablement which causes the inability to perform the particular activity or task at issue. If a claimant, for example, establishes mental disablement which results in fear or anxiety such that he is unable to undertake normal activities like visiting new places or engaging in social contact, there would seem to be no free-standing need to demonstrate 'overwhelming' fear or anxiety. From the wording of the whole phrase, the use of 'overwhelming' seems to add nothing once the other constituents are shown: if the shoe otherwise fits, this would in itself appear to demonstrate that the fear or anxiety is correctly described as 'overwhelming'." (para.11).

p.1222, *amendment to the Employment and Support Allowance Regulations 2008, Sch.6 (Housing costs), para.10 (General exclusions from paragraphs 8 and 9)*

2.100   With effect from June 28, 2010, reg.9(18) of the Social Security (Miscellaneous Amendments) (No.3) Regulations 2010 (SI 2010/840) substituted the words "the claimant or the claimant's partner" for the words "the claimant's partner" in para.10(1)(a).

p.1223, *amendment to the Employment and Support Allowance Regulations 2008, Sch.6 (Housing costs), para.13 (The standard rate)*

2.101   With effect from October 1, 2010, reg.2(1)(d) and (2) of the Social Security (Housing Costs) (Standard Interest Rate) Amendment Regulations 2010 (SI 2010/1811) substituted the following sub-paragraphs for sub-para.(2) in para.13:

"(2) Subject to the following provisions of this paragraph, the standard rate is to be the average mortgage rate published by the Bank of England in August 2010.

(2A) The standard rate is to be varied each time that sub-paragraph (2B) applies.

(2B) This sub-paragraph applies when, on any reference day, the Bank of England publishes an average mortgage rate which differs by

0.5% or more from the standard rate that applies on that reference day (whether by virtue of sub-paragraph (2) or of a previous application of this sub-paragraph).

(2C) The average mortgage rate published on that reference day then becomes the new standard rate in accordance with sub-paragraph (2D).

(2D) Any variation in the standard rate by virtue of sub-paragraphs (2A) to (2C) comes into effect—

(a) for the purposes of sub-paragraph (2B) (in consequence of its first and any subsequent application), on the day after the reference day referred to in subparagraph (2C);

(b) for the purpose of calculating the weekly amount of housing costs to be met under this Schedule, on the day specified by the Secretary of State.

(2E) In this paragraph—

"average mortgage rate" means the effective interest rate (non-seasonally adjusted) of United Kingdom resident banks and building societies for loans to households secured on dwellings published by the Bank of England in respect of the most recent period for that rate specified at the time of publication;

"reference day" means any day falling after 1st October 2010."

p.1233, *annotation to the Employment and Support Allowance Regulations 2008, Sch.6, para.10*

The amendment to para.10(1)(a) means that there will also be no waiting period for housing costs where it is the claimant who has reached the qualifying age for state pension credit. This brings the ESA provision into line with JSA (see para.8(1)(a) of Sch.2 to the Jobseeker's Allowance Regulations). 2.102

p.1233, *annotation to the Employment and Support Allowance Regulations 2008, Sch.6, para.13*

On the new para.13(2) to (2E), see the note to para.12 of Sch.3 to the Income Support (General) Regulations 1987, update to p.623, in Part III of this Supplement. 2.103

p.1235, *amendment to the Employment and Support Allowance Regulations 2008, Sch.7 (Sums to be disregarded in the calculation of earnings), para.5*

With effect from October 1, 2010, reg.5(4) of the Social Security (Miscellaneous Amendments) (No.4) Regulations 2010 (SI 2010/2126) substituted "£95" for "£93" in para.5. 2.104

p.1235, *amendment to the Employment and Support Allowance Regulations 2008, Sch.7 (Sums to be disregarded in the calculation of earnings), para.5A*

With effect from June 28, 2010, reg.9(19) of the Social Security (Miscellaneous Amendments) (No.3) Regulations 2010 (SI 2010/840) inserted the following new paragraph after para.5: 2.105

"**5A.** In the case of a claimant who receives a payment to which regulation 92(2) applies, £20, except where regulation 45(2) to (4) applies to the claimant, in which case the amounts specified in paragraph 6 shall apply, but only up to a maximum of £20."

p.1235, *amendment to the Employment and Support Allowance Regulations 2008, Sch.7 (Sums to be disregarded in the calculation of earnings), para.6*

2.106   With effect from October 1, 2010, reg.5(4) of the Social Security (Miscellaneous Amendments) (No.4) Regulations 2010 (SI 2010/2126) substituted "£95" for "£93" in para.6.

p.1235, *amendment to the Employment and Support Allowance Regulations 2008, Sch.7 (Sums to be disregarded in the calculation of earnings), para.7*

2.107   With effect from October 1, 2010, reg.5(4) of the Social Security (Miscellaneous Amendments) (No.4) Regulations 2010 (SI 2010/2126) substituted "£95" for "£93" in para.7.

p.1236, *annotation to the Employment and Support Allowance Regulations 2008, Sch.7, para.5A*

2.108   This provides for a £20 disregard to apply to royalties, copyright payments and public lending right payments. If a disregard in respect of exempt work already applies, the disregard under para.5A will depend on the amount by which the claimant's earnings fall below the relevant permitted work earnings limit, subject to the £20 maximum.

p.1238, *amendment to the Employment and Support Allowance Regulations 2008, Sch.8 (Sums to be disregarded in the calculation of income other than earnings), para.7*

2.109   With effect from June 28, 2010, reg.9(20)(a) of the Social Security (Miscellaneous Amendments) (No.3) Regulations 2010 (SI 2010/840) inserted the following new sub-paragraph after sub-para.(2) in para.7:

"(3) An increase under section 80 or 90 of the Contributions and Benefits Act."

p.1239, *amendment to the Employment and Support Allowance Regulations 2008, Sch.8 (Sums to be disregarded in the calculation of income other than earnings), para.15*

2.110   With effect from June 28, 2010, reg.9(20)(b) of the Social Security (Miscellaneous Amendments) (No.3) Regulations 2010 (SI 2010/840) inserted the words "or a jobseeker's allowance" after the words "employment and support allowance" in para.15(1)(a).

p.1241, *amendment to the Employment and Support Allowance Regulations 2008, Sch.8 (Sums to be disregarded in the calculation of income other than earnings), para.28*

With effect from November 1, 2010, reg.11(4)(a) of the Social Secu-   2.111
rity (Miscellaneous Amendments) (No.5) Regulations 2010 (SI
2010/2429) substituted the following paragraph for para.28:

"**28.** Any payment made to the claimant with whom a person is
accommodated by virtue of arrangements made—
  (a) by a local authority under—
      (i)   section 23(2)(a) of the Children Act 1989 (provision of
            accommodation and maintenance for a child whom they
            are looking after),
      (ii) section 26 of the Children (Scotland) Act 1995 (manner of
            provision of accommodation to child looked after by local
            authority), or
      (iii) regulations 33 or 51 of the Looked After Children (Scot-
            land) Regulations 2009 (fostering and kinship care allow-
            ances and fostering allowances); or
  (b) by a voluntary organisation under section 59(1)(a) of the 1989
       Act (provision of accommodation by voluntary organisa-
       tions)."

p.1242, *amendment to the Employment and Support Allowance Regulations 2008, Sch.8 (Sums to be disregarded in the calculation of income other than earnings), para.30*

With effect from November 1, 2010, reg.11(4)(b) of the Social Secu-   2.112
rity (Miscellaneous Amendments) (No.5) Regulations 2010 (SI
2010/2429) inserted "22," before "29" in para.30(1)(c).
  From the same date, reg.11(4)(c) of the same amending Regulations
inserted "22 or" before "29" in para.30(2).

p.1248, *annotation to the Employment and Support Allowance Regulations 2008, Sch.8, para.7*

Under the new para.7(3) child dependency increases paid with carer's   2.113
allowance, retirement pension, incapacity benefit, severe disablement
allowance and bereavement/widow's benefits are disregarded.

p.1248, *annotation to the Employment and Support Allowance Regulations 2008, Sch.8, para.15*

The amendment to para.15(1)(a) means that a training allowance paid   2.114
as a substitute for JSA is not disregarded. Under the previous form of
para.15(1)(a) only a training allowance paid as a substitute for ESA was
not disregarded.

pp.1258–1259, *amendment to the Employment and Support Allowance (Transitional Provisions) Regulations 2008, reg.2(2) (claim for an existing award)*

2.115   With effect from October 1, 2010, reg.23 of the Employment and Support Allowance (Transitional Provisions, Housing Benefit and Council Tax Benefit) (Existing Awards) (No.2) Regulations 2010 (SI 2010/1907) (the "Migration Regulations") amended para.(2)(a), (b) and (c) to read:

> "(2) Paragraph (1) does not apply to—
>   (a) [a claim made in respect of a period commencing before 31st January 2011] for incapacity benefit or severe disablement allowance relating to a period of incapacity for work which is one of two periods treated as one period of incapacity for work under section 30C(1)(c) of the Contributions and Benefits Act (linking rules);
>   (b) [a claim made in respect of a period commencing before 31st January 2011] made by a welfare to work beneficiary in accordance with regulation 13A of the Social Security (Incapacity for Work) (General) Regulations 1995 (welfare to work beneficiary);
>   (c) [a claim made in respect of a period commencing before 31st January 2011] for income support on the grounds of disability where—
>   (i) the claimant was previously entitled to income support on the grounds of disability, for a period of 4 or more consecutive days, and
>   (ii) the claimant ceased to be entitled to income support on the grounds of disability not more than 8 weeks before the commencement of the period in respect of which the current claim is made;".

p.1284, *amendment to the Social Security (General Benefit) Regulations 1982, reg.16 (earnings level for unemployability supplement)*

2.116   With effect from October 1, 2010, reg.2 of the Social Security (Miscellaneous Amendments) (No.4) Regulations 2010 (SI 2010/2126) increased the amount of earnings from £4,836 to £4,940.

pp.1346–1347, *annotation to the Social Security (Industrial Injuries) (Prescribed Diseases) Regulations 1985, Sch.1: II. "General matters" and "Any occupation involving"*

2.117   In *DM v SSWP (II)* [2010] UKUT (AAC), Judge Wikeley stressed that while the statutory words of prescription are always the starting point, a purposive approach had to be taken to them. "Any occupation involving" is not "a term of art" but requires a focus on the work activities performed rather than on the precise terms of the contract of employment ("the actual working test"), a proposition supported by

Secretary of State for Social Security v Davis [2001] EWCA Civ 105 (reported as *R(I) 2/01)*; *(R)I)2/79(T)* as well as *R(I) 3/78*.

pp.1348–1350, *annotation to the Social Security (Industrial Injuries) (Prescribed Diseases) Regulations 1985, Sch.1: PD A4 (Task-specific focal dystonia)*

In *SSWP v CS (II)* [2010] UKUT 198 (AAC), Judge Howell held that **2.118** cervical dystonia, which was work-related and which had been assessed at 30 per cent disablement, nonetheless did not fall within the governing prescription "task-related focal dystonia", since the medical evidence and IIAC Report indicated that, like its predecessor, it is limited to conditions affecting the hand and forearm.

p.1365, *annotation to the Social Security (Industrial Injuries) (Prescribed Diseases) Regulations 1985, Sch.1: PD A12 (carpal tunnel syndrome)*

FR v SSWP [2008] UKUT 12 (AAC) is reported as *R(I)1/09*. **2.119**

p.1366, *annotation to the Social Security (Industrial Injuries) (Prescribed Diseases) Regulations 1985, Sch.1: PD A14 (osteoarthritis of the knee)*

Extrapolating from a wide range of case authorities, Judge Wikeley, in **2.120** *DM v SSWP (II)* [2010] UKUT (AAC), has provided "some initial guidance on the interpretation and application of the relevant rules" in a context in which, while it was clear that the claimant (described by himself and the Coalboard Enquiry Service as an underground face electrician) had worked underground for at least 10 years, the question was whether he had done so in any of the relevant prescribed occupations. It was important to do so because there had been some 40,000 claims in the past year in respect of PD A14, many of which would generate appeals, and a significant number of which would turn on the issue now before him (para.4).

Judge Wikeley stressed that while the statutory words of prescription were the starting point, a purposive approach had to be taken to them. "Any occupation" is not "a term of art" but requires a focus on the work activities performed rather than on the precise terms of the contract of employment ("the actual working test") (paras 19–30) (see update to pp.1346–1347, above).

PD A14 provides two sets of relevant occupations. The first deals with periods before January 1, 1986. The second deals with periods on or after that date. The qualifying period might be all before that date, all after, or one spanning a period either side of that date. It need not have been in a single occupation (the words used are "at least 10 years in one or more of the following occupations"). The requisite occupation for periods before January 1, 1986 is working underground as a "coal miner", this term not being defined in social security legislation. Judge Wikeley, stressing the need to avoid an unduly restrictive construction, thought the new tribunal (whose decision it would be) might well have little difficulty in concluding that this claimant was a "coal miner" (para.34). Drawing by analogy on the definition in the now-repealed Stannaries Act 1887, as giving a flavour of what "coal miner" covered, he thought a tribunal might reasonably take the view that the term covered:

> "anyone working in or about a coal mine, in a skilled, semi-skilled or unskilled 'blue collar' capacity, but not, for example, a 'white collar' colliery manager, mining engineer or mining surveyor." (para.35).

But he also considered it impossible and unwise to attempt an exhaustive or comprehensive definition, referring here to the "elephant test"—difficult to describe but knowing it when you see it (para.36). Underground might usefully if colloquially be summed up as "down the pit" (paras 37–38).

The second set of relevant occupations cover the period on or after January 1, 1986 as a: (i) face worker on a non-mechanised coal face; (ii) development worker; (iii) face-salvage worker; (iv) conveyor belt cleaner; or (v) conveyor belt attendant. Again, the focus must be on what the claimant was actually doing in the periods relied on, and not on the contract of employment. Nor can simple reliance be placed on the claimant's pay grade or the label on his or her wage packet. The matter is ultimately one of fact for the tribunal (paras 61–63). But the question is whether in the period from 1986 onwards the claimant:

> "actually worked *in* one of the relevant occupations, and not whether he worked *in conditions similar to or indeed even identical to* those experienced by the listed occupations." (para.65).

PD A14 requires working underground in the relevant occupation(s) for a period, or aggregate periods, of 10 years. As Judge Wikeley noted, this could pose problems where the claimant has moved from pit to pit, or work underground is interspersed with work above ground or where, indeed, there was no work done at all because of a prolonged industrial dispute. He referred the new tribunal to which the appeal was remitted to the helpful guidance in *R(I) 3/78* and *R(I) 2/79(T)* on computing periods of work in scheduled occupations, remembering that the focus is to be "on what the claimant actually did" (paras 39–40).

Although PD A14 was inserted because of the risk of osteoarthritis as a result of kneeling and squatting, there was, however, no requirement in the terms of prescription (which he saw as clear and unambiguous) that the claimant's work underground involved periods of kneeling and squatting, prolonged or otherwise (paras 41–48, 54).

pp.1389–1390, *annotation to the Social Security (Industrial Injuries) (Regular Employment) Regulations 1990, regs 2 ("regular employment") and 3 ("circumstances in which a person . . . is to be regarded as having given up regular employment")*

2.121   That this can work harshly in respect of persons whose work is seasonal is shown in *SSWP v NH (II)* [2010] UKUT 84 (AAC). Here the claimant did seasonal work in a museum from March to October 2007, when the contract ended. In August 2007 he became 65. He next worked from March 11, 2008 at the museum. Judge Paines, agreeing in part with Judge Howell in *CI/16202/96* (applied in *CI/2517/01*) and partly with Judge Levenson in *CI/3224/04*, took the following approach to reg.3 read with reg.2:

"the question becomes, for the purposes of regulation 3 when read with regulation 2(a), whether the claimant was in employment under a contract (with, to put it loosely, average contractual hours of ten or more); for the purposes of regulation 2(b) the question is whether the claimant was in fact in gainful employment which he undertook for an average of ten hours measured over five consecutive weeks.

Viewing the questions in that way, it seems to me to be impossible to hold that a person is 'in' employment under a contract for the purposes of regulation 2(a) at a point in time at which the contract has ceased. In that regard I find Judge Howell's reasoning . . . compelling.

As far as regulation 2(b) is concerned, I agree with Judge Howell that it embraces both casual employment and self-employment. It is in addition self-evident that the employment or self-employment does not need to be full-time. The Regulations regard a person as being 'in employment' in a week provided at least that he performs enough hours of casual or self-employed work to maintain the required ten-hour average; that is so despite the fact that, if the work is casual, the claimant will probably not be in an employment relationship except during the hours that he performs it. It is against that background that I address the question whether for the purposes of regulation 2(b) there is (as Judge Howell suggested) an implicit requirement that the claimant must perform *some* work in each week.

I do not consider that there is such an implicit requirement. The question to be answered is whether, in the week under examination, the claimant is 'in' employment undertaken for an average of ten hours per week measured over five consecutive weeks. Where a claimant remains in the habit of taking employment, and moreover the five-week rolling average of ten hours' work per week is maintained, I do not find it necessary to hold that he is no longer in employment in a particular week merely because he performs no hours of work in that week.

If it were otherwise, a self-employed person could not take a week off without being regarded as giving up employment for the purposes of the Regular Employment Regulations. I find it impossible to conclude that, despite specifically providing for employees' holiday and other permitted absences to be disregarded for the purposes of the contractual hours calculation under regulation 2(a), the Regulations require self-employed persons to forego time off in order to avoid deemed giving up of employment. As a matter of language I have no difficulty in regarding a self-employed person taking time off as remaining 'in' self-employment. Similarly, I would regard a person as remaining 'in' self-employment even if no customers come his way in a particular week. Likewise I would regard a person who remains in the habit of taking casual employment as remaining 'in' casual employment during a week in which (whether because of a wish to take time off or because of the unavailability of work) he does not actually perform any work. This seems to me to be consistent with Judge Rowland's approach in *R(JSA) 1/03* to the concept of 'gainful employment' when used in the JSA Regulations; the same term is used in regulation 2 of the Regular Employment Regulations.

It seems to me to be a matter of giving the concept of being 'in' (for example) casual employment or self-employment its natural meaning. Following this approach, a casual employee or self-employed person will be regarded as giving up regular employment if he decides no longer to take work, or if his average hours fall below ten. The approach seems to me to be consistent with Judge Powell's approach in *CI/2517/01*, where the nurse's single week without agency work was not regarded as triggering regulation 3." (paras 21–26).

Consequently, reg.2(a) could not apply once the contract had ended in October 2007. Nor could the claimant avail himself of reg.2(b), because there was no suggestion that he undertook or planned to undertake any employment in the weeks immediately following October 30. Whereas, if his job at the museum had been all year round, rather than seasonal, he would have retained entitlement to REA while he continued working. Judge Lane noted the more flexible treatment of seasonal workers under JSA.

p.1410–1411, *revocation of the Vaccine Damage Payments (Specified Disease) Order 2009*

2.122 This Order was revoked with effect from September 1, 2010 by the Vaccine Damage Payments (Specified Disease) (Revocation and Savings) Order 2010 (SI 2010/1988) (see the "New Legislation" section of this Supplement). Influenza caused by the pandemic influenza A (H1N1) 2009 virus ("swine flu") thus ceases from that date to be one of the specified diseases to which the Act applies. Article 4 of the Order ensures, however, that protection under the Act remains applicable to anyone who received the vaccination against "swine flu" prior to September 1, 2010.

PART III

UPDATING MATERIAL
VOLUME II

INCOME SUPPORT, JOBSEEKER'S ALLOWANCE, STATE PENSION CREDIT AND THE SOCIAL FUND

Commentary by

Penny Wood

Richard Poynter

Nick Wikeley

David Bonner

p.37, *amendments to the Jobseekers Act 1995, s.2 (the contribution-based conditions)*

With effect from November 1, 2010, s.12 of the Welfare Reform Act   3.001
2009 amended s.2(1)–(3A) to read:

"**2.**—(1) The conditions referred to in section 1(2)(d) are that the claimant—

  (a) has actually paid Class 1 contributions in respect of one ("the base year") of the last two complete years before the beginning of the relevant benefit year and satisfies the additional conditions set out in subsection (2);

  (b) has, in respect of the last two complete years before the beginning of the relevant benefit year, either paid Class 1 contributions or been credited with earnings and satisfies the additional condition set out in subsection (3);

  (c) does not have earnings in excess of the prescribed amount; and

  (d) is not entitled to income support.

(2) The additional conditions mentioned in subsection (1)(a) are that—

  (a) the contributions have been paid before the week for which the jobseeker's allowance is claimed;

  [(b) the claimant's relevant earnings for the base year upon which primary Class 1 contributions have been paid or treated as paid are not less than the base year's lower earnings limit multiplied by 26.]

[(2A) Regulations may make provision for the purposes of subsection (2)(b) for determining the claimant's relevant earnings for the base year.

(2B) Regulations under subsection (2A) may, in particular, make provision—

  (a) for making that determination by reference to the amount of a person's earnings for periods comprised in the base year;

  (b) for determining the amount of a person's earnings for any such period by—

    (i) first determining the amount of the earnings for the period in accordance with regulations made for the purposes of section 3(2) of the Benefits Act, and

    (ii) then disregarding so much of the amount found in accordance with sub-paragraph (i) as exceeded the base year's lower earnings limit (or the prescribed equivalent).]

(3) The additional condition mentioned in subsection (1)(b) is that the earnings factor derived [from so much of the claimant's earnings as did not exceed the upper earnings limit and] upon which primary Class 1 contributions have been paid or treated as paid or from earnings credited is not less, in each of the two complete years, than the lower earnings limit for the year multiplied by 50.

(3A) Where primary Class 1 contributions have been paid or treated as paid on any part of a person's earnings, [subsection (3)] above shall have effect as if such contributions had been paid or treated as paid on so much of the earnings as did not exceed the upper earnings limit."

pp.38–39, *annotation to the Jobseekers Act 1995, s.2(1)(a) and (b), (2)–(4) (particular condition one: the contribution conditions)*

3.002   The changes effected by s.12 of the Welfare Reform Act 2009 and regulations made in consequence significantly tighten the contribution conditions for CBJSA. They mean that the requisite level of earnings in the tax year relied on for the first contribution condition is now 26 times that year's lower earnings limit, rather than 25, and the conditions now only count earnings at that lower earnings limit, so that new claimants will have to have worked for at least 26 weeks in one of the last two tax years. Prior to these amendments, when the level was 25 times the LEL and the scheme looked also to earnings between the lower and upper earnings limits, a high earner could qualify on less than four weeks' work in the tax year, and someone at the national minimum wage could qualify in about 12 weeks. The relevant regulations made under sub-s.(2A) are the Social Security (Contribution Conditions for Jobseeker's Allowance and Employment and Support Allowance) Regulations 2010 (SI 2010/2446), and amendments effected by them to the JSA Regulations are taken into account in the update to p.934 in this Part of the Supplement.

p.118, *annotation to the Jobseekers Act 1995, s.19(9) (national minimum wage rates)*

3.003   With effect from October 1, 2010, the hourly rates are £5.93 for those aged 21 and over (the Regulations effect a drop in eligible age from 22 to 21); £4.92 for those aged 18–20 (reflecting that drop); and £3.64 for those workers under 18 who have ceased to be of compulsory school age. The change in rates was effected by the National Minimum Wage Regulations 1999 (Amendment) Regulations 2010 (SI 2010/1901). Note that different rates apply for apprentices in the first year of their apprenticeship or who are under 19 (see reg.5 of the amending Regulations).

p.150, *annotation to the State Pension Credit Act 2002: Introduction and General Note*

3.004   *EC v SSWP* [2010] UKUT 93 (AAC) is reported as [2010] AACR 39.

p.152, *annotation to the State Pension Credit Act 2002, s.1*

3.005   *EC v SSWP* [2010] UKUT 93 (AAC) is reported as [2010] AACR 39.

p.203, *amendment to the Income Support (General) Regulations 1987, reg.2(1) (Interpretation: definition of "independent hospital")*

With effect from September 1, 2010, arts 2 and 5 of the Health and Social Care Act 2008 (Miscellaneous Consequential Amendments) Order 2010 (SI 2010/1881) amended reg.2(1) by substituting the following for the definition of "independent hospital": **3.006**

""independent hospital"—
  (a) in England, means a hospital as defined by section 275 of the National Health Service Act 2006 that is not a health service hospital as defined by that section;
  (b) in Wales, has the meaning assigned to it by section 2 of the Care Standards Act 2000; and
  (c) in Scotland, means an independent healthcare service as defined in section 2(5)(a) and (b) of the Regulation of Care (Scotland) Act 2001;"

p.207, *amendment to the Income Support (General) Regulations 1987, reg.2(1) (Interpretation: definition of "training allowance")*

With effect from September 1, 2010, art.3(1) and (2) of the Apprenticeships, Skills, Children and Learning Act 2009 (Consequential Amendments to Subordinate Legislation) (England) Order 2010 (SI 2010/1941) amended the definition of "training allowance" in reg.2(1) by substituting the words, "Young People's Learning Agency for England, the Chief Executive of Skills Funding" for the words, "Learning and Skills Council for England" in para.(a) of the definition. **3.007**

p.213, *annotation to the Income Support (General) Regulations 1987, reg.2(1) (Interpretation: care home)*

SA v SSWP (IS) [2010] UKUT 345 (AAC) confirms that if an establishment satisfies the conditions in the definition of "care home" then it falls to be treated as a care home even if it was also an educational establishment. Those terms are not mutually exclusive, and a care home does not cease to be a care home merely by virtue of fulfilling some other function. **3.008**

p.295, *annotation to the Income Support (General) Regulations 1987, reg.2(3ZA) (Special cases: patient—prisoner—person serving a sentence of imprisonment detained in hospital)*

The change in the law effected by the Social Security (Hospital In-Patients) Regulations 2005 (SI 2005/3360) with effect from April 10, 2006 (whereby convicted prisoners detained under certain provisions of the Mental Health Act 1983 lost the right to income support) does not infringe art.1 of Protocol 1 to the European Convention on Human Rights: see *JB v SSWP (IS)* [2010] UKUT 263 (AAC). **3.009**

p.305, *annotation to the Income Support (General) Regulations 1987, reg.21AA (Special cases: supplemental—persons from abroad—habitual residence test—EEA and Swiss nationals and their family members—the right to reside—residence permits and registration cards—reference to the ECJ in* Dias*)*

3.009.1 The opinion of the Advocate General in Case C-325/09 *Secretary of State for the Home Department v Dias* is now available. Mrs Dias (a Portuguese citizen) had resided legally in the UK for over five years between 1998 and 2003. She then continued to live here for slightly more than a year under a residence permit for which she no longer qualified but which had not been revoked. She then resided legally for a further period from April 2004 until after April 30, 2006. Advocate General Trstenjak advised the court that in those circumstances, Mrs Dias obtained a right of permanent residence on April 30, 2006 when the Directive came into force. The basis of that advice was that residence which is not based on the Directive or its predecessor provisions, but only on a residence permit granted by the national authorities, does not constitute legal residence within the meaning of art.16(1) of the Directive and cannot therefore be taken into account for the acquisition of a right of permanent residence. However, the period of non-legal residence on the basis of the residence permit did not terminate the right of permanent residence that had previously accrued under the principles established by Case C-162/09 *SSWP v Lassal* (see noter-up to p.330, below) by virtue of Mrs Dias' residence between 1998 and 2003. The final decision of the Court is still awaited.

pp.323–324, *annotation to the Income Support (General) Regulations 1987, reg.21AA (Special cases: supplemental—persons from abroad—habitual residence test—extended right of residence—self-employed persons—retention of self-employed status)*

3.010 The decision of the High Court in *Tilianu* has been confirmed by the Court of Appeal in *R. (Tilianu) v Secretary of State for Work and Pensions* [2010] EWCA Civ 1397. However, the issue whether a formerly self-employed person has to retain self-employed status only arises if that person has actually ceased to be self-employed. That is a question of fact in each case, see the decision of the Upper Tribunal in *Secretary of State for Work and Pensions v JS* [2010] UKUT 240 (AAC). Upper Tribunal Judge Jacobs stated (at para.5):

"5. I do not accept that a claimant who is for the moment doing no work is necessarily no longer self-employed. There will commonly be periods in a person's self-employment when no work is done. Weekends and holiday periods are obvious examples. There may also be periods when there is no work to do. The concept of self-employment encompasses periods of both feast and famine. During the latter, the person may be engaged in a variety of tasks that are properly seen as part of continuing self-employment: administrative work, such as maintaining the accounts; in marketing to generate more work; or developing the business in new directions. Self-employment is not confined to periods of actual work. It includes natural periods of rest and the vicissitudes of business life. This does not mean that self-employment survives regardless of how little work arrives. It does mean that the issue can only be decided in the context of the facts at any particular time. The amount of work is one factor. Whether the claimant is taking any other steps in the course of self-employment is also relevant. The claimant's motives and intentions must also be taken into account, although they will not necessarily be decisive."

p.324, *annotation to the Income Support (General) Regulations 1987, reg.21AA (Special cases: supplemental—persons from abroad—habitual residence test—extended right of residence—self-sufficient persons—sufficiency of resources)*

The application of the sufficient resources test was considered by the 3.011 Upper Tribunal in *SG v Tameside MBC (HB)* [2010] UKUT 243 (AAC). It decided that:

- The concept of "burden" in the phrase "not to become a burden on the social assistance system of the host Member State during their period of residence" in art.7(1)(b) of Directive 2004/38/EC (equivalent to reg.4(1)(c) of the 2006 Regulations) was not to be construed in the same way as "unreasonable burden" in recitals (10) and (16) to that Directive.
- As housing benefit and council tax benefit are forms of social assistance, they must be taken into account when applying the test in art.7(1)(b).
- Following the decision of the ECJ in Case C-408/03 *Commission v Kingdom of Belgium*, there was no requirement as to the origin of the resources, so that a person who had, for example, accommodation made available to them by a third party "is in principle entitled to have that taken into account towards determining the sufficiency of their resources".

p.324, *annotation to the Income Support (General) Regulations 1987, reg.21AA (Special cases: supplemental—persons from abroad—habitual residence test—extended right of residence—self-sufficient persons—comprehensive sickness insurance)*

In *SG v Tameside MBC* (HB) [2010] UKUT 243 (AAC), the claimant 3.012 was a Polish national who had living in Sweden for many years and was receiving Swedish invalidity benefit in the United Kingdom under the provisions of Regulation (EEC) No.1408/71. The Upper Tribunal accepted a concession from the Secretary of State that the claimant could rely on the United Kingdom's right to the reimbursement of healthcare costs under arts 27–34 of that Regulation and art.95 of Regulation (EEC) No.574/72 as meeting the requirement for comprehensive sickness insurance.

pp.325–326, *annotation to the Income Support (General) Regulations 1987, reg.21AA (Special cases: supplemental—persons from abroad—right to reside test—family members and extended family members—dependency)*

3.013   *VN (EEA rights—dependency) v Macedonia* [2010] UKUT 380 (IAC) confirms that the decision in *Pedro v Secretary of State for Work and Pensions* [2009] EWCA Civ 1358 applies to family members who are dependent direct relatives as defined by art.2(2)(d) of the Directive but not extended family members ("other family members" as defined by art.3.2(a) of the Directive). To establish a right of residence the extended family members are required to show both dependence in the country from which they have come and dependence in the United Kingdom.

pp.329–330, *annotation to the Income Support (General) Regulations 1987, reg.21AA (Special cases: supplemental—persons from abroad— habitual residence test—permanent right of residence—legal residence)*

3.014   The opinion of the Advocate-General in Case C-434/09 *McCarthy v Secretary of State for the Home Department* is now available. Advocate General Kokott suggests that the Court should answer the request for a preliminary ruling as follows:

> "Where a Union citizen is a national of two Member States of the European Union but has always lived in only one of those two States, she cannot claim a right of residence under Directive 2004/38/EC in that State."

In addition, the Advocate-General discussed the meaning of "resided legally" in art.16(1) of the Directive. He stated:

> "51. It is true that the preamble to Directive 2004/38 indicates that legal residence means, above all, residence 'in compliance with the conditions laid down in this Directive', that is to say, residence to which the person concerned was entitled by virtue of EU law. However, having regard to the context and objectives of Directive 2004/38, its provisions are not to be interpreted restrictively.
> 52. In providing for the right of permanent residence pursuant to Article 16 of Directive 2004/38, the European Union legislature had the aim of 'promoting social cohesion, which is one of the fundamental objectives of the Union' and of creating a 'genuine vehicle for integration into the society of the host Member State'. It is consistent with this objective for the group of persons entitled to permanent residence to be extended to those Union citizens whose residence entitlement in the host Member State results solely from the latter's domestic law on foreign nationals since, when assessing the degree of integration of a Union citizen in the host Member State, it is of secondary importance where his right of residence originates from.
> 53. The fact that there can be instances where a right of residence results solely from the host Member State's national law on foreign nationals is shown by Article 37 of Directive 2004/38, under which laws, regulations or administrative provisions laid down by a Member State which would be more favourable are expressly left unaffected.

There are also clearly instances in the case-law where residence of Union citizens in the relevant host Member State could not be based on EU law, but only on domestic law on foreign nationals. The Court has not in any way found such residence to be irrelevant, but on the contrary has linked conclusions under EU law to it.

54. 'Legal residence' for the purposes of Article 16(1) of Directive 2004/38 can nevertheless only mean residence which is founded on legal provisions on foreign nationals and not, by contrast, residence which is legal merely because the person concerned is a national of the host Member State. As already stated, (57) Directive 2004/38 serves to give effect to and facilitate the right of free movement of Union citizens. It is not intended to promote for example integration into the society of the host Member State of nationals of that State who have never exercised their right of free movement."

At the time of going to press, it is not known when the decision of the Court in *McCarthy* is to be expected.

pp.329–331, *annotation to Income Support (General) Regulations 1987, reg.21AA (Special cases: supplemental—persons from abroad—habitual residence test—right to reside—permanent right of residence—legal residence)*

In Case C-424/10 *Tomasz Ziolkowski v Land Berlin* and Case C-425/10   **3.015**
Marlon Szeja v Land Berlin, the Federal Administrative Court (Bundes-verwaltungsgericht) of the Federal Republic of Germany has referred the following questions to the ECJ for a preliminary ruling:

"Is the first sentence of Article 16(1) of Directive 2004/38/EC to be interpreted as conferring on Union citizens who have resided legally for more than five years on the basis only of national law in the territory of a Member State, but who did not during that period fulfil the conditions laid down in Article 7(1) of Directive 2004/38/EC, a right of permanent residence in that Member State?

Are periods of residence of Union citizens in the host Member State which took place before the accession of their Member State of origin to the European Union also to be counted towards the period of lawful residence under Article 16(1) of Directive 2004/38/EC?"

p.330, *annotation to the Income Support (General) Regulations 1987, reg.21AA (Special cases: supplemental—persons from abroad—habitual residence test—permanent right of residence—legal residence—residence before April 30, 2006)*

The decision of the European Court of Justice in Case C-162/09   **3.016**
SSWP v Lassal is now available. The Court ruled as follows:

"Article 16(1) and (4) of [the Citizenship Directive] must be interpreted as meaning that:
— continuous periods of five years' residence completed before the date of transposition of Directive 2004/38, namely 30 April 2006, in accordance with earlier European Union law instruments, must be taken into account for the purposes of

the acquisition of the right of permanent residence pursuant to Article 16(1) thereof, and

— absences from the host Member State of less than two consecutive years, which occurred before 30 April 2006 but following a continuous period of five years' legal residence completed before that date do not affect the acquisition of the right of permanent residence pursuant to Article 16(1) thereof."

p.331, *annotation to the Income Support (General) Regulations 1987, reg.21AA (Special cases: supplemental—persons from abroad—habitual residence test—permanent right of residence—legal residence—residence in prison)*

3.017   In *Carvalho v Secretary of State for the Home Department* [2010] EWCA Civ 1406, the Court of Appeal has confirmed that, as had been implied by *HR (Portugal) v Secretary of State for the Home Department* [2009] EWCA Civ 371, time spent in prison does not count towards the continuous period of five years that qualifies an EEA national for a permanent right of residence under reg.15 of the 2006 Regulations and art.16 of the Citizenship Directive.

pp.333–335, *annotation to the Income Support (General) Regulations 1987, reg.21AA (Special cases: supplemental—persons from abroad— habitual residence test—rights to reside of children in education and their principal carers:* Baumbast, Ibrahim *and* Teixeira—*A8 and A2 nationals)*

3.018   In *SSWP v JS (IS)* [2010] UKUT 347 (AAC), the Upper Tribunal held that an A8 national who had worked lawfully in the United Kingdom but had not completed 12 months' registered employment could assert a right to reside as the primary carer of her child in education. By implication the same is true of A2 nationals who are authorised workers.

pp.335–340, *annotation to the Income Support (General) Regulations 1987, reg.21AA (Special cases: supplemental—persons from abroad— habitual residence test—The special position of A8 and A2 nationals)*

3.019   In *SSWP v JS (IS)* [2010] UKUT 347 (AAC), the Upper Tribunal held that an A8 national who had worked lawfully in the United Kingdom but had not completed 12 months' registered employment could assert a right to reside as the primary carer of her child in education. By implication the same is true of A2 nationals who are authorised workers.

p.340, *annotation to the Income Support (General) Regulations 1987, reg.21AA (Special cases: supplemental—persons from abroad—habitual residence test—compatibility of the right to reside test with EC law—direct right of residence under art.21 TFEU)*

3.020   The circumstances in which it is permissible to conclude that there is a lacuna in Directive 2004/38/EC were considered further by the Upper Tribunal in *RM v SSWP (IS)* [2010] UKUT 238 (AAC).

pp.357–358, *annotation to the Income Support (General) Regulations 1987, reg.23, "Distinction between capital and income"*

In *Kingston upon Hull City Council v DLM (HB)* [2010] UKUT 234   3.021
(AAC) Judge Howell held that the compensation payment received by the claimant in settlement of a potential equal pay claim was clearly earnings (agreeing with *SSWP v JP* [2010] UKUT 90 (AAC) on this point). He disagreed, however, with the distinction endorsed in that case that had been made in *EM v Waltham Forest LBC* [2009] UKUT 245 (AAC) between equal pay settlements and those under the Part-time Workers (Prevention of Less Favourable Treatment) Regulations 2000 (SI 2000/1551). *EM v Waltham Forest LBC* had concluded that payments under the part-time workers legislation should be treated as capital. In Judge Howell's view there was no material distinction between the two types of payment as both were "catch-up redress for past failure to recognise the existence of claims to equal treatment in the matter of remuneration". Thus both counted as income.

DN v Leicester City Council (HB) [2010] UKUT 253 (AAC) discusses the nature of annuity payments. In that case the claimant's annuity payments, which were derived from a personal pension plan, paid annually and were subject to income tax, counted as income to be attributed over the whole year. In any event, however, reg.41(2) of the Housing Benefit Regulations 2006 (SI 2006/213) (which is in the same terms as reg.41(2) of the Income Support Regulations) was there to ensure that all annuity payments, whatever their complexion, were taken into account as income.

p.387, *annotation to the Income Support (General) Regulations 1987, reg.35(1)(b)*

See *Kingston upon Hull City Council v DLM (HB)* [2010] UKUT 234   3.022
(AAC) in the note to reg.23, update to pp.357–358, above.

p.415, *annotation to the Income Support (General) Regulations 1987, reg.41(2)*

See *DN v Leicester City Council (HB)* [2010] UKUT 253 (AAC) in the   3.023
note to reg.23, update to pp.357–358, above.

p.490, *amendment to the Income Support (General) Regulations 1987, reg.61(1) (Interpretation), definition of "access funds"*

With effect from September 1, 2010, art.3(3)(a) of the Apprentice-   3.024
ships, Skills, Children and Learning Act 2009 (Consequential Amendments to Subordinate Legislation) (England) Order 2010 (SI 2010/1941) substituted the words, "Young People's Learning Agency for England under sections 61 and 62 of the Apprenticeships, Skills, Children and Learning Act 2009 or the Chief Executive of Skills Funding under sections 100 and 101 of that Act" for the words, "Learning and Skills Council for England under sections 5, 6 and 9 of the Learning and Skills Act 2000" in para.(d) of the definition of "access funds".

p.491, *amendment to the Income Support (General) Regulations 1987, reg.61(1) (Interpretation), definition of "education authority"*

3.025   With effect from May 5, 2010, reg.5 of and para.13 of Sch.3 to the Local Education Authorities and Children's Services Authorities (Integration of Functions) (Local and Subordinate Legislation) Order 2010 (SI 2010/1172) substituted the words, "a local authority as defined in section 579 of the Education Act 1996 (interpretation)" for the words, "a local education authority as defined in section 114(1) of the Education Act 1944 (interpretation)" in the definition of "education authority" in reg.61(1).

p.492, *amendment to the Income Support (General) Regulations 1987, reg.61(1) (Interpretation), definition of "full-time course of advanced education"*

3.026   With effect from September 1, 2010, art.3(3)(b)(i) of the Apprenticeships, Skills, Children and Learning Act 2009 (Consequential Amendments to Subordinate Legislation) (England) Order 2010 (SI 2010/1941) substituted the words, "Young People's Learning Agency for England, the Chief Executive of Skills Funding" for the words, "Learning and Skills Council for England" in paras (a) and (b) (except para. (b)(i)) of the definition of "full-time course of advanced education".
From the same date, art.3(3)(b)(ii) of the same Order substituted the following sub-paragraph for sub-para.(i) in para.(b):

> "(i) in the case of a course funded by the Young People's Learning Agency for England or the Chief Executive of Skills Funding, in the student's learning agreement signed on behalf of the establishment which is funded by either of those bodies for the delivery of that course; or".

p.492, *amendment to the Income Support (General) Regulations 1987, reg.61(1) (Interpretation), definition of "full-time course of study"*

3.027   With effect from September 1, 2010, art.3(3)(c)(i) of the Apprenticeships, Skills, Children and Learning Act 2009 (Consequential Amendments to Subordinate Legislation) (England) Order 2010 (SI 2010/1941) substituted the words, "Young People's Learning Agency for England, the Chief Executive of Skills Funding" for the words, "Learning and Skills Council for England" in paras (a) and (b) (except para.(b)(i)) of the definition of "full-time course of study".
From the same date, art.3(3)(c)(ii) of the same Order substituted the following sub-paragraph for sub-para.(i) in para.(b):

> "(i) in the case of a course funded by the Young People's Learning Agency for England or the Chief Executive of Skills Funding, in the student's learning agreement signed on behalf of the establishment which is funded by either of those bodies for the delivery of that course; or".

p.528, *amendment to the Income Support (General) Regulations 1987, Sch.1B (Prescribed categories of person), para.1 (Lone parents)*

With effect from October 25, 2010, reg.4 of the Social Security (Lone   **3.028** Parents and Miscellaneous Amendments) Regulations 2008 (SI 2008/3051) substituted the following paragraph for para.1:

"Lone Parents

1. A person who is a lone parent and responsible for—
(a) a single child aged under 7, or
(b) more than one child where the youngest is aged under 7,
who is a member of that person's household."

p.529, *amendment to the Income Support (General) Regulations 1987, Sch.1B (Prescribed categories of person), para.7 (Persons treated as capable of work and persons entitled to statutory sick pay)*

With effect from November 1, 2010, reg.2(2)(a) of the Social Security   **3.029** (Miscellaneous Amendments) (No.5) Regulations 2010 (SI 2010/2429) substituted the words "the Contributions and Benefits Act" for the words "that Act" in para.7(c).

p.530, *amendment to the Income Support (General) Regulations 1987, Sch.1B (Prescribed categories of person), para.14 (Pregnancy)*

With effect from November 1, 2010, reg.2(2)(b) of the Social Security   **3.030** (Miscellaneous Amendments) (No.5) Regulations 2010 (SI 2010/2429) omitted the words, "seven weeks after the date on which her pregnancy ends where the expected week of confinement begins prior to 6th April 2003 or" and the words, "where the expected week of confinement begins on or after 6th April 2003" in para.14(b).

p.532, *amendment to the Income Support (General) Regulations 1987, Sch.1B (Prescribed categories of person), para.28 (Persons engaged in training)*

With effect from September 1, 2010, art.3(4) of the Apprenticeships,   **3.031** Skills, Children and Learning Act 2009 (Consequential Amendments to Subordinate Legislation) (England) Order 2010 (SI 2010/1941) substituted the words, "Young People's Learning Agency for England, the Chief Executive of Skills Funding" for the words, "Learning and Skills Council for England" in para.28.

pp.535–537, *annotation to the Income Support (General) Regulations 1987, Sch.1B, para.1*

On the new form of para.1 in force from October 25, 2010, see the   **3.032** notes to para.1 of Sch.1B in the main volume. Part 3 of the Schedule to the Social Security (Lone Parents and Miscellaneous Amendments)

Regulations 2008 (SI 2008/3051) contains special phasing-in arrangements that apply to certain claimants who have an existing entitlement under para.1 immediately before October 25, 2010 (and to whom no other paragraph in Sch.1B applies). For the effect of Part 3 see under *"Phase 3—lone parents with an only or youngest child aged 7 or over on October 25, 2010"* in the main volume.

p.582, *amendment to the Income Support (General) Regulations 1987, Sch.3 (Housing costs), para.12 (the standard rate)*

3.033 With effect from October 1, 2010, reg.2(1)(a) and (2) of the Social Security (Housing Costs) (Standard Interest Rate) Amendment Regulations 2010 (SI 2010/1811) substituted the following sub-paragraphs for sub-para.(2) in para.12:

"(2) Subject to the following provisions of this paragraph, the standard rate is to be the average mortgage rate published by the Bank of England in August 2010.

(2A) The standard rate is to be varied each time that sub-paragraph (2B) applies.

(2B) This sub-paragraph applies when, on any reference day, the Bank of England publishes an average mortgage rate which differs by 0.5% or more from the standard rate that applies on that reference day (whether by virtue of sub-paragraph (2) or of a previous application of this sub-paragraph).

(2C) The average mortgage rate published on that reference day then becomes the new standard rate in accordance with sub-paragraph (2D).

(2D) Any variation in the standard rate by virtue of sub-paragraphs (2A) to (2C) comes into effect—

(a) for the purposes of sub-paragraph (2B) (in consequence of its first and any subsequent application), on the day after the reference day referred to in sub-paragraph (2C);

(b) for the purpose of calculating the weekly amount of housing costs to be met under this Schedule, on the day specified by the Secretary of State.

(2E) In this paragraph—

"average mortgage rate" means the effective interest rate (non-seasonally adjusted) of United Kingdom resident banks and building societies for loans to households secured on dwellings published by the Bank of England in respect of the most recent period for that rate specified at the time of publication;

"reference day" means any day falling after 1st October 2010."

p.604, *annotation to the Income Support (General) Regulations 1987, Sch.3, para.3*

3.034 *SK v South Hants DC (HB)* [2010] UKUT 129 (AAC) is to be reported as [2010] AACR 40.

p.623, *annotation to the Income Support (General) Regulations 1987, Sch.3, para.12*

From October 1, 2010, the fixed standard interest rate of 6.08 per cent   **3.035** used to calculate the amount of interest on eligible loans has been replaced with a rate based on the "average mortgage rate" (defined in sub-para.(2E)) published by the Bank of England. According to the Explanatory Memorandum which accompanies this SI, the average mortgage rate is based on information from approximately 30 banks and building societies, representing more than 75 per cent of mortgage business, and is a weighted average of all existing loans to households secured on dwellings from banks and building societies in the sample.

Initially the standard interest rate from October 1, 2010 has been set at the average mortgage rate in August 2010 (see sub-para.(2)). The average mortgage rate in August 2010 was 3.63 per cent, which is considerably lower than the previous fixed rate of 6.08 per cent.

Changes in the standard interest rate will only be triggered when the average mortgage rate and the standard interest rate differ by 0.5 per cent or more (see sub-para.(2B)). When that occurs, the average mortgage rate becomes the new standard rate, but this will only take effect for the purpose of calculating the weekly amount of a claimant's housing costs on a day specified by the Secretary of State (see sub-para.(2D)). It apparently takes five to six weeks to implement a change to the standard rate in the Department's computer systems and thus to benefit awards (para.7.4 of the Explanatory Memorandum).

A footnote to the SI states that any new standard interest rate, and the day specified by the Secretary of State as the day on which it comes into effect, will be published on the Directgov website.

pp.634–635, *annotation to the Income Support (General) Regulations 1987, Sch.3, para.16(2)*

SSWP v AR (IS) [2010] UKUT 308 (AAC) considers the test for   **3.036** deciding whether repairs and improvements have been undertaken "with a view to maintaining the fitness of the dwelling for human habitation". Judge White concludes that it is whether they would have been carried out by a sensible and prudent householder properly advised as to the reasonable necessity of the repairs/improvements and the likely consequences if they were not undertaken (as opposed to measures that are undertaken principally out of choice or preference).

pp.637–641, *annotation to the Income Support (General) Regulations 1987, Sch.3, para.17*

In *SSWP v UP (JSA)* [2010] UKUT 262 (AAC), to be reported as   **3.037** [2011] AACR 12, the issue was whether payments made under home financing arrangements specifically designed to be compliant with Shari'a principles (i.e. not involving the payment of any interest) could constitute rent relating to a long tenancy and so qualify as a housing cost under para.16(1)(a) of Sch.2 to the Jobseeker's Allowance Regulations (the equivalent of para.17(1)(a) of Sch.3 to the Income Support Regulations). A "long tenancy" is defined as "a tenancy granted for a term of years certain exceeding 21 years" in reg.1(3) of the Jobseeker's Allowance Regulations; the same definition applies for the purposes of income support (see reg.2(1) of the Income Support Regulations). The arrangement in this case was that the bank bought the property and leased it to the purchaser for 25 years. Judge Mesher held that the rent could qualify for housing costs as rent relating to a long tenancy but only if the leasehold was registered at the Land Registry.

p.659, *amendment to the Income Support (General) Regulations 1987, Sch.9 (Sums to be disregarded in the calculation of income other than earnings), para.5B*

3.038   With effect from November 1, 2010, reg.2(3)(a) of the Social Security (Miscellaneous Amendments) (No.5) Regulations 2010 (SI 2010/2429) added the following sub-paragraph after sub-para.(2) in para.5B:

"(3) Any increase in respect of a dependent child or dependent young person under section 80 or 90 of the Contributions and Benefits Act where—
  (a) the claimant has a child or young person who is a member of the claimant's family for the purposes of the claimant's claim for income support, and
  (b) the claimant, or that claimant's partner, has been awarded a child tax credit."

p.663, *amendment to the Income Support (General) Regulations 1987, Sch.9 (Sums to be disregarded in the calculation of income other than earnings), para.26*

3.039   With effect from November 1, 2010, reg.2(3)(b) of the Social Security (Miscellaneous Amendments) (No.5) Regulations 2010 (SI 2010/2429) substituted the following paragraph for para.26:

"**26.** Any payment made to the claimant with whom a person is accommodated by virtue of arrangements made—
  (a) by a local authority under—
      (i) section 23(2)(a) of the Children Act 1989 (provision of accommodation and maintenance for a child whom they are looking after),
      (ii) section 26 of the Children (Scotland) Act 1995 (manner of provision of accommodation to child looked after by local authority), or
      (iii) regulations 33 or 51 of the Looked After Children (Scotland) Regulations 2009 (fostering and kinship care allowances and fostering allowances); or
  (b) by a voluntary organisation under section 59(1)(a) of the Children Act 1989 (provision of accommodation by voluntary organisations)."

p.664, *amendment to the Income Support (General) Regulations 1987, Sch.9 (Sums to be disregarded in the calculation of income other than earnings), para.28*

With effect from November 1, 2010, reg.2(3)(c)(i) of the Social Secu-   3.040
rity (Miscellaneous Amendments) (No.5) Regulations 2010 (SI 2010/2429) inserted "22," after the word "section" in para.28(1)(c).

From the same date, reg.2(3)(c)(ii) of the same amending regulations inserted "22 or" before "29" in para.28(2).

p.677, *annotation to the Income Support (General) Regulations 1987, Sch.9, para.5B*

The effect of the new sub-para.(3) added to para.5B of Sch.9 is that   3.041
any child dependency increase paid with another benefit, such as incapacity benefit or carer's allowance, is disregarded if the claimant has
been awarded child tax credit. The disregard does not apply to those
claimants who continue to receive amounts for their children as part of
their income support.

p.795, *modification of the Community Charges (Deductions from Income Support) (No.2) Regulations 1990, reg.1 (Citation, commencement and interpretation)*

Note that for the purpose of making "conversion decisions" under the   3.042
"Migration Regulations", from October 1, 2010, reg.1 is modified. See
reg.16(1) of and Sch.2, para.23 to those Regulations: the Employment
and Support Allowance (Transitional Provisions, Housing Benefit and
Council Tax Benefit) (Existing Awards) (No.2) Regulations 2010 (SI
2010/1907) (as amended) in the "New Legislation" section of this
Supplement.

p.802, *modification of the Fines (Deductions from Income Support) Regulations 1992, reg.1 (Citation, commencement and interpretation)*

Note that for the purpose of making "conversion decisions" under the   3.043
"Migration Regulations", from October 1, 2010, reg.1 is modified. See
reg.16(1) of and Sch.2, para.24 to those Regulations: the Employment
and Support Allowance (Transitional Provisions, Housing Benefit and
Council Tax Benefit) (Existing Awards) (No.2) Regulations 2010 (SI
2010/1907) (as amended) in the "New Legislation" section of this
Supplement.

p.811, *modification of the Council Tax (Deductions from Income Support) Regulations 1993, reg.1 (Citation, commencement and interpretation)*

Note that for the purpose of making "conversion decisions" under the   3.044
"Migration Regulations", from October 1, 2010, reg.1 is modified. See
reg.16(1) of and Sch.2, para.25 to those Regulations: the Employment
and Support Allowance (Transitional Provisions, Housing Benefit and

Council Tax Benefit) (Existing Awards) (No.2) Regulations 2010 (SI 2010/1907) (as amended) in the "New Legislation" section of this Supplement.

pp.846–847, *amendment to the Jobseeker's Allowance Regulations 1996, reg.1(3) (Citation, commencement and interpretation: definition of "full-time course of advanced education")*

3.045   With effect from September 1, 2010, art.5(1) and (2) of the Apprenticeships, Skills, Children and Learning Act 2009 (Consequential Amendments to Subordinate Legislation) (England) Order 2010 (SI 2010/1941) amended the definition of "full-time course of advanced education" in reg.1(3) to read as follows:

> ""full-time course of advanced education" means a course of advanced education which is—
>> (a) a full-time course of study which is not funded in whole or in part by the [Young People's Learning Agency for England, the Chief Executive of Skills Funding] or by the Welsh Ministers or a full-time course of study which is not funded in whole or in part by the Secretary of State for Scotland at a college of further education or a full-time course of study which is a course of higher education and is funded in whole or in part by the Secretary of State for Scotland;
>> (b) a course of study which is funded in whole or in part by the [Young People's Learning Agency for England, the Chief Executive of Skills Funding] or by the Welsh Ministers if it involves more than 16 guided hours per week for the student in question, according to the number of guided learning hours per week for that student set out—
>>> [(i) in the case of a course funded by the Young People's Learning Agency for England or the Chief Executive of Skills Funding, in the student's learning agreement signed on behalf of the establishment which is funded by either of those bodies for the delivery of that course; or]
>>> (ii) in the case of a course funded by the Welsh Ministers, in a document signed on behalf of the establishment which is funded by the National Council for Education and Training for Wales for the delivery of that course; or,
>> (c) a course of study (not being higher education) which is funded in whole or in part by the Secretary of State for Scotland at a college of further education if it involves—
>>> (i) more than 16 hours per week of classroom-based or workshop-based programmed learning under the direct guidance of teaching staff according to the number of hours set out in a document signed on behalf of the college; or

(ii) 16 hours or less per week of classroom-based or work-shop-based programmed learning under the direct guidance of teaching staff and it involves additional hours using structured learning packages supported by the teaching staff where the combined total of hours exceeds 21 per week, according to the number of hours set out in a document signed on behalf of the college;".

p.847, *amendment to the Jobseeker's Allowance Regulations 1996, reg.1(3) (Citation, commencement and interpretation: definition of "full-time student")*

With effect from September 1, 2010, art.5(1) and (2) of the Apprenticeships, Skills, Children and Learning Act 2009 (Consequential Amendments to Subordinate Legislation) (England) Order 2010 (SI 2010/1941) amended the definition of "full-time student" in reg.1(3) to read as follows: 3.046

""full-time student" means a person, other than a person in receipt of a training allowance or a person who is a qualifying young person or child within the meaning of section 142 of the Benefits Act (child and qualifying young person), who is—

(a) aged less than 19 and attending or undertaking a full-time course of advanced education or

(b) aged 19 or over but under pensionable age and—

    (i) attending or undertaking a full-time course of study which is not funded in whole or in part by the [Young People's Learning Agency for England, the Chief Executive of Skills Funding] or by the Welsh Ministers or a full-time course of study which is not funded in whole or in part by the Secretary of State for Scotland at a college of further education or a full-time course of study which is a course of higher education and is funded in whole or in part by the Secretary of State for Scotland;

    (ii) attending or undertaking a course of study which is funded in whole or in part by the [Young People's Learning Agency for England, the Chief Executive of Skills Funding] or by the Welsh Ministers if it involves more than 16 guided hours per week for the student in question, according to the number of guided learning hours per week for that student set out—

    [(aa) in the case of a course funded by the Young People's Learning Agency for England or the Chief Executive of Skills Funding, in the student's learning agreement signed on behalf of the establishment which is funded by either of those bodies for the delivery of that course; or,] (bb) in the case of a course funded by the National Council for Education and Training for Wales, in a document signed on behalf of the establishment which is funded by the Welsh Ministers for the delivery of that course; or

  (iii) attending or undertaking a course of study (not being higher education) which is funded in whole or in part by the Secretary of State for Scotland at a college of further education if it involves—

   (aa) more than 16 hours per week of classroom-based or workshop-based programmed learning under the direct guidance of teaching staff according to the number of hours set out in a document signed on behalf of the college; or

   (bb) 16 hours or less per week of classroom or workshop based programmed learning under the direct guidance of teaching staff and it involves additional hours using structured learning packages supported by the teaching staff where the combined total of hours exceeds 21 per week, according to the number of hours set out in a document signed on behalf of the college;".

p.848, *amendment to the Jobseeker's Allowance Regulations 1996, reg.1(3) (Citation, commencement and interpretation: definition of "independent hospital")*

3.047 With effect from September 1, 2010, arts 2 and 8 of the Health and Social Care Act 2008 (Miscellaneous Consequential Amendments) Order 2010 (SI 2010/1881) amended reg.2(1) by substituting the following for the definition of "independent hospital":

""independent hospital"—

  (a) in England, means a hospital as defined by section 275 of the National Health Service Act 2006 that is not a health service hospital as defined by that section;

  (b) in Wales, has the meaning assigned to it by section 2 of the Care Standards Act 2000; and

  (c) in Scotland, means an independent healthcare service as defined in section 2(5)(a) and (b) of the Regulation of Care (Scotland) Act 2001;".

p.852, *amendment to the Jobseeker's Allowance Regulations 1996, reg.1(3) (Citation, commencement and interpretation: definition of "training allowance")*

3.048 With effect from September 1, 2010, art.5(1) and (2) of the Apprenticeships, Skills, Children and Learning Act 2009 (Consequential Amendments to Subordinate Legislation) (England) Order 2010 (SI 2010/1941) amended the definition of "full-time student" in reg.1(3) by substituting the words, "Young People's Learning Agency for England, the Chief Executive of Skills Funding" for the words, "Learning and Skills Council for England" in para.(a) of the definition.

p.871, *amendment to the Jobseeker's Allowance Regulations 1996, reg.5 (exceptions to requirement to be available immediately)*

With effect from April 26, 2010, reg.2(2) of the Jobseeker's Allowance **3.049** (Lone Parents) (Availability for Work) Regulations 2010 (SI 2010/837) amended para.(4) by inserting ", 13A" after "13", and amended para.(5) by replacing "or 13" with ", 13 or 13A".

p.874, *amendment to the Jobseeker's Allowance Regulations 1996, reg.6 (employment of at least 40 hours per week)*

With effect from April 26, 2010, reg.2(3) of the Jobseeker's Allowance **3.050** (Lone Parents) (Availability for Work) Regulations 2010 (SI 2010/837) amended each para. of reg.6 by replacing "13 or" with "13, regulation 13A or".

p.875, *amendment to the Jobseeker's Allowance Regulations 1996, reg.7(1) (restriction of hours . . . to 40 hours per week)*

With effect from April 26, 2010, reg.2(4) of the Jobseeker's Allowance **3.051** (Lone Parents) (Availability for Work) Regulations 2010 (SI 2010/837) amended reg.7(1) by replacing "regulation 13 and in regulation 17(2)" with "regulations 13, 13A and 17(2)".

p.880, *amendment to the Jobseeker's Allowance Regulations 1996, reg.8 (Other restrictions on availability)*

With effect from April 26, 2010, reg.2(5) of the Jobseeker's Allowance **3.052** (Lone Parents) (Availability for Work) Regulations 2010 (SI 2010/837) amended reg.8 by inserting "13A" before "or 17(2)".

p.882, *amendment to the Jobseeker's Allowance Regulations 1996, reg.11(1) (Part-time students)*

With effect from April 26, 2010, reg.2(6) of the Jobseeker's Allowance **3.053** (Lone Parents) (Availability for Work) Regulations 2010 (SI 2010/837) amended reg.11(1)(b) by inserting "13A" before "or 17(2)".

p.884, *amendment to the Jobseeker's Allowance Regulations 1996, reg.12(1) (Volunteers)*

With effect from April 26, 2010, reg.2(7) of the Jobseeker's Allowance **3.054** (Lone Parents) (Availability for Work) Regulations 2010 (SI 2010/837) amended reg.12(1)(a) by inserting "13A" before "or 17(2)".

p.885, *amendment to the Jobseeker's Allowance Regulations 1996, reg.13(2) (Additional restrictions on availability for certain groups)*

3.055   With effect from April 26, 2010, reg.2(8) of the Jobseeker's Allowance (Lone Parents) (Availability for Work) Regulations 2010 (SI 2010/837) amended reg.13(2) by inserting ", regulation 13A or" after "paragraph (3), (3A) or (4) of this regulation".

p.889, *amendment to the Jobseeker's Allowance Regulations 1996: insertion of new reg.13A*

3.056   With effect from April 26, 2010, reg.2(9) of the Jobseeker's Allowance (Lone Parents) (Availability for Work) Regulations 2010 (SI 2010/837) inserted between regs 13 and 14 a new reg.13A to read:

"Additional restrictions on availability for lone parents

13A. A lone parent who in any week is responsible for, and a member of the same household as, a child under the age of 13 may restrict his availability for employment to the child's normal school hours."

p.891, *amendment to the Jobseeker's Allowance Regulations 1996, reg.14(2A) (Circumstances in which a person is to be treated as available)*

3.057   With effect from April 26, 2010, reg.2(10) of the Jobseeker's Allowance (Lone Parents) (Availability for Work) Regulations 2010 (SI 2010/837) amended para.(2A) by inserting ", 13A" before "or 17(2)" in the two places in which "or 17(2)" appears.

p.930, *amendment to the Jobseeker's Allowance Regulations 1996, reg.31(c) (Contents of Jobseeker's Agreement)*

3.058   With effect from April 26, 2010, reg.2(11) of the Jobseeker's Allowance (Lone Parents) (Availability for Work) Regulations 2010 (SI 2010/837) amended para.(c) by inserting ", or 13A" after "13".

p.934, *amendment to the Jobseeker's Allowance Regulations 1996: insertion of new reg.45A*

3.059   With effect from November 1, 2010, reg.2 of the the Social Security (Contribution Conditions for Jobseeker's Allowance and Employment and Support Allowance) Regulations 2010 (SI 2010/2446) inserted a new reg.45A between the heading ("OTHER CONDITIONS OF ENTITLEMENT") and reg.46, to read:

"The contribution-based conditions and relevant earnings

45A.—(1) A claimant's relevant earnings for the purposes of section 2(2)(b) of the Act are the total amount of the claimant's earnings at the lower earnings limit for the base year.

(2) For the purposes of paragraph (1), earnings which exceed the lower earnings limit are to be disregarded."

As noted in the updates to pp.37 and 38–39, above, the changes effected by s.12 of the Welfare Reform Act 2009 and this regulation made in consequence significantly tighten the contribution conditions for CBJSA. Together they mean that the requisite level of "relevant earnings" in the tax year relied on for the first contribution condition is now 26 times that year's lower earnings limit, rather than 25. This new regulation defines "relevant earnings" to cover only earnings at that lower earnings limit, so that new claimants will have to have worked for at least 26 weeks in one of the last two tax years (April 6 to April 5) complete before the start of the benefit year (beginning in early January) which includes the first day of claim in the relevant jobseeking period.

p.936, *amendment to the Jobseeker's Allowance Regulations 1996, reg.47(4)(b)(ii) (Jobseeking period)*

With effect from April 1, 2010, reg.11(2) of the Social Security (Loss of Benefit) (Amendment) Regulations 2010 (SI 2010/1160) amended para.(4)(b)(ii) by inserting in the penultimate line of the sub-para."6B," between "section" and "7". 3.060

p.957, *amendment to the Jobseeker's Allowance Regulations 1996, reg.57(1) (Interpretation of Part IV: definition of "training")*

With effect from September 1, 2010, art.5(1) and (4) of the Apprenticeships, Skills, Children and Learning Act 2009 (Consequential Amendments to Subordinate Legislation) (England) Order 2010 (SI 2010/1941) amended the definition of "training" in reg.57(1) by substituting the words, "Young People's Learning Agency for England, the Chief Executive of Skills Funding" for the words, "Learning and Skills Council for England". 3.061

p.958, *amendment to the Jobseeker's Allowance Regulations 1996, reg.57(1) (Interpretation of Part IV)*

With effect from September 1, 2010, reg.2 of the Education and Inspections Act 2006 and Education and Skills Act 2008 (Consequential Amendments to Subordinate Legislation) (England) Regulations 2010 (SI 2010/1939) amended reg.57(1) by substituting the following for the definition of "the Connexions Service": 3.062

""the Connexions Service" means a service made available by a local authority in accordance with section 68 of the Education and Skills Act 2008;".

p.982, *annotation to the Jobseeker's Allowance Regulations 1996, reg.69 (Prescribed period for purposes of section 19(2))*

SSWP v JB (JSA) [2010] UKUT 4 (AAC) is reported as [2010] AACR 25. 3.063

p.985, *amendment to the Jobseeker's Allowance Regulations 1996, reg.72(2)(a) (Good cause)*

3.064   With effect from April 26, 2010, reg.2(12) of the Jobseeker's Allowance (Lone Parents) (Availability for Work) Regulations 2010 (SI 2010/837) amended para.(2)(a) by inserting ", or 13A" after "13".

p.1082, *amendment to the Jobseeker's Allowance Regulations 1996, reg.130 (Interpretation), definition of "access funds"*

3.065   With effect from September 1, 2010, art.5(6) of the Apprenticeships, Skills, Children and Learning Act 2009 (Consequential Amendments to Subordinate Legislation) (England) Order 2010 (SI 2010/1941) substituted the words, "Young People's Learning Agency for England under sections 61 and 62 of the Apprenticeships, Skills, Children and Learning Act 2009 or the Chief Executive of Skills Funding under sections 100 and 101 of that Act" for the words, "Learning and Skills Council for England under sections 5, 6 and 9 of the Learning and Skills Act 2000" in para.(d) of the definition of "access funds".

p.1082, *amendment to the Jobseeker's Allowance Regulations 1996, reg.130 (Interpretation), definition of "education authority"*

3.066   With effect from May 5, 2010, art.5 of and para.27(3) of Sch.3 to the Local Education Authorities and Children's Services Authorities (Integration of Functions) (Local and Subordinate Legislation) Order 2010 (SI 2010/1172) substituted the words, "a local authority as defined in section 579 of the Education Act 1996" for the words, "a local education authority as defined in section 114(1) of the Education Act 1944" in the definition of "education authority" in reg.130.

p.1123, *amendment to the Jobseeker's Allowance Regulations 1996, reg.170 (Persons in receipt of a training allowance)*

3.067   With effect from September 1, 2010, art.5(5) of the Apprenticeships, Skills, Children and Learning Act 2009 (Consequential Amendments to Subordinate Legislation) (England) Order 2010 (SI 2010/1941) substituted the words, "Young People's Learning Agency for England, the Chief Executive of Skills Funding" for the words, "Learning and Skills Council for England" in reg.170(2).

p.1125, *amendment to the Jobseeker's Allowance Regulations 1996, Sch.A1 (Categories of members of a joint-claim couple who are not required to satisfy the conditions in section 1(2B)(b)), para.6 (Member incapable of work)*

3.068   With effect from November 1, 2010, reg.4(2)(a)(i) of the Social Security (Miscellaneous Amendments) (No.5) Regulations 2010 (SI 2010/2429) revoked sub-paras (a) and (b) of para.6, subject to the saving provision in reg.4(3) and (4).

From the same date, reg.4(2)(b) of the same amending Regulations substituted the following heading for the heading to para.6:

"Member treated as capable of work, or member entitled to statutory sick pay".

From the same date, reg.4(2)(c) of the same amending Regulations substituted the words "the Benefits Act" for the words "that Act" in para.6(c).

p.1126, *amendment to the Jobseeker's Allowance Regulations 1996, Sch.A1 (Categories of members of a joint-claim couple who are not required to satisfy the conditions in section 1(2B)(b)), para.9 (Disabled students)*

With effect from November 1, 2010, reg.4(2)(a)(ii) of the Social   3.069
Security (Miscellaneous Amendments) (No.5) Regulations 2010 (SI 2010/2429 revoked sub-para.9, subject to the saving provision in reg.4(3) and (4).

p.1126, *amendment to the Jobseeker's Allowance Regulations 1996, Sch.A1 (Categories of members of a joint-claim couple who are not required to satisfy the conditions in section 1(2B)(b)), para.10 (Deaf students)*

With effect from November 1, 2010, reg.4(2)(a)(iii) of the Social   3.069.1
Security (Miscellaneous Amendments) (No.5) Regulations 2010 (SI 2010/2429) revoked sub-para.10, subject to the saving provision in reg.4(3) and (4).

p.1126, *amendment to the Jobseeker's Allowance Regulations 1996, Sch.A1 (Categories of members of a joint-claim couple who are not required to satisfy the conditions in section 1(2B)(b)), para.11 (Blind members)*

With effect from November 1, 2010, reg.4(2)(a)(iv) of the Social   3.069.2
Security (Miscellaneous Amendments) (No.5) Regulations 2010 (SI 2010/2429) revoked sub-para.11, subject to the saving provision in reg.4(3) and (4).

p.1127, *amendment to the Jobseeker's Allowance Regulations 1996, Sch.A1 (Categories of members of a joint-claim couple who are not required to satisfy the conditions in section 1(2B)(b)), para.16 (Young persons in training)*

With effect from September 1, 2010, art.5(5) of the Apprenticeships,   3.070
Skills, Children and Learning Act 2009 (Consequential Amendments to Subordinate Legislation) (England) Order 2010 (SI 2010/1941) substituted the words, "Young People's Learning Agency for England, the Chief Executive of Skills Funding" for the words, "Learning and Skills Council for England" in para.16.

p.1128, *annotation to the Jobseeker's Allowance Regulations 1996, Sch.A1, paras 6, 9, 10 and 11*

3.071   Many of the categories in Sch.A1 are similar to those in Sch.1B to the Income Support Regulations (people eligible for IS). In order to mirror the changes to Sch.1B to the Income Support Regulations made as a result of the introduction of ESA, paras 6(a) and (b), 9, 10 and 11 are revoked. This will not, however, apply to joint-claim claimants who immediately before November 1, 2010 were entitled to JSA and to whom one of those provisions applied (reg.4(3) of the Social Security (Miscellaneous Amendments) (No.5) Regulations 2010 (SI 2010/2429)). This savings provision ceases to apply when the JSA award to which the couple were entitled before November 1, 2010 ends (reg.4(4) of the 2010 Regulations).

p.1154, *amendment to the Jobseeker's Allowance Regulations 1996, Sch.2 (Housing costs), para.11 (The standard rate)*

3.072   With effect from October 1, 2010, reg.2(1)(b) and (2) of the Social Security (Housing Costs) (Standard Interest Rate) Amendment Regulations 2010 (SI 2010/1811) substituted the following sub-paragraphs for sub-para.(2) in para.11:

"(2) Subject to the following provisions of this paragraph, the standard rate is to be the average mortgage rate published by the Bank of England in August 2010.

(2A) The standard rate is to be varied each time that sub-paragraph (2B) applies.

(2B) This sub-paragraph applies when, on any reference day, the Bank of England publishes an average mortgage rate which differs by 0.5% or more from the standard rate that applies on that reference day (whether by virtue of sub-paragraph (2) or of a previous application of this sub-paragraph).

(2C) The average mortgage rate published on that reference day then becomes the new standard rate in accordance with sub-paragraph (2D).

(2D) Any variation in the standard rate by virtue of sub-paragraphs (2A) to (2C) comes into effect—
   (a) for the purposes of sub-paragraph (2B) (in consequence of its first and any subsequent application), on the day after the reference day referred to in sub-paragraph (2C);
   (b) for the purpose of calculating the weekly amount of housing costs to be met under this Schedule, on the day specified by the Secretary of State.

(2E) In this paragraph—
"average mortgage rate" means the effective interest rate (non-seasonally adjusted) of United Kingdom resident banks and building societies for loans to households secured on dwellings

published by the Bank of England in respect of the most recent period for that rate specified at the time of publication;
"reference day" means any day falling after 1st October 2010."

p.1164, *annotation to the Jobseeker's Allowance Regulations 1996, Sch.2, para.11*

On the new para.11(2) to (2E), see the note to para.12 of Sch.3 to the 3.073
Income Support (General) Regulations 1987, update to p.623, above.

p.1184, *amendment to the Jobseeker's Allowance Regulations 1996, Sch.7 (Sums to be disregarded in the calculation of income other than earnings), para.6B*

With effect from November 1, 2010, reg.4(5)(a) of the Social Security 3.074
(Miscellaneous Amendments) (No.5) Regulations 2010 (SI 2010/2429)
added the following sub-paragraph after sub-para.(2) in para.6B:

"(3) Any increase in respect of a dependent child or dependent young person under section 80 or 90 of the Benefits Act where—
  (a) the claimant has a child or young person who is a member of the claimant's family for the purposes of the claimant's claim for income-based jobseeker's allowance, and
  (b) the claimant, or that claimant's partner, has been awarded a child tax credit."

p.1188, *amendment to the Jobseeker's Allowance Regulations 1996, Sch.7 (Sums to be disregarded in the calculation of income other than earnings), para.27*

With effect from November 1, 2010, reg.4(5)(b) of the Social Security 3.075
(Miscellaneous Amendments) (No.5) Regulations 2010 (SI 2010/2429)
substituted the following paragraph for para.27:

"**27.** Any payment made to the claimant with whom a person is accommodated by virtue of arrangements made—
  (a) by a local authority under—
      (i) section 23(2)(a) of the Children Act 1989 (provision of accommodation and maintenance for a child whom they are looking after),
      (ii) section 26 of the Children (Scotland) Act 1995 (manner of provision of accommodation to child looked after by local authority), or
      (iii) regulations 33 or 51 of the Looked After Children (Scotland) Regulations 2009 (fostering and kinship care allowances and fostering allowances); or
  (b) by a voluntary organisation under section 59(1)(a) of the Children Act 1989 (provision of accommodation by voluntary organisations)."

p.1188, *amendment to the Jobseeker's Allowance Regulations 1996, Sch.7 (Sums to be disregarded in the calculation of income other than earnings), para.29*

3.076   With effect from November 1, 2010, reg.4(5)(c)(i) of the Social Security (Miscellaneous Amendments) (No.5) Regulations 2010 (SI 2010/2429) inserted "22," after the word "section" in para.29(1)(c).

From the same date, reg.4(5)(c)(ii) of the same amending Regulations inserted "22 or" before "29" in para.29(2).

p.1197, *annotation to the Jobseeker's Allowance Regulations 1996, Sch.7, para.6B*

3.077   On the new sub-para.(3) added to para.6B of Sch.7, see the note to para.5B of Sch.9 to the Income Support (General) Regulations 1987, update to p.677, above.

p.1217, *amendment to the State Pension Credit Regulations 2002, reg.1(2)*

3.078   With effect from October 1, 2010, Health and Social Care Act 2008 (Miscellaneous Consequential Amendments) Order 2010 (SI 2010/1881) substituted the following definition for the definition of "independent hospital" in reg.1(2):

""independent hospital"—
    (a) in England, means a hospital as defined by section 275 of the National Health Service Act 2006 that is not a health service hospital as defined by that section;
    (b) in Wales, has the meaning assigned to it by section 2 of the Care Standards Act 2000; and
    (c) in Scotland, means an independent healthcare service as defined in section 2(5)(a) and (b) of the Regulation of Care (Scotland) Act 2001;".

p.1223, *annotation to the State Pension Credit Regulations 2002, reg.2*

3.079   *EC v SSWP* [2010] UKUT 93 (AAC) is reported as [2010] AACR 39; the Court of Appeal's decision in *Pedro v SSWP* is reported as [2010] AACR 18. On the importance of fact-finding where there is a claim of dependency on a relative, see *LA v SSWP* [2010] UKUT 109 (AAC). For a discussion of what may be needed to lose habitual residence, see *KS v SSWP* [2010] UKUT 156 (AAC), holding that a VSO volunteer who went to India for more than two years had not lost his UK habitual residence.

p.1249, *amendment to the State Pension Credit Regulations 2002, reg.17B(4)*

3.080   With effect from November 1, 2010, reg.6 of the Social Security (Miscellaneous Amendments) (No.5) Regulations 2010 (SI 2010/2429) substituted, "the following paragraph shall be added after paragraph (1)" in place of, "for paragraph (2), the following provision shall have effect" in reg.17B(4)(b), and for sub-para.(b) of the new para.(2) to be added to reg.12 (earnings of self-employed earners) of the Social Security Benefits (Computation of Earnings) Regulations 1996, substituted the following:

"(b) any payment made by a local authority to a claimant with whom a person is accommodated by virtue of arrangements made under—

  (i) section 23(2)(a) of the Children Act 1989 (provision of accommodation and maintenance for a child whom they are looking after),

  (ii) section 26 of the Children (Scotland) Act 1995 (manner of provision of accommodation to child looked after by local authority), or

  (iii) regulations 33 or 51 of the Looked After Children (Scotland) Regulations 2009 (fostering and kinship care allowances and fostering allowances);".

p.1259, *annotation to the State Pension Credit Regulations 2002, reg.23*

For a valuable reminder that in cases where capital is held jointly, "the market value of such an interest in circumstances such as these is not by any means the same thing as half the entire value of the freehold with vacant possession", see *AM v SSWP* [2010] UKUT 134 (AAC) (at para.5), applying *R(IS) 5/07*.   3.081

p.1273, *amendments to the State Pension Credit Regulations 2002, Sch.2, para.9*

With effect from October 1, 2010, Social Security (Housing Costs) (Standard Interest Rate) Amendment Regulations 2010 (SI 2010/1811) substituted the following sub-paragraphs for sub-para.(2):   3.082

"(2) Subject to the following provisions of this paragraph, the standard rate is to be the average mortgage rate published by the Bank of England in August 2010.

(2A) The standard rate is to be varied each time that sub-paragraph (2B) applies.

(2B) This sub-paragraph applies when, on any reference day, the Bank of England publishes an average mortgage rate which differs by 0.5% or more from the standard rate that applies on that reference day (whether by virtue of sub-paragraph (2) or of a previous application of this sub-paragraph).

(2C) The average mortgage rate published on that reference day then becomes the new standard rate in accordance with sub-paragraph (2D).

(2D) Any variation in the standard rate by virtue of sub-paragraphs (2A) to (2C) comes into effect—

(a) for the purposes of sub-paragraph (2B) (in consequence of its first and any subsequent application), on the day after the reference day referred to in sub-paragraph (2C);

(b) for the purpose of calculating the weekly amount of housing costs to be met under this Schedule, on the day specified by the Secretary of State.

(2E) In this paragraph—

"average mortgage rate" means the effective interest rate (non-seasonally adjusted) of United Kingdom resident banks and building societies for loans to households secured on dwellings published by the Bank of England in respect of the most recent period for that rate specified at the time of publication;

"reference day" means any day falling after 1st October 2010."

p.1278, *annotation to the State Pension Credit Regulations 2002, Sch.II, para.3*

3.083   See further *AH v SSWP* [2010] UKUT 353 (AAC).

p.1293, *annotation to the State Pension Credit Regulations 2002, Sch. V, para.10*

3.084   See further *AB v SSWP* [2010] UKUT 343 (AAC), where the claimant wrote to the DWP asking for a recalculation of his pension credit and for it to be backdated, as he now realised that on his claim form he had declared details of the surrender value of a life insurance policy which should not have been counted as part of his capital resources. His benefit was recalculated as from the date of the letter. Judge Ovey held that the tribunal had erred in treating the information supplied by the claimant as a notification of a change of circumstances rather than revelation of a mistake in the calculation of the original award, and had further failed to consider whether there had been an official error in the making of that award.

p.1294, *annotation to the State Pension Credit Regulations 2002, Sch. V, paras 17–19*

3.085   See *DH v SSWP* [2010] UKUT 241 (AAC), confirming that for the purposes of the disregard in paras 17(b) and 19, time runs from the actual date of receipt of the funds, regardless of whether the claimant is actually in the United Kingdom at the time in question.

p.1303, *amendment to the Social Fund Cold Weather Payments (General) Regulations 1988, reg.1(2) (Interpretation: definition of "the Act")*

3.086   With effect from November 1, 2010, reg.2(1) and (2)(a) of the Social Fund Cold Weather Payments (General) Amendment Regulations 2010 (SI 2010/2442) substituted the following for the definition of "the Act" in reg.1(2):

""the Act" means the Social Security Contributions and Benefits Act 1992;".

p.1304, *amendment to the Social Fund Cold Weather Payments (General) Regulations 1988, reg.1(2) (Interpretation: definition of "child")*

With effect from November 1, 2010, reg.2(1) and (2)(b) of the Social Fund Cold Weather Payments (General) Amendment Regulations 2010 (SI 2010/2442) revoked the definition of "child" in reg.1(2).   **3.087**

p.1304, *amendment to the Social Fund Cold Weather Payments (General) Regulations 1988, reg.1(2) (Interpretation: definition of "cold weather payment")*

With effect from November 1, 2010, reg.2(1) and (2)(e) of the Social Fund Cold Weather Payments (General) Amendment Regulations 2010 (SI 2010/2442) inserted the following definition of "cold weather payment" immediately after the definition of "claimant" in reg.1(2):   **3.088**

> ""cold weather payment" means a payment to meet expenses for heating made out of the social fund under section 138(2) of the Act and these Regulations;".

p.1304, *amendment to the Social Fund Cold Weather Payments (General) Regulations 1988, reg.1(2) (Interpretation: definition of "family")*

With effect from November 1, 2010, reg.2(1) and (2)(c) of the Social Fund Cold Weather Payments (General) Amendment Regulations 2010 (SI 2010/2442) substituted the following for the definition of "family" in reg.1(2):   **3.089**

> ""family" has the meaning given to it in section 137 of the Act and the General Regulations;".

p.1304, *amendment to the Social Fund Cold Weather Payments (General) Regulations 1988, reg.1(2) (Interpretation: definition of "income support")*

With effect from November 1, 2010, reg.2(1) and (2)(d) of the Social Fund Cold Weather Payments (General) Amendment Regulations 2010 (SI 2010/2442) substituted the following for the definition of "income support" in reg.1(2):   **3.090**

> ""income support" means income support under Part 7 of the Act;".

p.1304, *amendment to the Social Fund Cold Weather Payments (General) Regulations 1988, reg.1(2) (Interpretation: definition of "polygamous marriage")*

With effect from November 1, 2010, reg.2(1) and (2)(b) of the Social Fund Cold Weather Payments (General) Amendment Regulations 2010   **3.091**

(SI 2010/2442) revoked the definition of "polygamous marriage" in reg.1(2).

p.1305, *amendment to the Social Fund Cold Weather Payments (General) Regulations 1988, reg.1(2) (Interpretation: definition of "winter period")*

3.092   With effect from November 1, 2010, reg.2(1) and (2)(e) of the Social Fund Cold Weather Payments (General) Amendment Regulations 2010 (SI 2010/2442) inserted the following definition of "winter period" immediately after the definition of "station" in reg.1(2):

> ""winter period" means the period beginning on 1st November in any year and ending on 31st March in the following year."

p.1306, *amendment to the Social Fund Cold Weather Payments (General) Regulations, reg.1A(3)(b) (Prescribed description of persons: definition of "independent hospital")*

3.093   With effect from September 1, 2010, arts 2 and 6 of the Health and Social Care Act 2008 (Miscellaneous Consequential Amendments) Order 2010 amended reg.1A(3)(b) by substituting the following for the definition of "independent hospital":

> ""independent hospital"—
> > (i) in England, means a hospital as defined by section 275 of the National Health Service Act 2006 that is not a health service hospital as defined by that section;
> > (ii) in Wales, has the meaning assigned to it by section 2 of the Care Standards Act 2000; and
> > (iii) in Scotland, means an independent healthcare service as defined in section 2(5)(a) and (b) of the Regulation of Care (Scotland) Act 2001;".

p.1306, *amendment to the Social Fund Cold Weather Payments (General) Regulations 1988, reg.1A (Prescribed definition of persons)*

3.094   With effect from November 1, 2010, reg.2(1) and (3) of the Social Fund Cold Weather Payments (General) Amendment Regulations 2010 (SI 2010/2442) and reg.3(1) of the Social Fund Cold Weather Payments (General) Amendment (No.2) Regulations 2010 (SI 2010/2591) substituted the following for reg.1A:

"Prescribed description of persons

1A.—(1) A cold weather payment may be made in the circumstances prescribed by regulation 2 to a person who satisfies the following conditions.

(2) The first condition is that, in respect of at least one day during the recorded or the forecasted period of cold weather specified in regulation 2(1)(a), the person has been awarded—
(a) state pension credit;
(b) income support;

(c) an income-based jobseeker's allowance; or

(d) an income-related employment and support allowance.

(3) The second condition (which applies only if the person ("P") falls within paragraph (2)(b), (c) or (d)) is that, in respect of the day to which paragraph (2) relates—

(a) P's family includes a member aged less than 5;

(b) where P has been awarded income support, P's applicable amount includes one or more of the premiums specified in paragraphs 9 to 14 of Part 3 of Schedule 2 to the General Regulations;

(c) where P has been awarded a jobseeker's allowance, P's applicable amount includes one or more of the premiums specified in paragraphs 10 to 16 of Part 3 of Schedule 1 to the Jobseeker's Allowance Regulations 1996;

(d) P's child tax credit includes an individual element referred to in regulation 7(4)(a), (b), (d) or (e) of the Child Tax Credit Regulations 2002; or

(e) where P has been awarded an employment and support allowance, P's applicable amount includes—

　(i) one or more of the premiums specified in paragraphs 5 to 7 of Schedule 4 to the Employment and Support Allowance Regulations 2008, or

　(ii) an amount under section 4(2)(b) of the Welfare Reform Act.

(4) The third condition (which does not apply to a person who comes [within] paragraph (3)(a) or (d)) is that the person does not reside in—

(a) a care home;

(b) an independent hospital;

(c) an establishment run by the Abbeyfield Society or by a body corporate or incorporate which is affiliated to that Society; or

(d) accommodation provided under section 3(1) of, and Part 2 of the Schedule to, the Polish Resettlement Act 1947 (provision by the Secretary of State of accommodation in camps).

(5) In paragraph (4)—

(a) "care home" in England and Wales has the meaning assigned to it by section 3 of the Care Standards Act 2000, and in Scotland means a care home service as defined by section 2(3) of the Regulation of Care (Scotland) Act 2001;

(b) "independent hospital"—

　(i) in England, means a hospital as defined by section 275 of the National Health Service Act 2006 that is not a health service hospital as defined by that section;

　(ii) in Wales, has the meaning assigned to it by section 2 of the Care Standards Act 2000; and

　(iii) in Scotland, means an independent healthcare service as defined in section 2(5)(a) and (b) of the Regulation of Care (Scotland) Act 2001."

p.1307, *amendment to the Social Fund Cold Weather Payments (General) Regulations 1988, reg.2 (Prescribed circumstances)*

3.095   With effect from November 1, 2010, reg.2(1) and (4) of the Social Fund Cold Weather Payments (General) Amendment Regulations 2010 (SI 2010/2442) amended reg.2 to read as follows:

"Prescribed circumstances

2.—(1) The prescribed circumstances in which [a cold weather payment may be made] are—

(a) subject to paragraphs (1A), (1B), (3), (4) [, (5) and (6)]—

   (i) there is a recorded period of cold weather at a station identified in column (1) of Schedule 1 to these Regulations; or

   (ii) there is a forecasted period of cold weather at a station identified in column (1) of Schedule 1 to these Regulations; and

   (iii) . . .

(b) the home of the claimant is, or by virtue of paragraph (2)(b) is treated as, situated in a postcode district in respect of which the station mentioned in sub-paragraph (a)(i) or, as the case may be, (a)(ii) is the designated station.

(c) . . .

(1A) For the purposes of paragraph (1)(a)(i), where a station identified in column (1) of Schedule 1 to these Regulations (in this paragraph and in paragraph (1B) referred to as "the primary station") is unable to provide temperature information in respect of a particular day, the mean daily temperature on that day—

(a) at the alternative station for that primary station specified in column (2) of Schedule 2 to these Regulations; or

(b) where there is no such alternative station specified, at the nearest station to that primary station able to provide temperature information in respect of that day, shall be used to determine whether or not there is a recorded period of cold weather at the relevant primary station.

(1B) For the purposes of paragraph (1)(a)(ii), where the Meteorological Office is unable to produce a forecast in respect of a particular period at a primary station, any forecast produced in respect of that period—

(a) at the alternative station for that primary station specified in column (2) of Schedule 2 to these Regulations; or

(b) where there is no such alternative station specified, at the nearest station to that primary station able to provide temperature information for that period, shall be used to determine whether or not there is a forecasted period of cold weather at the relevant primary station.

(2) For the purposes of this regulation—

(a) the station identified in column (1) of Schedule 1 to these Regulations is the designated station for the postcode districts identified in the corresponding paragraph in column (2) of that Schedule;

(b) where the home of the claimant is not situated within a post-code district identified in column (2) of that Schedule, it shall be treated as situated within the postcode district nearest to it identified in that column.

(3) Subject to paragraphs (4) and (5) where a recorded period of cold weather is joined by an overlap period to a forecasted period of cold weather a payment under paragraph (1) may only be made in respect of the forecasted period of cold weather.

(4) Where—

(a) there is a continuous period of forecasted periods of cold weather, each of which is linked by an overlap period; and

(b) the total number of recorded periods of cold weather during that continuous period is greater than the total number of forecasted periods of cold weather, a payment in respect of the last recorded period of cold weather may also be made under paragraph (1).

[(5) Where—

(a) a claimant satisfies the conditions in regulation 1A and para-graph (1) in respect of a recorded period of cold weather, and

(b) a payment in respect of the recorded period of cold weather does not fall to be made by virtue of paragraph (4), and

(c) the claimant does not satisfy the conditions in regulation 1A in respect of the forecasted period of cold weather which is linked to the recorded period of cold weather by an overlap period,

a cold weather payment may be made in respect of that recorded period of cold weather.

(6) A cold weather payment may not be made after the end of the period of 26 weeks beginning with the last day of the winter period in which the period of cold weather concerned falls.]"

p.1310, *amendment to the Social Fund Cold Weather Payments (General) Regulations 1988, reg.3 (Prescribed amount)*

With effect from November 1, 2010, reg.2(1) and (6) of the Social Fund Cold Weather Payments (General) Amendment Regulations (No.2) 2010 (SI 2010/2591) amended reg.3 by substituting "£25" for "£8.50". 3.096

pp.1311–1313, *amendment to the Social Fund Cold Weather Payments (General) Regulations 1988, Sch.1 (Identification of stations and postcode districts)*

With effect from November 1, 2010, reg.2(1) and (5) of the Social Fund Cold Weather Payments (General) Amendment Regulations 2010 (SI 2010/2442) substituted the following for Sch.1: 3.097

Income Support, Jobseeker's Allowance, etc.

"[Regulation 2(1)(a) and (2)

SCHEDULE 1

IDENTIFICATION OF STATIONS AND POSTCODE DISTRICTS

Column (1) *Meteorological Office Station*	Column (2) *Postal Districts*
1. Aberporth	SA35–48, SA64–65.
2. Albemarle	DH1–7, DH9, DL4–5, DL14–17, NE1–13, NE15–18, NE20–21, NE23, NE25–46, SR1–7, TS21, TS28–29.
3. Andrewsfield	CB1–5, CB10–11, CB21–25. CM1–9, CM11–24, CM77, CO9, RM4, SG8–11.
4. Aultbea	IV21–22, IV26.
5. Aviemore	AB37, PH19–26.
6. Bedford	MK1–19, MK40–46, NN1–16, NN29, PE19, SG5–7, SG15–19.
7. Bingley	BB4, BB8–12, BB18, BD1–24, BL0, BL7–8, DL8, DL11, HD3, HD7–9, HX1–7, LS21, LS29, OL1–5, OL11–16, S36, SK13.
8. Bishopton	G1–5, G11–15, G20–23, G31–34, G40–46, G51–53, G60–62, G64, G66, G69, G71–78, G81–84. KA1–18, KA20–25, KA28–30, ML1–5, PA1–27, PA32.
9. Boscombe Down	BA12, RG28, SO20–23, SP1–5, SP7, SP9–11.
10. Boulmer	NE22, NE24, NE61–70.
11. Braemar	AB33–36, PH10–11, PH18.
12. Brize Norton	OX1–6, OX8, OX10–14, OX18, OX20, OX25–29, OX33, OX44, SN7.
13. Capel Curig	LL24–25, LL41.
14. Cardinham (Bodmin)	PL13–18, PL22–35, TR9.
15. Carlisle	CA1–8, DG12, DG16.
16. Cassley	IV27–28, KW11, KW13.
17. Charlwood	BN5–6, BN44, GU5–6, ME6, ME14–20, RH1–20, TN1–20, TN22, TN27.

Column (1) Meteorological Office Station	Column (2) Postal Districts
18. Charterhall	NE71, TD1–6, TD8, TD10–15.
19. Chivenor	EX22, EX31–34, EX39.
20. Coleshill	B1–21, B23–38, B40, B42–50, B60–80, B90–98, CV1–12, CV21–23, CV31–35, CV37, CV47, DY1–14. LE10, WS1–15, WV1–16.
21. Crosby	CH41–49, CH60–66, FY1–8, L1–40, PR1–9, PR25–26, WA1–2, WA4–12, WN1–6, WN8.
22. Culdrose	TR1–8, TR10–20, TR26–27.
23. Dundrennan	DG1–2, DG5–7.
24. Dunkeswell Aerodrome	DT6–8, EX1–5, EX8–15, EX24, TA21.
25. Dunstaffnage	PA30–31, PA34–35, PA37–38, PA62–65, PA68–72.
26. Dyce	AB10–16, AB21–25, AB30–32, AB39, AB41–43, AB51–54, DD8–9.
27. Edinburgh Gogarbank	EH1–42, EH47–49, EH51–55, FK1–7, FK9–10, KY3, KY11–13.
28. Eskdalemuir	DG3–4, DG10–11, DG13–14, ML12, TD7, TD9.
29. Filton	BS1–11, BS13–16, BS20–24, BS29–32, BS34–37, BS39–41, BS48–49, GL11–13, NP16, NP26.
30. Fylingdales	YO13, YO18, YO21–22, YO62.
31. Gravesend	BR5–8, CM0, DA1–18, ME1–5, ME7–8, RM1–3, RM5–20, SS0–17.
32. Hawarden Airport	CH1–8, LL11–14, SY14.
33. Heathrow	BR1–4, CR0, CR2–9, E1–18, E1W, EC1–4, EN1–5, EN7–11, HA0–9, IG1–11, KT1–24, N1–22, NW1–11, SE1–28, SL0, SL3, SM1–7, SW1–20, TW1–20, UB1–10, W1–14, WC1–2, WD1–2.
34. Hereford-Credenhill	GL1–6, GL10, GL14–20, GL50–53, HR1–9, NP7–8, NP15, NP25, SY8, WR1–11, WR13–15.
35. Herstmonceux, West End	BN7–8, BN20–24, BN26–27, TN21, TN31–40.
36. High Wycombe	HP5–23, HP27, OX9, OX39, OX49, RG9, SL7–9.
37. Hurn (Bournemouth Airport)	BH1–25, BH31, DT1–2, DT11, SP6.
38. Isle of Portland	DT3–5.

Column (1) *Meteorological Office Station*	Column (2) *Postal Districts*
39. Keele	CW1–3, CW5, ST1–8, ST11–12, ST14–21.
40. Kinloss	AB38, AB44–45, AB55–56, IV1–3, IV5, IV7–20, IV30–32, IV36.
41. Kirkwall	KW15–17.
42. Lake Vyrnwy	LL20–21, LL23, SY10, SY15–17, SY19, SY21–22.
43. Leconfield	DN14, HU1–20, YO11–12, YO14–17, YO25.
44. Leek	DE4, DE45, S32–33. SK17, SK22–23. ST9–10, ST13.
45. Lerwick	ZE1–3.
46. Leuchars	DD1–7, DD10–11, KY1–2, KY4–10, KY15–16, PH12, PH14.
47. Linton on Ouse	DL1–3, DL6–7, DL9–10, HG1–5, LS1–20, LS22–28, TS9, TS15–16, YO1, YO7–8, YO10, YO19, YO23–24, YO26, YO30–32, YO41–43, YO51, YO60–61.
48. Liscombe	EX16, EX35–36, TA22, TA24.
49. Little Rissington	CV36, GL54–56, OX7, OX15–17, WR12.
50. Loch Glascarnoch	IV4, IV6, IV23–24, IV63.
51. Loftus	SR8, TS1–8, TS10–14, TS17–20, TS22–27.
52. Lusa	IV40–49, IV51–56, PH36, PH38–41.
53. Lyneham	BA1–3, BA11, BA13–15, GL7–9, RG17, SN1–6, SN8–16, SN25–26.
54. Machrihanish	KA27, PA28–29, PA41–49, PA60.
55. Manston	CT1–21, ME9–13, TN23–26, TN28–30.
56. Marham	CB6–7, IP24–28, PE12–14, PE30–38.
57. Mona	LL33–34, LL42–49, LL51–78.
58. North Wyke	EX6–7, EX17–22, EX37–38, PL19–21, TQ1–6, TQ9–14.
59. Norwich Airport	NR1–35.
60. Nottingham Watnall	CV13, DE1–3, DE5–7, DE11–15, DE21–24, DE55–56, DE65, DE72–75, LE1–9, LE11–14, LE16–19, LE65, LE67, NG1–22, NG25, NG31–34.
61. Pembrey Sands	SA1–8, SA14–18, SA31–34, SA61–63, SA66–73.

Column (1) *Meteorological Office Station*	Column (2) *Postal Districts*
62. Plymouth	PL1–12, TQ7–8.
63. Redesdale	CA9, DH8, DL12–13, NE19, NE47–49.
64. Rhyl	LL15–19, LL22, LL26–32.
65. Rothamsted	AL1–10, EN6, HP1–4, LU1–7, SG1–4, SG12–14, WD3–7, WD17–19, WD23–25.
66. St. Athan	CF3, CF5, CF10–11, CF14–15, CF23–24, CF31–36, CF61–64, CF71–72, NP10, NP18–20, SA10–13.
67. St. Bees Head	CA13–15, CA18–28.
68. St. Catherine's Point	PO30, PO38–41.
69. Salsburgh	EH43–46. G65, G67–68, ML6–11.
70. Scilly, St. Mary's	TR21–25.
71. Sennybridge	LD1–8, SA19–20, SY7, SY9, SY18.
72. Shap	CA10–12, CA16–17, LA8–10, LA22–23.
73. Shawbury	SY1–6, SY11–13, TF1–13.
74. Sheffield	DN1–8, DN11–12, HD1–2, HD4–6, S1–14, S17–18, S20–21, S25–26, S35, S40–45, S60–66, S70–75, S80–81, WF1–17.
75. South Farnborough	GU1–4, GU7–35, GU46–47, GU51–52, RG1–2, RG4–8, RG10, RG12, RG14, RG18–27, RG29–31, RG40–42, RG45, SL1–2, SL4–6, SO24.
76. Stonyhurst	BB1–3, BB5–7, LA2, LA6–7.
77. Stornoway Airport	HS1–9.
78. Strathallan	FK8, FK11–19, G63, KY14, PH1–7, PH13.
79. Thorney Island	BN1–3, BN9–18, BN25, BN41–43, BN45, PO1–22, PO31–37, SO14–19, SO30–32, SO40–43, SO45, SO50–53.
80. Tiree	PA61, PA66–67, PA73–78. PH42–44.
81. Trawsgoed	LL35–40, SY20, SY23–25.
82. Tredegar	CF37–48, CF81–83, NP4, NP11–13, NP22–24, NP44, SA9.
83. Tulloch Bridge	FK 20–21, PA33, PA36, PA40, PH8–9, PH15–17, PH30–35, PH37, PH49–50.
84. Waddington	DN9–10, DN13, DN15–22, DN31–41, LN1–13, NG23–24, PE10–11, PE20–25.

Column (1) *Meteorological Office Station*	Column (2) *Postal Districts*
85. Walney Island	LA1, LA3–5, LA11–21.
86. Wattisham	CB8–9, CO1–8, CO10–16. IP1–23, IP29–33.
87. West Freugh	DG8–9, KA19, KA26.
88. Wick Airport	IV25, KW1–3, KW5–10, KW12, KW14.
89. Wittering	LE15, NN17–18, PE1–9, PE15–17, PE26–29.
90. Woodford	BL1–6, BL9, CW4, CW6–12, M1–9, M11–35, M38, M40–41, M43–46, M50, M90, OL6–10, SK1–12, SK14–16, WA3, WA13–16, WN7.
91. Yeovilton	BA4–10, BA16, BA20–22, BS25–28, DT9–10, SP8, TA1–20, TA23.]"

"

p.1314, *amendment to the Social Fund Cold Weather Payments (General) Regulations 1988, Sch.2 (Specified alternative stations)*

3.098   With effect from November 1, 2010, reg.2(1) and (6) of the Social Fund Cold Weather Payments (General) Amendment Regulations 2010 (SI 2010/2442) substituted the following for Sch.2:

"**[Regulation 2(1A)(a) and 2(1B)(a)**

SCHEDULE 2

SPECIFIED ALTERNATIVE STATIONS

Column (1) *Meteorological Office Station*	Column (2) *Specified Alternative Station*
Capel Curig	Lake Vyrnwy
Cardinham	North Wyke
Carlisle	Keswick
Charlwood	Kenley Airfield
Coleshill	Pershore College
Crosby	Rhyl
Dunstaffnage	Lusa
Gravesend	Kenley
Hawarden Airport	Crosby
Heathrow	Gravesend

134

Column (1) *Meteorological Office Station*	Column (2) *Specified Alternative Station*
Hereford-Credenhill	Pershore College
High Wycombe	Rothamsted
Keele	Shawbury
Kinloss	Lossiemouth
Linton on Ouse	Church Fenton
Liscombe	North Wyke
Mona	Rhyl
North Wyke	Okehampton
Rhyl	Crosby
St. Athan	Mumbles
Sennybridge	Tredegar
Shap	Keswick
Sheffield	Nottingham Watnall
Tiree	Lusa
Woodford	Keele]"

p.1316, *amendment to the Income Support (General) Regulations 1987, reg.1(2) (Citation, commencement and interpretation: definition of "independent hospital")*

With effect from September 1, 2010, arts 2 and 10 of the Health and Social Care Act 2008 (Miscellaneous Consequential Amendments) Order 2010 (SI 2010/1881) amended reg.1(2) by substituting the following for the definition of "independent hospital":   **3.099**

""independent hospital"—
- (a) in England, means a hospital as defined by section 275 of the National Health Service Act 2006 that is not a health service hospital as defined by that section;
- (b) in Wales, has the meaning assigned to it by section 2 of the Care Standards Act 2000; and
- (c) in Scotland, means an independent healthcare service as defined in section 2(5)(a) and (b) of the Regulation of Care (Scotland) Act 2001;".

p.1320, *annotation to the Social Fund Winter Fuel Payment Regulations 2000, reg.2 (Social fund winter fuel payments)*

Regulation 2 of the Social Fund Winter Fuel Payment (Temporary Increase) Regulations 2010 (SI 2010/1161) has not been revoked following the change of government in May 2010, and the temporary increase   **3.100** for the 2010–11 winter has taken effect. Accordingly, the £100 rate in reg.2(1)(b)(ii) and (2)(b) continues to be modified to £125; the £200 rate in reg.2(1)(b)(i), (2)(a) and (3) continues to be modified to £250; the £200 rate in reg.2(2)(b) continues to be modified to £275; the £150 rate in reg.2(2)(b) continues to be modified to £200; and the £300 rate in reg.2(2)(a) and (3) continues to be modified to £400.

p.1328, *annotation to the Social Fund Maternity and Funeral Expenses (General) Regulations 2005, reg.3 (Interpretation: definition of "family element")*

3.101   The definition of "family element" in reg.3 was considered in detail by the Upper Tribunal in *AM v SSWP (SF)* [2010] UKUT 344 (AAC). Following *CSG/607/2004* and *CIS/2303/2008*, Judge Wikeley held that child tax credit is payable at a rate higher than the family element when the level of the award is such that, after the application of the first taper (i.e. the 39 per cent (formerly 37 per cent) taper provided for by Steps 3–7 of reg.8(3) of the Tax Credits (Income Thresholds and Determination of Rates) Regulations 2002, as amended), includes a sum attributable to an individual child element of CTC and not just sums attributable to the family element. That is so even if the actual cash amount of CTC paid appears to be just over the prescribed family element as a result of rounding by HMRC. Judge Wikeley also points out that the statement in the Main Volume that:

> "In practice, CTC will only be payable at a rate at or below the level of the family element if the family's income (calculated in accordance with the Tax Credits (Definition and Calculation of Income) Regulations 2002) is over £50,000 *per annum* (see reg.8(3) of the Tax Credits (Income Thresholds and Determination of Rates) Regulations 2002, particularly Steps 8–10)."

confuses that first taper with the second taper of 6.67 per cent that is applied to the family element once annual income exceeds £50,000 pa under Steps 8–10 of reg.8(3), and disregards the "plateau effect" that occurs where a claimant's income is sufficient to reduce the individual child elements to nil under the first taper but does not exceed £50,000. He suggests that the commentary "would be more accurate, if perhaps more long-winded, if it read:

> "Under reg.5(1)(a)(v), CTC must be payable at a rate higher than this in order to count as a qualifying benefit for a maternity grant. In practice, CTC will only be payable at a rate above the family element (i.e. including at least some individual child element) where the family's income (calculated in accordance with the Tax Credits (Definition and Calculation of Income) Regulations 2002) is either below or at least (and depending on the precise circumstances) not very far above the initial threshold of £16,040 *per annum*, given the impact of the first taper of 37 [now 39] pence in the pound (see reg.8(3) of the Tax Credits (Income Thresholds and Determination of Rates) Regulations 2002, and particularly Steps 3–7)."

pp.1336–1337, *annotation to Social Fund Maternity and Funeral Expenses (General) Regulations 2005, reg.7(4) (Funeral payments: entitlement—entitlement to a qualifying benefit)*

In *RM v SSWP (IS)* [2010] UKUT 220 (AAC), the deceased was   3.102
Jewish and a member of an orthodox synagogue. He had no family or friends to arrange his funeral, and the claimant, who was the deceased's solicitor and personal representative and a member of the same synagogue, arranged the funeral in his professional capacity. The deceased's estate was insolvent and the claimant's claim for a funeral payment was refused because he was not in receipt of a qualifying benefit. The Upper Tribunal confirmed that decision and that the failure of the scheme to provide for the personal representative of an insolvent estate to be eligible for a payment was neither irrational nor an infringement of the claimant's Convention Rights.

p.1337, *annotation to the Social Fund Maternity and Funeral Expenses (General) Regulations 2005, reg.7 (Funeral payments: entitlement—responsible person)*

In *VC v SSWP (IS)* [2010] UKUT 189 (AAC), the Upper Tribunal   3.103
stressed the importance of making sufficient findings of fact as to the nature of any agreement between the claimant and any other putative responsible person.

PART IV

UPDATING MATERIAL
VOLUME III

ADMINISTRATION, ADJUDICATION AND
THE EUROPEAN DIMENSION

Commentary by

Mark Rowland and Robin White

p.53, *annotations to the Social Security Administration Act 1992, s.71, para.1.87 (Recovery at common law)*

In *CPAG v SSWP* [2010] UKSC 54, the Supreme Court has dis- 4.001
missed the appeal by the Secretary of State, and held that s.71 of the
Administration Act provides the only route to recovery of social security
benefits overpayments to the exclusion of any common law rights.

Para.1.88

FW v SSWP (IS) [2010] UKUT 374 (AAC) reminds us that it is for
the Secretary of State to establish the statutory conditions for the recovery of overpaid benefit. Where the Secretary of State has been given
every opportunity to prove the statutory conditions, but has manifestly
failed to do so, and does not appear before a First-tier Tribunal (in this
case after an adjournment with directions), then it is entirely appropriate
to find against the Secretary of State.

SSWP v AM [2010] UKUT 428 (AAC) is an instructive case for those
situations where an overpayment arises as a result of a determination that
a couple has been living together as husband and wife. Tribunals need to
be alert to the way in which the Secretary of State has made decisions.
A simple determination that a couple is living together as husband and
wife is merely the starting point. Once that determination is made, there
must be an outcome decision to determine the effect on the benefit
entitlements of each member of the couple. Following a proper outcome
decision, there may be a recoverability decision. The decision also
reminds us that a later tribunal is not bound by a decision of an earlier
tribunal, but is obliged, where it does not follow the conclusions of an
earlier tribunal, to give cogent reasons for its different conclusions.
Where there are arguments about the quality of two competing tribunal
decisions, it is not a matter of determining which is reasoned more
effectively, but rather of testing whether the reasoning in the decision
under appeal is, or is not, erroneous in law. It only has to be good
enough; it does not have to be in any sense better reasoned than the
earlier decision.

AG v SSWP [2010] UKUT 291 (AAC) considers the effect of a
tribunal decision that an overpayment is irrecoverable, and warns that it
is necessary in such cases to consider exactly what the decision of an
earlier tribunal did. In this case, a tribunal had determined that an
overpayment was not recoverable because there was no entitlement
decision prior to the recoverability decision. Subsequently the decision-
maker had started all over again and made an entitlement decision
followed immediately by a recoverability decision. The claimant
appealed on the grounds that the Secretary of State was precluded by the
earlier decision from resurrecting the recoverability of the overpayment
for the substantial periods for which the two decisions overlapped. The
Upper Tribunal judge, relying on *R(IS) 13/05*, ruled that since the
original tribunal decision had ruled the overpayment was *then* not recoverable because the required entitlement decision did not exist, this did
not preclude the Secretary of State from correcting that omission and

proceeding to seek recovery on the basis of a properly drawn entitlement decision followed by a fresh recoverability decision.

Para.1.95

The reference to *CJSA/1423/1999* is incorrect. It should be a reference to *CIS/1423/1997*, which is now reported as *R(IS) 6/01*.

Para.1.98

JM v SSWP [2010] UKUT 135 (AAC) illustrates the need to analyse carefully what is in issue in an overpayment recoverability decision. The claimant had been in receipt of the lowest rate of the care component on the grounds that she could not cook a main meal for herself. She subsequently asked for the mobility component to be added, but raised no issue relating to the care component. The mobility component was added. It was then established that she was working as a cleaning supervisor and that her mobility was, in fact, far in excess of the description of her walking ability on which the award had been based. Those circumstances also called into question her entitlement to the care component. An entitlement decision was made removing entitlement to both components from their initial award, and an overpayment decision was made seeking recovery. A First-tier Tribunal confirmed the entitlement decision, and the Upper Tribunal judge on appeal found no fault with it. But the First-tier Tribunal had not sufficiently examined the basis for recovery of the overpaid benefit. It was accepted that there had been a serious misrepresentation of her walking ability by the claimant, which was "simply and obviously far beyond any genuine margin of error or imprecise description" (para.22). But the appellant had not made any representations beyond statements made at the time of the original award of just the care component, and that had been based on her claim supported only by her GP. The First-tier Tribunal had, in the opinion of the Upper Tribunal judge, been right to conclude that an overpayment of the care component could only arise if the Secretary of State could establish that there had been a failure to disclose a material fact. The Upper Tribunal judge observes:

> "What the evidence showed was that in making her application in early November 2004 to have the mobility component added to her existing disability living allowance award, the claimant simply said nothing about her care needs because she was not asked to. On her own admission and the tribunal's findings, she knew she could in fact cook a main meal for herself all along, and knew the basis for her existing award of care component was a mistaken assumption that she could not reasonably do so. What she did then was simply to keep mum, and not volunteer any information to the department from which they could see they had made a mistake." (para.27).

The Upper Tribunal judge noted that prior to *R(IS) 9/06 B v SSWP*, disclosure by the appellant would have been regarded as reasonably to be expected, but following that decision, the proper enquiry was to ask whether she had been required to disclose her knowledge that she had been awarded the care component on a mistaken basis. The judge concluded that none of the requirements imposed on the appellant required her to disclose information concerning her care needs or specifically on her ability to cook a main meal for herself. In all the circumstances the Secretary of State had not shown a required basis for recovery of the overpaid care component of the disability living allowance.

pp.160–197, *application of the Social Security (Recovery of Benefits) Act 1997*

By reg.16 of the Employment and Support Allowance (Transitional Provisions, Housing Benefit and Council Tax Benefit) (Existing Awards) (No.2) Regulations 2010 (SI 2010/1907), the 1997 Act is applied with effect from October 1, 2010 for the purposes of enabling the Secretary of State to recover employment and support allowance paid in consequence of a "conversion decision" if a compensation payment is made. This is achieved by treating a conversion decision as though it were a decision as to a person's entitlement to an employment and support allowance which had been made on a claim. Whether it was really necessary to include this Act within the scope of reg.16 seems doubtful.   4.002

pp.204–266, *application of the Social Security Act 1998, ss.8 to 39*

By regs 6 and 16 of the Employment and Support Allowance (Transitional Provisions, Housing Benefit and Council Tax Benefit) (Existing Awards) (No.2) Regulations 2010 (SI 2010/1907), the whole of Ch.II of Pt I of the 1998 Act is applied with effect from October 1, 2010 for the purposes of enabling the Secretary of State to make, revise and supersede a "conversion decision" moving a claimant from incapacity benefit to employment and support allowance and to enable "any other matter to be determined in connection with any person's entitlement or continuing entitlement to an award of an employment and support allowance by virtue of these Regulations". This is achieved by treating a conversion decision as though it were a decision as to a person's entitlement to an employment and support allowance which had been made on a claim. Note the modification to Sch.3, see below.   4.003

pp.241–243, *annotation to the Social Security Act 1998, s.17(2)*

In *Secretary of State for Work and Pensions v AM (IS)* [2010] UKUT 428 (AAC), the judge took a subtly different approach from *CIS/1330/2002* (mentioned in the main work) and held that "an entitlement decision necessarily establishes that there has been an overpayment, because it proves that the amount paid during a particular period was more than the claimant was entitled to" although he also held, consistently with *CIS/1330/2002*, that "when making findings of fact, the effect of section 17(2) of the 1992 Act is that the decision maker or tribunal dealing with the overpayment recoverability decision cannot be bound by the findings in relation to those facts made in the course of   4.003.1

dealing with the entitlement decision". The difference in approach is therefore of little, if any, practical importance.

In *LS v Lambeth LBC (HB)* [2010] UKUT 461 (AAC), the three-judge panel was invited to consider whether the First-tier Tribunal had been bound by a decision of a legally qualified panel member of an appeal tribunal to admit an appeal that it considered ought not to have been admitted because the legally qualified panel member had had no power to admit it. The majority held that it was unnecessary to decide whether the First-tier Tribunal had had discretion to reconsider the legally qualified panel member's decision because it found the First-tier Tribunal's decision to be erroneous in point of law on another ground and substituted a decision that the legally qualified panel member's decision would not be reconsidered. The implication is that the First-tier Tribunal was at least not bound to reconsider the legally qualified panel member's decision. The issue arose because, in *Watt v Ahsan* [2007] UKHL 51; [2008] A.C. 696, the House of Lords held that an employment tribunal had been bound by a decision of the Employment Appeal Tribunal, dismissing an appeal from the employment tribunal's ruling made in the same proceedings to the effect that it had jurisdiction to consider the case before it, notwithstanding that a subsequent decision of the Court of Appeal in different proceedings had overruled the Employment Appeal Tribunal's decision. It may just be arguable that the legally qualified panel member's determination would have been a "determination embodied in or necessary to such a decision" so as to have brought s.17(2) of the Social Security Act 1998 into play had the issue arisen in the context of an ordinary social security decision, but there is no equivalent to s.17(2) in para.11 of Sch.7 to the Child Support, Pensions and Social Security Act 2000, which provides for the finality of decisions in housing benefit cases, and so the point did not arise in *LS v Lambeth LBC (HB)*. On the other hand, the First-tier Tribunal's power under r.5(3)(e) of the Tribunal procedure (First-tier Tribunal) (Social Entitlement Chamber) Rules 2008 to deal with an issue as a preliminary issue would be undermined if a decision on a preliminary issue were not binding in the same proceedings. Section 17 appears generally to be more concerned with whether a decision made in one set of proceedings is binding on a decision-maker or tribunal concerned with another set of proceedings.

p.274, *amendments to the Social Security Act 1998, Sch.3*

4.004   With effect from April 6, 2010, para.3(da) is amended by s.33(4) of the Welfare Reform Act 2009. "8 or" is inserted after "section", so as to create a right of appeal against a decision imposing a sanction for failing to attend an interview.

By reg.16 of and para.5 of Sch.2 to the Employment and Support Allowance (Transitional Provisions, Housing Benefit and Council Tax Benefit) (Existing Awards) (No.2) Regulations 2010 (SI 2010/1907), as amended by reg.15 of the Employment and Support Allowance (Transitional Provisions, Housing Benefit and Council Tax Benefit) (Existing Awards) (No.2) (Amendment) Regulations 2010 (SI 2010/2430), Sch.3

of the 1998 Act is modified with effect from October 1, 2010 for the purpose of migrating claimants from incapacity benefit to employment and support allowance. It is to be read as though there were inserted:

> *"Conversion of certain existing awards into awards of an employment and support allowance*
> **8E.** A conversion decision within the meaning of the Employment and Support Allowance (Transitional Provisions, Housing Benefit and Council Tax Benefit) (Existing Awards) (No. 2) Regulations 2010."

p.329, *Social Security (Claims and Information) Regulations 2007, reg.1*

With effect from June 28, 2010, the Social Security (Miscellaneous Amendments) (No.3) Regulations 2010 (SI 2010/840), reg.8 amends reg.1(3) by inserting after "disability living allowance": **4.005**

"(ee)   employment and support allowance;".

p.338, *Social Security (Claims and Payments) Regulations 1987, reg.3(j) and annotation*

With effect from June 28, 2010, the Social Security (Miscellaneous Amendments) (No.3) Regulations 2010 (SI 2010/840), reg.2 amends reg.3(j) to read as follows: **4.006**

> "(j)   in the case of an employment and support allowance where—
>> (i)   the beneficiary has made and is pursuing an appeal against a decision of the Secretary of State that embodies a determination that the beneficiary does not have limited capability for work, and
>> (ii)   that appeal relates to a decision to terminate or not to award a benefit for which a claim was made."

With effect from November 2, 2010, the Social Security (Exemption from Claiming Retirement Pension) Regulations 2010 (SI 2010/1794), reg.2 amends reg.3 by inserting the following provision before reg.3(a):

> "(za)   in the case of a Category A or B retirement pension, where the beneficiary is a person to whom regulation 3A applies;".

The same provision inserts reg.3A after reg.3 as follows:

> **"Notification that claim not required for entitlement to a Category A or B retirement pension**
>
> **3A.**—(1) Subject to paragraph (4), this regulation applies to a beneficiary who has received, on or before the day provided for in paragraph (2), a written notification from the Secretary of State that no claim is required for a Category A or B retirement pension.
> (2) The day referred to in paragraph (1) is—
>> (a) the day which falls 2 weeks before the day on which the beneficiary reaches pensionable age; or
>> (b) such later day as the Secretary of State may consider reasonable in any particular case or class of case.

(3) The Secretary of State may give a notification under paragraph (1) only in a case where, on the day which falls 8 weeks before the day on which the beneficiary reaches pensionable age, the beneficiary—

(a) is in receipt of an exempt benefit, or would be in receipt of it but for that benefit not being payable as a result of the application of any of the legislation listed in paragraph (7); and

(b) is neither entitled to, nor awaiting the determination of a claim for, a non-exempt benefit.

(4) Receipt of a written notification under paragraph (1) does not affect the requirement that a beneficiary who—

(a) before reaching pensionable age, informs the Secretary of State that they want their entitlement to a Category A or B retirement pension to be deferred in accordance with section 55(3)(a) of the Contributions and Benefits Act; or

(b) after reaching pensionable age, elects to be treated as not having become entitled to either a Category A or B retirement pension in accordance with regulation 2 of the Social Security (Widow's Benefit and Retirement Pensions) Regulations 1979,

must make a claim in order subsequently to be entitled to a Category A or B retirement pension.

(5) For the purposes of paragraph (3)(a), a beneficiary who is in receipt of an exempt benefit includes a beneficiary who—

(a) has been awarded such a benefit on or before the day which falls 8 weeks before the day on which the beneficiary reaches pensionable age; and

(b) has not yet received the first payment of that benefit.

(6) For the purposes of this regulation—

"exempt benefit" means any of the following—

(a) an employment and support allowance;

(b) income support;

(c) a jobseeker's allowance;

(d) long-term incapacity benefit;

(e) state pension credit; and

"non-exempt benefit" means any of the following—

(a) carer's allowance;

(b) short-term incapacity benefit;

(c) severe disablement allowance;

(d) widowed mother's allowance;

(e) widow's pension.

(7) The legislation referred to in paragraph (3)(a) is—

(a) section 19 of the Jobseekers Act (circumstances in which a jobseeker's allowance is not payable);

(b) section 20A of that Act (denial or reduction of joint-claim jobseeker's allowance);

(c) regulations made by virtue of any of the following provisions of the Jobseekers Act—

(i) section 8(2)(a) (attendance, information and evidence);

(ii) section 17A(5)(d) (schemes for assisting persons to obtain employment: "work for your benefit" schemes etc.);

    (iii) paragraph 7(1)(a) of Schedule A1 (persons dependent on drugs etc.);
(d) regulation 18 of the Social Security (Incapacity for Work) (General) Regulations 1995 (disqualification for misconduct etc.); and
(e) regulation 157 of the Employment and Support Allowance Regulations (disqualification for misconduct etc.)."

Note that Pt 4 of Sch.2 to the Employment and Support Allowance (Transitional Provisions, Housing Benefit and Council Tax Benefit) (Existing Awards) (No.2) Regulations 2010 (SI 2010/1907) (as amended), set out in the "New Legislation" section of this Supplement, contains modifications of reg.3 for the purposes of the transition to employment and support allowance.

p.341, *Social Security (Claims and Payments) Regulations 1987, reg.4*

With effect from July 29, 2010, the Social Security (Claims and Payments) Amendment (No.3) Regulations 2010 (SI 2010/1676), reg.2 amend reg.4(11) by: **4.007**

(a) substituting the words ", a retirement pension, a bereavement benefit or a social fund payment for funeral expenses" for the words "or retirement pension";
(b) substituting the words "a telephone number specified by the Secretary of State for the purpose of the benefit for which the claim is made" for the words "the telephone number specified by the Secretary of State".

p.400, *correction to the Social Security (Claims and Payments) Regulations 1987, reg.19*

Regulation 19(7)(e)(i) should read as follows: **4.007.1**

"(i) the expiry of entitlement to income support ignoring any period in which entitlement resulted from the person entitled not being treated as engaged in remunerative work by virtue of paragraphs (2) and (3), or paragraphs (5) and (6) of regulation 6 of the Income Support (General) Regulations 1987; or"

Regulation 19(7)(f) should read as follows:

"(f) except in the case of a claim for working families tax credit or disabled persons' tax credit, the claimant has ceased to be a member of a married or unmarried couple within the period of one month before the claim is made;"

p.425, *modification to the Social Security (Claims and Payments) Regulations 1987, reg.26C*

Note that Pt 4 of Sch.2 to the Employment and Support Allowance (Transitional Provisions, Housing Benefit and Council Tax Benefit) (Existing Awards) (No.2) Regulations 2010 (SI 2010/1907) (as   **4.008** amended), set out in the "New Legislation" section of this Supplement, contains modifications of reg.26C for the purposes of the transition to employment and support allowance.

p.434, *annotation to the Social Security (Claims and Payments) Regulations 1987, reg.32, annotations*

4.009   Note that Pt 3 of Sch.1 and Pt 4 of Sch.2 to the Employment and Support Allowance (Transitional Provisions, Housing Benefit and Council Tax Benefit) (Existing Awards) (No.2) Regulations 2010 (SI 2010/1907) (as amended), set out in the "New Legislation" section of this Supplement, contains modifications of reg.32 for the purposes of the transition to employment and support allowance.

p.467, *amendment of the Social Security (Claims and Payments Regulations 1987, Sch.9*

4.010   With effect from April 1, 2010, the Housing and Regeneration Act 2008 (Consequential Provisions) (No.2) Order 2010 (SI 2010/671) art.4 and Sch.1, amends para.1(b)(i) by substituting the words, "the Regulator of Social Housing or the Welsh Ministers" for the words, "the Housing Corporation established by the Housing Act 1964".

With effect from April 30, 2010, the Social Security (Claims and Payments) Amendment (No.2) Regulations 2010, (SI 2010/870), reg.2 amends para.7C(9) by inserting the words, "under this paragraph" after the words, "eligible benefit".

The same regulation inserts a new para.7E after para.7D as follows:

"Tax credits overpayment debts and self-assessment debts

7E.—(1) In this paragraph—
"self-assessment debt" means any debt which—
   (a) has arisen from submission of a self-assessment to Her Majesty's Revenue and Customs under section 9 of the Taxes Management Act 1970 (returns to include self-assessment); and
   (b) is recoverable under Part 6 of that Act;
"tax credits overpayment debt" means any debt which is recoverable under section 29 of the Tax Credits Act 2002 (recovery of overpayments).

(2) Where the conditions set out in sub-paragraph (3) are met, the Secretary of State may deduct from a specified benefit to which the beneficiary is entitled a sum which is up to a maximum of 3 times 5 per cent of the personal allowance for a single claimant aged not less than 25 and pay that sum to Her Majesty's Revenue and Customs towards discharge of any outstanding tax credits overpayment debt or self-assessment debt owed by the beneficiary to Her Majesty's Revenue and Customs.

(3) The conditions mentioned in sub-paragraph (2) are—

(a) that the beneficiary has given written consent to Her Majesty's Revenue and Customs for deductions to be made from a specified benefit towards discharge of any outstanding tax credits overpayment debt or self-assessment debt owed by the beneficiary to Her Majesty's Revenue and Customs; and

(b) no sum is being deducted under this paragraph.

(4) The Secretary of State shall cease making deductions from a specified benefit under this paragraph if—

(a) there is no longer sufficient entitlement to a specified benefit to enable deductions to be made;

(b) entitlement to all specified benefits has ceased;

(c) the beneficiary withdraws consent for the Secretary of State to make deductions from a specified benefit; or

(d) the beneficiary is no longer liable to repay any tax credits overpayment debt or self-assessment debt.

(5) The Secretary of State shall notify the beneficiary in writing of the total sums deducted under this paragraph—

(a) on receipt of a written request for such information from the beneficiary; or

(b) on the termination of deductions.

(6) Where a deduction is made under this paragraph from a specified benefit, paragraph 8 (maximum amount of payment to third parties) is to have effect as if—

(a) in sub-paragraph (1) for "and 7A" there were substituted ", 7A and 7E"; and

(b) in sub-paragraph (2) for "and 7D" there were substituted ", 7D and 7E"."

The same regulation amends para.9(1)(A)(a) by substituting the words "7A, 7C or 7E" for the words "7A or 7C"; and after paragraph 9(1)(B)(h) inserts the following provision:

"(i) any liability mentioned in paragraph 7E (tax credits overpayment debts and self-assessment debts.)".

With effect from October 1, 2010, the Employment and Support Allowance (Transitional Provisions, Housing Benefit and Council Tax Benefit) (Existing Awards) (No.2) Regulation 2010 (SI 2010/1907), reg.26 and Sch.4 amend para.8 of Sch.9 by substituting the following provision for sub-para.(iv):

"(iv) in the case of an employment and support allowance, the applicable amount for the family as is awarded under paragraph (1)(a) and (b) of regulation 67 (prescribed amounts) or paragraph (1)(a) to (c) of regulation 68 (polygamous marriages) of the Employment and Support Allowance Regulations; or".

p.482, *amendment to the Social Security (Claims and Payments) Regulations 1987, Sch.9A*

With effect from April 1, 2010, the Housing and Regeneration Act 2008 (Consequential Provisions) (No.2) Order 2010 (SI 2010/671) **4.011** art.4 and Sch.1 amend para.1(b)(i) by substituting the words, "Regulator of Social Housing" for the words, "Housing Corporation".

With effect from November 1, 2010, the Social Security (Miscellaneous Amendments) (No.5) Regulations 2010 (SI 2010/2429), reg.3 amends Sch.9A by inserting after para.(c) in the definition of "relevant benefits" the following provision:

"(ca) contribution-based jobseeker's allowance where—
    (i) both income-based jobseeker's allowance and contribution-based jobseeker's allowance are in payment, and
    (ii) the income-based jobseeker's allowance alone is insufficient for the purposes of this Schedule;"

and inserts after para.(e), the following provision:

"(f) contributory employment and support allowance where—
    (i) both income-related employment and support allowance and contributory employment and support allowance are in payment, and
    (ii) the income-related employment and support allowance alone is insufficient for the purposes of this Schedule;".

p.500, *amendment to the Social Security and Child Support (Decisions and Appeals) Regulations 1999, reg.1(3)*

4.012   The definition of "the Breach of Community Order Regulations", which is misplaced in this work, is omitted by reg.4(1) and (2) of the Welfare Reform Act 2009 (Section 26) (Consequential Amendments) Regulations 2010 (SI 2010/424), with effect from March 22, 2010.

pp.507–514, *amendments to the Social Security and Child Support (Decisions and Appeals) Regulations 1999, reg.3*

4.013   New paras (5E) and (5F) are inserted by reg.7(1) and (2) of the Social Security (Miscellaneous Amendments) (No.3) Regulations 2010 (SI 2010/840), with effect from June 28, 2010:

"(5E) A decision under section 8 or 10 awarding an employment and support allowance may be revised if—
    (a) the decision of the Secretary of State awarding an employment and support allowance was made on the basis that the claimant had made and was pursuing an appeal against a decision of the Secretary of State that the claimant did not have limited capability for work ("the original decision"); and
    (b) the appeal to the First-tier Tribunal in relation to the original decision is successful.

(5F) A decision under section 8 or 10 awarding an employment and support allowance may be revised if—
    (a) the person's current period of limited capability for work is treated as a continuation of another such period under regulation 145(1) and (2) of the Employment and Support Allowance Regulations; and

(b) regulation 7(1)(b) of those Regulations applies."

For the purposes of the Work for Your Benefit pilot scheme, reg.3(6) is to be read as though the words ", or with regulations made under section 17A of that Act" were inserted after "Jobseekers Act" (reg.20(a) of the Jobseeker's Allowance (Work for Your Benefit Pilot Scheme) Regulations 2010 (SI 2010/1222), with effect from November 22, 2010).

Paragraph (8A) is omitted by reg.4(1) and (3) of the Welfare Reform Act 2009 (Section 26) (Consequential Amendments) Regulations 2010 (SI 2010/424), with effect from March 22, 2010.

For the purpose of the migration of claimants from incapacity benefit to employment and support allowance, regs 6 and 16 of, and Sch.3 to, the Employment and Support Allowance (Transitional Provisions, Housing Benefit and Council Tax Benefit) (Existing Awards) (No.2) Regulations 2010 (SI 2010/1907) apply the 1999 Regulations to "conversion decisions", treating a conversion decision as though it were a decision as to entitlement to employment and support allowance made on a claim. Regulation 17, as amended by reg.9 of the Employment and Support Allowance (Transitional Provisions, Housing Benefit and Council Tax Benefit) (Existing Awards) (No.2) (Amendment) Regulations 2010 (SI 2010/2430), provides:

"Where, on or after the effective date of any person's conversion decision, the Secretary of State is notified of any change of circumstances or other relevant event which occurred before that date and would have been relevant to the existing award or awards, the Secretary of State—

(a) must treat any award—
    (i) converted by virtue of regulation 14(2) (conversion decision that existing award qualifies for conversion), or
    (ii) terminated by virtue of regulation 14(2B)(a) (termination of an existing award of incapacity benefit or severe disablement allowance where entitlement to award of income support continues), regulation 14(3) (termination of award of an employment and support allowance where that entitlement already exists) or regulation 15(2) (termination of existing awards which do not qualify for conversion),
as if that award had not been converted or terminated;

(b) must treat any entitlement to be credited with earnings terminated by virtue of regulation 14(5) or 15(3) as if it had not been terminated;

(c) must treat any entitlement to a disability premium terminated by virtue of regulations 14(2B)(b), 15(2B) or 15(6) as if it had not been terminated;

(d) must take account of the change of circumstances or other relevant event for the purposes of determining whether to revise or supersede a decision ("the earlier decision") relating to the award or awards in respect of which the conversion decision was made;

151

(e) in an appropriate case, must revise or supersede the earlier decision;

(f) if any earlier decision is revised or superseded, must determine whether to revise the conversion decision made in relation to P; and

(g) in an appropriate case, must revise that conversion decision."

Paragraph 25A(1) of Sch.2 to SI 2010/1907, as amended by reg.17(1) and (12) of SI 2010/2430, specifically provides that, with effect from October 1, 2010, reg.3 of the 1999 Regulations "is to be read as if—

(a) in the case of a revision of a decision to award jobseeker's allowance made following the reinstatement of an existing award in accordance with regulation 15(5) of the Employment and Support Allowance (Transitional Provisions, Housing Benefit and Council Tax Benefit) (Existing Awards) (No. 2) Regulations 2010 ("the 2010 Regulations"), the words "within one month of the date of notification of the original decision" in paragraph (1)(a) were omitted;

(b) in the case of a conversion decision where there has been a change of circumstances to which regulation 12(4) of the 2010 Regulations (calculation of transitional addition) applies, paragraph (9)(a) were omitted; and

(c) in paragraph (9)(a), for "in the case of an advance award under regulation 13, 13A or 13C of the Claims and Payments Regulations" there were substituted, "in the cases of an advance award under regulation 13, 13A or 13C of the Claims and Payments Regulations or a conversion decision within the meaning of regulation 5(2)(a) of the 2010 Regulations"."

pp.523–527, *amendments to the Social Security and Child Support (Decisions and Appeals) Regulations 1999, reg.6*

4.014   For the purpose of the migration of claimants from incapacity benefit to employment and support allowance, regs 6 and 16 of, and Sch.3 to, the Employment and Support Allowance (Transitional Provisions, Housing Benefit and Council Tax Benefit) (Existing Awards) (No.2) Regulations 2010 (SI 2010/1907) apply the 1999 Regulations to "conversion decisions", treating a conversion decision as though it were a decision as to entitlement to employment and support allowance made on a claim. For the terms of reg.17 to the 2010 Regulations, see the supplementary annotation to reg.3, above. Paragraph 25A(2) of Sch.2 to the 2010 Regulations, as amended by reg.17(1) and (12) of the Employment and Support Allowance (Transitional Provisions, Housing Benefit and Council Tax Benefit) (Existing Awards) (No.2) (Amendment) Regulations 2010 (SI 2010/2430) provides that, with effect from October 1, 2010, reg.6(2)(a)(i) of the 1999 Regulations is to be read as if for "in the case of an advance award under regulation 13, 13A or 13C of the Claims and Payments Regulations or regulation 146 of the Employment and Support Allowance Regulations" there were substituted "in the cases of an advance award under regulation 13, 13A or 13C of the Claims and

Payments Regulations or regulation 146 of the Employment and Support Allowance Regulations or a conversion decision within the meaning of regulation 5(2)(a) of the 2010 Regulations".

By virtue of reg.20(b) of the Jobseeker's Allowance (Work for Your Benefit Pilot Scheme) Regulations 2010 (SI 2010/1222), reg.6(2) is to be read for the purposes of the Work for Your Benefit pilot scheme from November 22, 2010 as though there were a sub-para.(fa):

> "(fa) is a decision that a jobseeker's allowance is payable to a claimant where that allowance ceases to be payable or is reduced by virtue of regulations made under section 17A of the Jobseekers Act;".

Sub-paragraph (2)(i) is omitted by reg.4(1) and (4) of the Welfare Reform Act 2009 (Section 26) (Consequential Amendments) Regulations 2010 (SI 2010/424), with effect from March 22, 2010.

Sub-paragraph (2)(r) is substituted by reg.7(1) and (3) of the Social Security (Miscellaneous Amendments) (No.3) Regulations 2010 (SI 2010/840), with effect from June 28, 2010 so as to read:

> "(r) is an employment and support allowance decision where, since the decision was made, the Secretary of State has—
>> (i) received medical evidence from a health care professional approved by the Secretary of State, or
>> (ii) made a determination that the claimant is to be treated as having limited capability for work in accordance with regulation 20, 25, 26 or 33(2) of the Employment and Support Allowance Regulations."

pp.537–547, *amendments to the Social Security and Child Support (Decisions and Appeals) Regulations 1999, reg.7*

By virtue of reg.20(c) of the Jobseeker's Allowance (Work for Your 4.015 Benefit Pilot Scheme) Regulations 2010 (SI 2010/1222), reg.7 is to be read for the purposes of the Work for Your Benefit pilot scheme from November 22, 2010 as though there were a para.(8ZA) after para.(8):

> "(8ZA) A decision to which regulation 6(2)(fa) applies shall take effect as from the beginning of the period specified in regulation 8(11) of the Jobseeker's Allowance (Work for Your Benefit Pilot Scheme) Regulations 2010."

Paragraph (27) is omitted by reg.4(1) and (5) of the Welfare Reform Act 2009 (Section 26) (Consequential Amendments) Regulations 2010 (SI 2010/424), with effect from March 22, 2010.

Paragraph (38) is substituted and para.(40) is added by reg.7(1) and (4) of the Social Security (Miscellaneous Amendments) (No.3) Regulations 2010 (SI 2010/840), with effect from June 28, 2010.

> "(38) A decision made in accordance with regulation 6(2)(r) that embodies a determination that the claimant has—
>> (a) limited capability for work; or
>> (b) limited capability for work-related activity; or

> (c) limited capability for work and limited capability for work-related activity
>
> which is the first such determination shall take effect from the beginning of the 14th week of entitlement."

> "(40) A decision made in accordance with regulation 6(2)(r) that embodies a determination that the claimant has—
>
> (a) limited capability for work; or
> (b) limited capability for work-related activity; or
> (c) limited capability for work and limited capability for work-related activity
>
> where regulation 5 of the Employment and Support Allowance Regulations (assessment phase—previous claimants) applies shall take effect from the beginning of the 14th week of the person's continuous period of limited capability for work."

These paragraphs ensure that the decision is effective from the end of the "assessment phase", with para.(40) dealing with cases where there are linked periods of claim. Note that reg.6(2)(r) has been substituted (see above).

p.553, *amendment to the Social Security and Child Support (Decisions and Appeals) Regulations 1999, reg.7A(1)*

4.016   Regulation 7(1) and (5) of the Social Security (Miscellaneous Amendments) (No.3) Regulations 2010 (SI 2010/840) inserts ", 6(2)(r)" after "6(2)(g)", with effect from June 28, 2010.

p.568, *amendment to the Social Security and Child Support (Decisions and Appeals) Regulations 1999, reg.17(5)*

4.017   By reg.7(1) and (6) of the Social Security (Miscellaneous Amendments) (No.3) Regulations 2010 (SI 2010/840) "(f)" is substituted for "(e)", with effect from June 28, 2010.

p.588, *annotation to the Social Security and Child Support (Decisions and Appeals) Regulations 1999, reg.38A*

4.018   *SSWP v TB (RP)* [2010] UKUT 88 (AAC) has been reported at [2010] AACR 38.

p.593, *amendment to the Social Security and Child Support (Decisions and Appeals) Regulations 1999, Sch.2*

4.019   Paragraph 19A and the preceding heading are omitted by reg.4(1) and (6) of the Welfare Reform Act 2009 (Section 26) (Consequential Amendments) Regulations 2010 (SI 2010/424), with effect from March 22, 2010.

p.614, *amendment to the Social Security (Incapacity Benefit Work-focused Interviews) Regulations 2008, reg.11*

With effect from November 1, 2010, the Social Security (Miscellaneous Amendments) (No.5) Regulations 2010 (SI 2010/2429), reg.12 amends reg.9 as follows:　　　　　　　　　　　　　　　　　　　4.020

(a) by inserting in para.(1)(a) before "50%" the words "an amount equivalent to"; and

(b) by inserting in paras (1)(b) and (12)(c) after "by" the words "an amount equivalent to".

p.618, *amendment to the Social Security (Jobcentre Plus Interviews) Regulations 2002, reg.2*

With effect from May 5, 2010, the Local Education Authorities and Children's Services Authorities (Integration of Functions) (Local and Subordinate Legislation) Order 2010 (SI 2010/1172), Sch.3, para.45 amends the definition of "the Careers Service" by substituting the words "local authority" for the words "local education authority".　　4.021

p.623, *amendment to the Social Security (Jobcentre Plus Interviews) Regulations 2002, reg.4A*

With effect from October 25, 2010, the Social Security (Lone Parents and Miscellaneous Amendments) Regulations 2008 (SI 2008/3051), reg.10 amends reg.4A by substituting the number "6" for the words "6, 7, 8 or 9" in both places.　　　　　　　　　　　　　　　　4.022

p.675, *amendment to the Social Security (Payments on account, etc.) Regulations 1988, reg.5*

With effect from June 28, 2010, the Social Security (Miscellaneous Amendments) (No.3) Regulations 2010 (SI 2010/840), reg.3 amends reg.5 by inserting the words ", employment and support allowance for those persons with limited capability for work in relation to youth in accordance with paragraph 4 of Schedule 1 to the Welfare Reform Act 2007," after the words "severe disablement allowance".　　4.023

p.644, *amendment to the Social Security (Loss of Benefit) Regulations 2001, reg.3*

In para.(1), "and (3)" is substituted for "to (4)" and para.(4) is omitted by reg.7(1) and (2) of the Welfare Reform Act 2009 (Section 26) (Consequential Amendments) Regulations 2010 (SI 2010/424), with effect from March 22, 2010.　　　　　　　　　　　　　　4.024

For the purposes of these Regulations, reg.16 of, and Sch.3 to, the Employment and Support Allowance (Transitional Provisions, Housing Benefit and Council Tax Benefit) (Existing Awards) (No.2) Regulations 2010 (SI 2010/1907) treat a "conversion decision", migrating a claimant from incapacity benefit to employment and support allowance, as though it were a decision as to entitlement to employment and support allowance.

p.648, *amendment to the Social Security (Loss of Benefit) Regulations 2001, reg.5(3)*

4.025   By reg.7(1) and (2) of the Welfare Reform Act 2009 (Section 26) (Consequential Amendments) Regulations 2010 (SI 2010/424) the "or" is moved to the end of sub-para.(a) and sub-para.(c) is omitted, with effect from March 22, 2010.

pp.698–708, *amendments to the Employment Protection (Recoupment of Jobseeker's Allowance and Income Support) Regulations 1996*

4.026   Regulation 5 of the Social Security (Miscellaneous Amendments) (No.5) Regulations 2010 (SI 2010/2429) inserts ", income-related employment and support allowance" after "allowance" in the definition of "recoupable benefit" in reg.2(1) and in each of regs 4(1) and (8), 8(1), (2)(b) and (3)(b) and 10(1) and (2), with effect from November 1, 2010.

p.739, *amendment to the Social Security (Work-focused Interviews for Lone Parents) Regulations 2000, reg.2ZA*

4.027   With effect from October 25, 2010, the Social Security (Lone Parents and Miscellaneous Amendments) Regulations 2008 (SI 2008/3051), reg.7 amends reg.2ZA by substituting the number "6" for the words "6, 7, 8 or 9" in both places.

p.759, *substitution of the Child Benefit and Guardian's Allowance (Administration) Regulations 2003, regs 16 and 17*

4.028   With effect from November 1, the Child Benefit and Guardian's Allowance (Administration) (Amendment) Regulations 2010 (SI 2010/2459), reg.2 substitutes the following provisions for regs 16 and 17 and the headings immediately preceding them:

"Payment by direct credit transfer

16.—(1) Child benefit or guardian's allowance shall be paid in accordance with paragraphs (2) to (6) unless paid in accordance with regulation 17.

(2) Payment of child benefit or guardian's allowance to a person shall be made by direct credit transfer into a bank or other account that has been notified to the Board for the purpose of payment of—
   (a) a benefit described in section 5(2) of the Social Security Administration Act 1992;
   (b) a benefit described in section 5(2) of the Social Security Administration (Northern Ireland Act) 1992; or
   (c) a tax credit described in section 1 of the Tax Credits Act 2002, to which that person is entitled.

(3) If a person entitled to child benefit is also entitled to guardian's allowance, the allowance shall be paid into the same bank or other account as that into which the child benefit is paid under this regulation.

(4) The bank account or other account into which the Board may make payment of the allowance or benefit must be—

(a) in the name of—
    (i) the person entitled to the benefit or allowance ("the person"),
    (ii) the person's partner, or
    (iii) a person acting on behalf of the person; or

(b) in the joint names of the person and—
    (i) the person's partner, or
    (ii) a person acting on the person's behalf.

(5) Subject to paragraph (6), the benefit or allowance shall be paid within seven days of the last day of each successive period of entitlement.

(6) The Board may make a particular payment by direct credit transfer otherwise than is provided by paragraph (5) if it appears to them appropriate to do so for the purpose of—

(a) paying any arrears of benefit or allowance, or

(b) making a payment in respect of a terminal period of an award for any similar purpose.

Payment by other means

17.—(1) Child benefit or guardian's allowance may be paid by a means other than by direct credit transfer where it appears to the Board to be appropriate to do so in the circumstances of a particular case.

(2) If a person entitled to child benefit is also entitled to guardian's allowance, the allowance shall be paid in the same manner as that in which the child benefit is paid under this regulation.

(3) An instrument of payment issued by the Board pursuant to this regulation shall—

(a) remain the property of the Board, and

(b) be returned immediately to the Board (or such person as the Board may direct) if the person who has the instrument—
    (i) is required to do so by the Board; or
    (ii) ceases to be entitled to any part of the benefit or allowance to which the instrument relates."

p.764, *amendment of the Child Benefit and Guardian's Allowance (Administration) Regulations 2003, reg.25(a)*

With effect from November 1, 2010, the Child Benefit and Guardian's   4.029
Allowance (Administration) (Amendment) Regulations 2010 (SI 2010/2459), reg.2 substitutes in reg.25(a) the words "Regulation 16" for the words "Regulation 17".

p.764, *amendment of the Child Benefit and Guardian's Allowance (Administration) Regulations 2003, reg.27(2)(a)*

4.030   With effect from November 1, 2010, the Child Benefit and Guardian's Allowance (Administration) (Amendment) Regulations 2010 (SI 2010/2459), reg.2 substitutes in reg.27(2)(a) the words "Regulation 16" for the words "Regulation 17".

p.765, *amendment of the Child Benefit and Guardian's Allowance (Administration) Regulations 2003, reg.29(4)(a)*

4.031   With effect from November 1, 2010, the Child Benefit and Guardian's Allowance (Administration) (Amendment) Regulations 2010 (SI 2010/2459), reg.2 substitutes in reg.29(4)(a) the words "Regulation 16" for the words "Regulation 17".

p.768, *amendment of the Child Benefit and Guardian's Allowance (Administration) Regulations 2003, reg.35*

4.032   With effect from November 1, 2010, the Child Benefit and Guardian's Allowance (Administration) (Amendment) Regulations 2010 (SI 2010/2459), reg.2 substitutes in reg.35(1)(a) the words "Regulation 16" for the words "Regulation 17".

The same regulation amends reg.35(2)(b) by substituting the words, "before the Board made the arrangement for the payment of child benefit or guardian's allowance into that account" for the words, "before he agreed to the arrangement".

p.844, *annotation to art.21 TFEU*

4.033   *RM v SSWP* [2010] UKUT 238 (AAC) considers the claim of a Polish national to a right of residence flowing from art.21 (formerly art.18 EC). The claimant is a young woman who had spent the best part of ten years in the United Kingdom, initially as a child when her father came to the United Kingdom, but latterly in her own right. She had undertaken some short-term work, but had then become pregnant and had to cease work. Her claim was that she had a right of residence under the *Baumbast* principles since there was a lacuna in the scheme in the Treaty, and it would be unfair or disproportionate to refuse to recognise her right of residence in the United Kingdom. The judge reminds us that there is a difference between a lacuna in the scheme of the Treaty (and its implementing legislation) and a deliberate omission. In this case it could not be said that there was an accidental omission—and this was all the clearer since the claimant was an A8 national. But the judge does refer to the unsatisfactory position under which a claimant who is a national of the one of the Member States cannot establish their immigration status in the United Kingdom. He says that there "is a clear need for the benefit authorities to be able to refer arguable cases to the immigration authorities for a decision that will be effective from the date from which benefit was claimed . . . " (para.15).

p.854, *annotations to art.45 TFEU*

The Commission announced at the end of October 2010 that it had 4.033.1
opened infringement proceedings against the United Kingdom by issu-
ing a reasoned opinion that the provisions of the Worker Registration
Scheme which have the effect of excluding A8 nationals from eligibility
for certain benefits breach the European Union law prohibition on
discrimination on grounds of nationality. The United Kingdom has two
months from receipt of the reasoned opinion to bring its legislation in
line with the Commission's view of European Union law, or to persuade
the Commission that its provisions are not in breach of European Union
law. If the Commission is not so satisfied, it may bring the United
Kingdom before the Court of Justice under art.258 TFEU.

p.896, *annotation to art.2 Dir.2004/38/EC*

The decision in *BB v Secretary of State for Work and Pensions* [2010] 4.034
UKUT 126 (AAC), in which the judge held that an A8 national who had
worked for more than a year in work which was not registered was not
working lawfully and so did not fall within the scope of those with a right
to reside under European Union law, has been upheld by the Court of
Appeal in *Miskovic and Blazej v Secretary of State for Work and Pensions*
[2011] EWCA Civ 16 on this point. However, an argument that the
requirement for a claimant in the circumstances of the appellant to have
a right to reside in the United Kingdom or Ireland amounts to direct
discrimination on grounds of nationality or unjustified indirect discrimination contrary to art.3 of Regulation 1408/71 was stayed pending the
decision of the Supreme Court on this point in *Patmalniece v Secretary of
State for Work and Pensions*.

p.903, *annotation to art.7 Dir.2004/38/EC*

For a decision exploring the requirement of sufficiency of resources 4.035
under art.7(1)(b) in the context of a claim for housing benefit and
council tax benefit, see *SG v Tameside MBC* [2010] UKUT 243 (AAC).
This judgment also records a concession by the Secretary of State (who
had been joined in the appeal to the Upper Tribunal) that the appellant
had adequate health insurance under arrangements applicable because
she held an exported invalidity benefit from Sweden which entitled her
to medical treatment within the NHS (paras 20–28 of the Decision).
JS v Secretary of State for Work and Pensions [2010] UKUT 240 (AAC)
discusses the circumstances in which a person remains a self-employed
person notwithstanding that there is no current work being undertaken
in that capacity. The judge points out that although art.7 includes
provisions on the retention of worker status (that is, status as an
employee) under the Treaty, art.7 is silent on the retention of self-
employed status. Whether self-employed status has been abandoned or
lost, or retained, will depend on the particular circumstances of each
case, and the significance of any change in the self-employed person's
personal circumstances: see para.8 of the decision.

The appeal against the decision of the Administrative Court in *R. (Tilianu) v Secretary of State for Work and Pensions* has failed in the Court of Appeal, see [2010] EWCA Civ 1397.

p.913, *annotation to art.16 Dir.2004/38/EC*

4.036   In its judgment of October 7, 2010 in Case C-162/09 *Secretary of State for Work and Pensions v Lassal,* the European Court of Justice has followed the Opinion of its Advocate-General in ruling that continuous periods of residence completed before the entry into force of the Directive on April 30, 2006 are to be taken into account in computing the five years of lawful residence required in order to acquire a right of permanent residence. Furthermore, absences from the host Member State of less than two consecutive years prior to April 30, 2006 but following a continuous period of lawful residence of five years completed before April 30, 2006 do not affect the acquisition of permanent residence status following entry into force of the Directive.

The Advocate-General has, on November 25, 2010, issued her Opinion in Case C-434/09 *McCarthy.* She suggests that the Court should rule that a person with dual nationality who has always lived in one of the two Member States in question cannot claim a right of residence under the Directive in that Member State. While "legal residence" for the purposes of art.16 can result from the application of national law or European Union law, "legal residence" for the purposes of art.16 does not arise in relation to a person who has always been resident only in the Member State of their nationality on the basis of that nationality.

p.913, *annotation to art.16 Dir.2004/38/EC*

4.036.1   For a comment on the Advocate General's Opinion of February 17, 2011 in Case C-325/09 *Secretary of State for the Home Department v Dias,* see update to p.305 of Vol.II at para.3.009.1, above.

p.1004, *annotation to reg.883/2004, art.70*

4.037   In *SC v SSWP* [2010] UKUT 108 (AAC), the judge found that Italian civil invalidity benefit is a "special non-contributory benefit", and so receipt of this benefit could not count towards the 364 days of entitlement to an equivalent of short-term incapacity benefit in order to qualify for long-term incapacity benefit.

p.1220, *annotation to art.14 European Convention on Human Rights*

4.038   *JM v United Kingdom* (37060/06) Judgment of September 28, 2010 concerned the differential treatment of the assets of a homosexual couple as compared with an unmarried heterosexual couple in the determination of the liability of a mother to contribute to the maintenance of her children. The applicant complained that the calculation of her housing costs did not take account of her homosexual relationship with another woman, whereas were her new relationship to be with a man her housing costs would be calculated at a higher level.

The Strasbourg Court concluded that the computation of a liability to maintain children in the circumstances of this case clearly fell within the ambit of art.1 of Protocol 1 (and that it was not necessary to determine whether it also fell within the ambit of art.8). Furthermore, there was differential treatment of individuals based on sexual preference, which could not be justified.

For a decision in which the judge decides that social fund payments for funeral expenses do not discriminate unfairly between those with resources and those without resources, in the context of the particular requirements for Jewish burials, see *RM v Secretary of State for Work and Pensions* [2010] UKUT 220 (AAC).

For confirmation that there is no sustainable argument that the cessation of income support entitlement for those detained as a hospital in-patient amounts to a violation of art.14 when read with art.1 of Protocol 1, see *JB v Secretary of State for Work and Pensions* [2010] UKUT 263 (AAC).

p.1234, *annotation to art.1 of Protocol 1 European Convention on Human Rights*

Note that a complaint that the suspension of payment of the state pension during any period when the beneficiary is in prison violates art.1 of Protocol 1 was declared to be manifestly ill-founded in *Szrabjer v United Kingdom* (27004/95 and 27011/95), Decision of October 23, 1997.   4.039

p.1253, *annotation to the Tribunals, Courts and Enforcement Act 2007, s.3(1)*

The approach taken in *Evans v Secretary of State for Social Services* (reported as *R(I) 5/94*) and *Butterfield v Secretary of State for Defence* [2002] EWHC 2247 (Admin), both mentioned in the main work, has been followed in *MB v DSD (II)* [2010] NICom 133, where an appeal tribunal made new findings as a consequence of a medical examination and it was held that fairness required the claimant to have an opportunity to comment on those findings after the examination.   4.039.1

p.1256, *annotation to the Tribunals, Courts and Enforcement Act 2007, s.3(2)*

In *Secretary of State for Justice v RB* [2010] UKUT 454 (AAC), a three-judge panel of the Upper Tribunal has held that, when applying the law of England and Wales, the Upper Tribunal is not bound by decisions of the High Court exercising the supervisory jurisdiction of the High Court over inferior tribunals where an appeal to the Upper Tribunal is for practical purposes the successor to that supervisory role. It would, however, be bound to follow decisions of the High Court exercising its supervisory role over the Upper Tribunal if the decision in   4.040

R. (Cart) v Upper Tribunal (Public Law Project intervening) [2010] EWCA Civ 859; [2011] 2 W.L.R. 50 is upheld by the Supreme Court. Moreover, a single judge of the Upper Tribunal will follow a decision of a divisional court (i.e. two or more judges of the High Court sitting together) as a matter of judicial comity (*Salisbury Independent Living v Wirral MBC (HB)* [2011] UKUT 44 (AAC).

Secretary of State for Work and Pensions v Deane [2010] EWCA Civ 699 has been reported at [2010] AACR 42.

p.1260, *annotation to the Tribunals, Courts and Enforcement Act 2007, s.3(5)*

4.041   In *Eba v Advocate General for Scotland* [2010] CSIH 78, the Inner House of the Court of Session allowed the claimant's appeal against the Lord Ordinary's decision that the Upper Tribunal was amenable to judicial review only in exceptional circumstances and decided that there was no such restriction. The Advocate General for Scotland has been given permission to appeal to the Supreme Court, and the appeal is to be heard in March 2011 with Mr Cart's appeal against the decision of the Court of Appeal in *R. (Cart) v Upper Tribunal (Public Law Project Intervening)* [2010] EWCA Civ 859; [2011] 2 W.L.R. 50 (mentioned in the main work).

pp.1261–1262, *annotation to the Tribunals, Courts and Enforcement Act 2007, s.7*

4.042   The First-tier Tribunal and Upper Tribunal (Chambers) Order 2008 has been replaced by the First-tier Tribunal and Upper Tribunal (Chambers) Order 2010 (SI 2010/2655) with effect from November 29, 2010. There is no practical difference as regards social security cases and, in particular, art.6 of the 2010 Order replicates art.3 of the 2008 Order with only some renumbering of sub-paragraphs. Articles 2, 6, 7, 8 and 11 of the 2008 Order are replaced respectively by arts 2, 9, 10, 13 and 15 of the 2010 Order. Judge Colin Bishopp has been appointed Chamber President of the Tax Chamber of the First-tier Tribunal.

p.1264, *annotation to the Tribunals, Courts and Enforcement Act 2007, s.9(1) to (3)*

4.043   *R. (RB) v First-tier Tribunal (Review)* [2010] UKUT 160 (AAC) has been reported at [2010] AACR 41.

pp.1274–1275, *annotation to the Tribunals, Courts and Enforcement Act 2007, s.11(2)*

4.044   A witness is not a "party" and so cannot challenge by way of an appeal a refusal by the First-tier Tribunal to set aside a summons issued by it. However, the refusal could be challenged in judicial review proceedings and, in England and Wales, the proceedings could be brought in the Upper Tribunal because they would fall within the scope of the practice direction made by the Lord Chief Justice under s.18(6) of this Act (*CB v Suffolk CC (Enforcement Reference)* [2010] UKUT 413 (AAC)).

KC v Lewisham LBC (SEN) [2010] UKUT 96 (AAC) has been reported at [2010] AACR 36.

In *LS v Lambeth LBC (HB)* [2010] UKUT 461 (AAC), a three-judge panel has decided that there is a right of appeal under s.11 against any decision of the First-tier Tribunal that is not an "excluded decision". It was pointed out that, by making an order under subs.(5)(f) and (6)(b), the Lord Chancellor could have preserved the effect of *Morina v Secretary of State for Work and Pensions* [2007] EWCA Civ 749; [2007] 1 W.L.R. 3033 (mentioned in the main work) in social security cases but had not done so.

Nonetheless, interlocutory appeals have not been encouraged. The duty under r.33(2)(c) of the Tribunal Procedure (First-tier Tribunal) (Social Entitlement Chamber) Rules to inform a person of the right of appeal applies only to a decision which finally disposes of all issues in the proceedings and the three-judge panel itself said that:

> "it will be open to both the First-tier Tribunal and the Upper Tribunal to refuse permission to bring an interlocutory appeal on the ground that it is premature. The circumstances of the individual case must be considered. It is one thing to grant permission for an interlocutory appeal in a case where the final hearing may last for a fortnight. It is another to do so where the final hearing is likely to last about an hour, as is often the case in social security appeals. Moreover, as was suggested in *Dorset Healthcare NHS Foundation Trust v MH* [2009] UKUT 4 (AAC) at [19], where case-management decisions are being challenged, the First-tier Tribunal can treat an application for permission to appeal as an application for a new direction if it is satisfied that the challenged direction is not appropriate."

It must follow that parties will not be prejudiced by waiting until there has been a final decision in the case and then relying on an error in an interlocutory decision as grounds of appeal against the final decision.

p.1282, *annotation to the Tribunals, Courts and Enforcement Act 2007, s.13*

In *Miskovic v Secretary of State for Work and Pensions* [2011] EWCA Civ 16, the Court of Appeal rejected an argument that it was precluded from considering points not argued before the Upper Tribunal and accepted that it could do so, provided it would not be unfair to the other party. The Court also said that it might be reluctant to consider a new point unless all the facts potentially relevant to the correct determination of the point had been found. However, in a jurisdiction where an appeal lies only on a point of law, which includes a failure to find material facts, and where the Court can remit the matter to a tribunal to make further findings, it is not easy to see why there should be such reluctance as long as the absence of findings does not make the determination of the point of law too speculative.

4.045

In *RH v South London and Maudsley NHS Foundation Trust* [2010] EWCA Civ 1273; [2011] AACR 14 the Court of Appeal has made it clear that if only one of a number of grounds of appeal raises an important point of principle or practice, the Upper Tribunal should carefully consider whether the grant of permission should be limited to that ground. Moreover, if a ground is raised that was not advanced on the appeal before the Upper Tribunal, the Upper Tribunal should consider obtaining the other party's view on it before granting permission.

pp.1295–1296, *annotation to the Tribunals, Courts and Enforcement Act 2007, s.25*

4.046   *MD v SSWP (Enforcement Reference)* [2010] UKUT 202 (AAC) is now reported at [2011] AACR 5.

In *CB v Suffolk CC (Enforcement Reference)* [2010] UKUT 413 (AAC) the Upper Tribunal fined a witness £500 for ignoring a summons issued by the Health, Education and Social Care Chamber of the First-tier Tribunal and, under s.16(3) of the Contempt of Court Act 1981, specified a term of imprisonment of seven days to be served if the fine was not paid within the time allowed.

p.1319, *annotation to First-tier Tribunal and Upper Tribunal (Composition of Tribunal) Order 2008, art.8*

4.047   Tribunal Procedure Rules do not require that either a decision notice or a statement of reasons should indicate whether a decision was unanimous. However, in *SSWP v SS (DLA)* [2010] UKUT 384 (AAC) it was held that there was a material error of law when a decision notice said that a decision was unanimous but the statement of reasons said it had been reached by a majority, without acknowledging the error. Moreover, the judge said that, although there was generally no duty to include in a statement of reasons the reasons for any dissent, if a decision notice did state that a decision was by a majority, there was a duty to include the reasons of the dissenting member, and that the same approach applied if a decision notice stated that a decision was unanimous when in fact it had been reached by a majority.

p.1322, *amendment to Tribunal Procedure (First-tier Tribunal) (Social Entitlement Chamber) Rules 2008, r.1(2)*

4.048   Rule 1(2) has been substituted by r.5(1) and (2) of the Tribunal Procedure (Amendment No.3) Rules 2010 (SI 2010/2653), with effect from November 29, 2010, so that it reads:

"(2) These Rules apply to proceedings before the Social Entitlement Chamber of the First-tier Tribunal."

pp.1325–1326, *annotation to Tribunal Procedure (First-tier Tribunal) (Social Entitlement Chamber) Rules 2008, r.2*

4.048.1   *AT v SSWP (ESA)* [2010] UKUT 430 (AAC) is another case where it has been suggested that r.2 largely reinforces principles that already existed, so that a failure expressly to refer to it is unlikely to be an error of law in itself. Moreover, while a tribunal must consider those factors in para.(2) that are relevant, not every factor will be relevant in every case.

p.1328, *annotation to Tribunal Procedure (First-tier Tribunal) (Social Entitlement Chamber) Rules 2008, r.5(3)(a)*

R. (CD) v First-tier Tribunal (CIC) [2010] UKUT 181 (AAC) has been reported at [2011] AACR 1.   **4.049**

pp.1329–1332, *annotation to Tribunal Procedure (First-tier Tribunal) (Social Entitlement Chamber) Rules 2008, r.5(3)(h)*

The approach taken in *Evans v Secretary of State for Social Services*   **4.049.1**
(reported as *R(I) 5/94*) and *Butterfield v Secretary of State for Defence* [2002] EWHC 2247 (Admin), both mentioned in the main work, has been followed in *MB v DSD (II)* [2010] NICom 133, where an appeal tribunal made new findings as a consequence of a medical examination and it was held that fairness required the claimant to have an opportunity to comment on those findings after the examination.

Although it has been held in *LS v Lambeth LBC (HB)* [2010] UKUT 61 (AAC) that there is a right of appeal against including interlocutory decisions (other than an "excluded decision" within the scope of s.11(5) of the Tribunals, Courts and Enforcement Act 2007), the three-judge panel did not encourage interlocutory appeals and it remains the case that an unfair refusal to adjourn may be challenged by way of an appeal against the final decision. It was said that permission to appeal against an interlocutory decision before the final decision had been given might be refused on the ground that any appeal was premature.

pp.1332–1333, *annotation to Tribunal Procedure (First-tier Tribunal) (Social Entitlement Chamber) Rules 2008, r.5(3)(l)*

There is no automatic right to a suspension in any particular case. In   **4.049.2**
Carmarthenshire CC v MW (SEN) [2010] UKUT 348 (AAC) which was concerned with the Upper Tribunal's power to suspend the effect of a decision of the First-tier Tribunal, it was held that there has to be balancing exercise, taking into account the practical consequences of suspending the decision on one side and the practical consequences of not doing so on the other. The chances of the appeal succeeding would be relevant but it was doubted whether a good prospect of the appeal succeeding could operate as a threshold condition, particularly in a case of urgency where the grounds of appeal might not have been formulated.

p.1335, *annotation to Tribunal Procedure (First-tier Tribunal) (Social Entitlement Chamber) Rules 2008, r.7(3)*

MD v Secretary of State for Work and Pensions (Enforcement Reference)   **4.050**
[2010] UKUT 202 (AAC) is now reported at [2011] AACR 5.

p.1336, *amendment to Tribunal Procedure (First-tier Tribunal) (Social Entitlement Chamber) Rules 2008, r.8(8)*

4.051   The words, "and may summarily determine any or all issues against that respondent" have been added to the end of r.8(8) by r.5(1) and (3) of the Tribunal Procedure (Amendment No.3) Rules 2010 (SI 2010/2653), with effect from November 29, 2010, thus making it clear that, in an appropriate case, barring a respondent can have the same effect on a respondent that striking out the proceedings has on an appellant.

pp.1337–1338, *annotation to Tribunal Procedure (First-tier Tribunal) (Social Entitlement Chamber) Rules 2008, r.8*

4.052   *LS v Lambeth LBC (HB)* [2010] UKUT 461 (AAC), in which it has been held that there is a right of appeal against any decision of the First-tier Tribunal (other than an "excluded decision" within the scope of s.11(5) of the Tribunals, Courts and Enforcement Act 2007), removes the doubt there had been as to whether there was a right of appeal against a decision under this rule. Note, however, that where an appeal is automatically struck out under para.(1), the striking out is not itself a decision. Before considering an appeal, it will usually be necessary to apply for reinstatement under para.(5) and then, if necessary, it will be possible to appeal against a refusal to reinstate the appeal. However, where a party knows that compliance will be impossible or there has been admitted non-compliance, an alternative approach would be to appeal against the earlier direction insofar as it stated that failure to comply with it would lead to the appeal being struck out (as was done in *Salisbury Independent Living v Wirral MBC (HB)* [2011] UKUT 44 (AAC)).

AW v Essex CC (SEN) [2010] UKUT 74 (AAC) has been reported at [2010] AACR 35.

In *Camden LBC v FG (SEN)* [2010] UKUT 249 (AAC) it was suggested that case management directions containing a warning that a failure to comply with them might result in the First-tier Tribunal's use of its powers to strike out a case under r.8 ought to have referred specifically to the equivalents of paras (3)(a), (7) and (8) of this rule and, more importantly, that an order under the equivalent of r.8(3)(a) addressed to a respondent ought to have referred to the equivalent of para.(7) and also to the equivalent of paras (5) and (6), which confer the right to apply for the lifting on a bar. However, in the particular case, the failure was not important because the respondent did protest and its letter was treated as an application for a lifting of the bar. The decision refusing to lift the bar was communicated by telephone initially, and then it appears that a letter was sent, again "pp'd" on behalf of the judge. The Upper Tribunal recommended that such a decision should be in the form of an order signed by the judge and that it ought to draw attention to the right to make an application under the equivalent of Pt 4 of these Rules, although such notice does not appear to be mandatory where

barring a respondent does not dispose of all issues in the proceedings
(see r.33).

p.1349, *annotation to Tribunal Procedure (First-tier Tribunal) (Social
Entitlement Chamber) Rules 2008, r.16*

In *CB v Suffolk CC (Enforcement Reference)* [2010] UKUT 413 (AAC) **4.053**
the Upper Tribunal has emphasised that it is wrong to draw the impres-
sion from *MD v Secretary of State for Work and Pensions (Enforcement
Reference)* [2010] UKUT 202 (AAC) (now reported at [2011] AACR
5):

> "that a person on whom a witness summons has been served can
> simply sit back, await any reference to the Upper Tribunal and only
> then argue that the witness summons was not appropriately issued."

An application may be made to the First-tier Tribunal for a summons to
be set aside (see para.(4)(a)) and a refusal to set it aside may be challenged by way of an application to the Upper Tribunal for judicial review.
If a summons is not successfully challenged, it must be obeyed. In that
case, the Upper Tribunal fined the witness £500 for failing to comply
with a summons issued by the Health, Education and Social Care
Chamber of the First-tier Tribunal. It also commented that the scheme
of expenses for witnesses operated by the Tribunals Service, which is the
same as that for jurors and covers travel expenses and loss of earnings up
to a fixed limit, was sufficient for compliance with r.16(2)(b) and that it
was not necessary to compensate for all financial loss.

In *Camden LBC v FG (SEN)* [2010] UKUT 249 (AAC) it was
suggested that a summons should be signed by a judge "rather than
being pp'd (as happened here) on his or her behalf", but the summons
was nonetheless held valid.

p.1358, *annotation to Tribunal Procedure (First-tier Tribunal) (Social
Entitlement Chamber) Rules 2008, r.25(2)*

In *MB v DSD (II)* [2010] NICom 133, it was held that, where a **4.053.1**
tribunal makes new findings of significance in consequence of a medical
examination, fairness may require all parties to the proceedings to have
an opportunity to comment on those findings, even if that sometimes
involves an adjournment to allow the claimant to seek advice. See also
Evans v Secretary of State for Social Services (reported as *R(I) 5/94*).

pp.1360–1366, *annotation to Tribunal Procedure (First-tier Tribunal)
(Social Entitlement Chamber) Rules 2008, r.27(1) to (3)*

In the past, there was a standard "record of proceedings" for "paper **4.054**
hearings" in which a judge ticked boxes to confirm not only that the
claimant had made such an election but also that the chairman was
satisfied that a hearing was not required. Now that that form is no longer
used, it may be necessary for a judge to explain why the case was dealt
with on the papers and without an adjournment if asked to provide a

statement of reasons for the decision. Rule 27(1)(b) expressly requires the First-tier Tribunal to be satisfied that it is able to decide the matter without a hearing. In *MH v Pembrokeshire CC (HB)* [2010] UKUT 28 (AAC), the First-tier Tribunal declined to accept a claimant's assertion that he suffered from a mental disorder, saying that he had not produced medical evidence and had elected a paper hearing. The decision was set aside by the Upper Tribunal because the First-tier Tribunal had given no indication that it had considered adjourning. The judge drew attention to the overriding objective in r.2. No-one had told the claimant that he needed to produce medical evidence or ask for a hearing.

However, it is clear from *AT v Secretary of State for Work and Pensions (ESA)* [2010] UKUT 430 (AAC), in which *MH* was distinguished, that a failure expressly to refer to the overriding objective is unlikely to be an error of law in itself and, while a tribunal must consider those factors in paragraph (2) that are relevant, not every factor will be relevant in every case.

In *DG v Secretary of State for Work and Pensions (ESA)* [2010] UKUT 409 (AAC), a decision made on the papers was set aside where a mentally ill claimant had not sought a hearing after being given advice from the jobcentre that he need not do anything, which was held to have been misleading when the claimant had not been made aware of the consequences of the choice.

p.1368, *annotation to Tribunal Procedure (First-tier Tribunal) (Social Entitlement Chamber) Rules 2008, r.30(3)*

4.054.1   *Independent News and Media Ltd v A* [2010] EWCA Civ 343 has now been reported at [2010] 1 W.L.R. 2262.

In *KP v Hertfordshire CC (SEN)* [2010] UKUT 119 (AAC), the Upper Tribunal was not persuaded that there was any duty to hold a hearing of a directions application when no request for a hearing had been made.

Although care must be taken when considering whether to hear evidence from a child, there can be no presumption against a child giving evidence and regard must be had to the fairness of the proceedings as well as the interests of the child (In *re W (Children) (Family Proceedings: Evidence)* [2010] UKSC 12; [2010] 1 W.L.R. 701).

pp.1373–1381, *annotation to Tribunal Procedure (First-tier Tribunal) (Social Entitlement Chamber) Rules 2008, r.34(2) to (5)*

4.055   Whether reasons are needed for an interlocutory decision is likely to depend on the context. Although an appeal lies against interlocutory decisions (*LS v Lambeth LBC (HB)* [2010] UKUT 461 (AAC)), there is no statutory requirement to give reasons for decisions that do not finally dispose of all issues in the proceedings (see r.34(5)) and no general common law requirement to do so either, although a decision may be set aside on the ground of a failure to provide reasons if a discretion has been exercised in a particularly unusual manner (*Jones v Governing Body of Burdett Coutts School* [1999] I.C.R. 38, 47) or the decision appears aberrant (*R. v Higher Education Funding Council, Ex p. Institute of Dental Surgery* [1994] 1 W.L.R. 242 at 263).

For the need to give reasons for deciding a case without a hearing, see the supplementary annotation to r.27, above.

Where reasons for interlocutory decisions are requested, they are sometimes conveyed in a letter signed by the clerk to the tribunal. This is not improper, provided that the reasons are those of the tribunal (*R. v Stoke City Council, Ex p. Highgate Projects* (1993) 26 H.L.R. 551) and, indeed, it would not necessarily be improper for a clerk to assist in the drafting of reasons (*Virdi v Law Society (Solicitors Disciplinary Tribunal intervening)* [2010] EWCA Civ 100; [2010] 1 W.L.R. 2840).

In *Sandhu v Secretary of State for Work and Pensions* [2010] EWCA Civ 962 the Court of Appeal held reasons to be flawed for inconsistency when at one point the First-tier Tribunal said that it accepted that the claimant could not put any weight on his right leg and then at another point it found he could walk with crutches. In *Secretary of State for Work and Pensions v SS (DLA)* [2010] UKUT 384 (AAC) it was held that there was a material error of law when a decision notice said that a decision was unanimous but the statement of reasons said it had been reached by a majority, without acknowledging the error. Moreover, the judge said that, although there was generally no duty to include in a statement of reasons the reasons for any dissent, if a decision notice did state that a decision was by a majority, there was a duty to include the reasons of the dissenting member, and that the same approach applied if a decision notice stated that a decision was unanimous when in fact it had been reached by a majority.

The mere fact that another tribunal has given more detailed reasons when considering the same issue does not render the briefer reasons of a second tribunal inadequate, particularly when they are based on a clear finding of credibility (*Secretary of State for Work and Pensions v AM (IS)* [2010] UKUT 428 (AAC)).

pp.1388–1390, annotation to *Tribunal Procedure (First-tier Tribunal) (Social Entitlement Chamber) Rules 2008, r.40*

R. (RB) v First-tier Tribunal (Review) [2010] UKUT 160 (AAC) has been reported at [2010] AACR 41.   4.056

p.1390, amendment to *Tribunal Procedure (First-tier Tribunal) (Social Entitlement Chamber) Rules 2008, Sch.1*

The first entry in the Schedule is substituted by r.5(1) and (4) of the Tribunal Procedure (Amendment No.3) Rules 2010 (SI 2010/2653), with effect from November 29, 2010, so that it reads: 4.057

"Cases other than those listed below.
The latest of—
   (a) one month after the date on which notice of the decision being challenged was sent to the appellant;
   (b) if a written statement of reasons for the decision was requested within that month, 14 days after the later of—

(i) the end of that month; or

(ii) the date on which the written statement of reasons was provided; or

(c) if the appellant made an application for revision of the decision under—

(i) regulation 17(1)(a) of the Child Support (Maintenance Assessment Procedure) Regulations 1992,

(ii) regulation 3(1) or (3) or 3A(1) of the Social Security and Child Support (Decision and Appeals) Regulations 1999, or

(iii) regulation 4 of the Housing Benefit and Council Tax Benefit (Decisions and Appeals) Regulations 2001,

and that application was unsuccessful, one month after the date on which notice that the decision would not be revised was sent to the appellant."

This makes it clearer that a written statement of reasons must be requested within a month of the decision if time is to be extended under sub-para.(b).

pp.1403–1404, *annotation to Tribunal Procedure (Upper Tribunal) Rules 2008, r.5(3)*

4.057.1 In *Carmarthenshire CC v MW (SEN)* [2010] UKUT 348 (AAC), it was held that the power conferred by r.5(3)(m) to suspend the effect of a decision of the First-tier Tribunal required a balancing exercise, taking into account the practical consequences of suspending the decision on one side and the practical consequences of not doing so on the other. The chances of the appeal succeeding would be relevant but it was doubted whether a good prospect of the appeal succeeding could operate as a threshold condition, particularly in a case of urgency where the grounds of appeal might not have been formulated.

p.1405, *annotation to Tribunal Procedure (Upper Tribunal) Rules 2008, r.7*

4.058 *MD v Secretary of State for Work and Pensions (Enforcement Reference)* [2010] UKUT 202 (AAC) is now reported at [2011] AACR 5.

p.1449, *insertion of Tribunal Procedure (Upper Tribunal) Rules 2008, r.48*

4.059 A new r.48 is inserted by r.8 of the Tribunal Procedure (Amendment No.3) Rules 2010 (SI 2010/2653), with effect from November 29, 2010. It is in the same terms as r.41 of the First-tier Tribunal Rules (see p.1390 of the main work) and provides:

"Power to treat an application as a different type of application

48. The Tribunal may treat an application for a decision to be corrected, set aside or reviewed, or for permission to appeal against a decision, as an application for any other one of those things."

PART V

UPDATING MATERIAL
VOLUME IV

TAX CREDITS AND HMRC-ADMINISTERED SOCIAL SECURITY BENEFITS

Commentary by

Nick Wikeley, David Williams and Ian Hooker

p.37, *annotation to the Social Security Contributions and Benefits Act 1992, s.146*

In *Commissioners for HMRC v Ruas* [2010] EWCA Civ 291; [2010]   5.001
AACR 31 the claimant, a Portuguese national, had come to the United
Kingdom from Portugal in 2000 with his wife and youngest child. His
two elder children had remained living in Portugal with a relative. The
claimant worked in the United Kingdom and paid national insurance
contributions until he became unable to work due to ill-health in 2004.
He remained living in the United Kingdom and in 2006 applied for child
benefit for all three of his children, when he was in receipt of DLA and
income support and qualified for national insurance credits on the
ground of incapacity for work. The Court of Appeal held (dismissing the
appeal of the Secretary of State against the decision of Judge Mesher in
CF/2266/2007) that the claimant was entitled to claim child benefit in the
United Kingdom for his children resident in Portugal. The effect of
s.146, which restricts child benefit to children resident in Great Britain,
had to be disapplied by virtue of art.73 of Council Regulation (EEC)
1408/71, which was directly effective in the United Kingdom, conferring
on the claimant an entitlement to UK child benefit (*Martinez Sala v
Freistaat Bayern* (C-85/96) [1998] E.C.R. I-2691 ECtHR followed).

p.49, *annotation to the Social Security Contributions and Benefits Act 1992, s.163*

GENERAL NOTE   5.002

Subsection (2) defines "normal weekly earnings" by reference to "the average
weekly earnings which in the relevant period have been paid to him". A First-tier
Tribunal in the Tax Chamber has ruled that where an employer unlawfully failed
to pay an employee her wages in the relevant period it followed that the employee
had no entitlement to SSP, even if she later succeeded in an employment tribunal
claim for unlawful deduction of wages: *Seaton v Commissioners for HMRC* [2010]
UKFTT 270 (TC).

p.120, *annotation to the Tax Credits Act 2002, s.3*

In *CTC/1853/2009* it was held that claimants resident not in the   5.003
United Kingdom but elsewhere in the European Union could not claim
child tax credit under art.77 of Council Regulation (EEC) 1408/71. This
was agreed in *EM v HMRC (TC)* [2010] UKUT 323 (AAC), although
it was commented that in some circumstances there might be a claim
under other European legislation. However, both judges noted that the
Regulation was replaced by Council Regulation (EC) 883/2004 as from
May 2010. HMRC will now pay child tax credit to claimants such as
those in these appeals (payment having been stopped in both cases).

HMRC is reminding all claimants by letter of the need to report a
change of circumstances, including in particular whether a claim should
be a joint claim. This followed recognition that in 2008–09 150,000
claims (2.5 per cent of the total) were incorrect single claims.

p.130, *annotation to the Tax Credits Act 2002, s.7(4)*

5.004 *CTC/2270/2007* was followed by an Upper Tribunal judge in *PD v HMRC (TC)* [2010] UKUT 159 (AAC).

p.131, *annotation to the Tax Credits Act 2002, s.8*

5.005 The question whether claimants caring for children elsewhere in the European Union were entitled to child tax credit has been considered by the Upper Tribunal in two appeals. See note to s.3(3), above.

p.367, *amendments to the Working Tax Credit (Entitlement and Maximum Rate) Regulations 2002, reg.5*

5.006 With effect from November 14, 2010, reg.3(2)–(4) of the Tax Credits (Miscellaneous Amendments) (No.2) Regulations 2010 (SI 2010/2494) amended reg.5 by substituting "ordinary statutory paternity pay" for "statutory paternity pay" in para.(1)(d), inserting "(da) is paid additional statutory paternity pay," after para.(1)(d) and substituting a new para.(1)(e) as follows:

"(e) is absent from work during an ordinary paternity leave period under sections 80A or 80B of the Employment Rights Act 1996 or Articles 112A or 112B of the Employment Rights (Northern Ireland) Order 1996,".

With effect from the same date, reg.3(5) inserted a new sub-paragraph after para.(1)(e) as follows:

"(ea) is absent from work during an additional paternity leave period under sections 80AA or 80BB of the Employment Rights Act 1996 or Articles 112AA or 112BB of the Employment Rights (Northern Ireland) Order 1996,".

p.368, *amendments to the Working Tax Credit (Entitlement and Maximum Rate) Regulations 2002, reg.5*

5.007 With effect from November 14, 2010, reg.3(6) and (7) of the Tax Credits (Miscellaneous Amendments) (No.2) Regulations 2010 (SI 2010/2494) amended reg.5 by substituting "paragraphs (3) and (3A)" for "paragraph (3)" in para.(2) and inserting after para.(3) the following new paragraph:

"(3A) A person shall only be treated as being engaged in qualifying remunerative work by virtue of paragraph (1)(ea) for such period as that person would have been paid additional statutory paternity pay had the conditions of entitlement in Parts 2 or 3 of the Additional Statutory Paternity Pay (General) Regulations 2010 or Parts 2 or 3 of the Additional Statutory Paternity Pay (General) Regulations (Northern Ireland) 2010 been satisfied."

p.412, *amendment to the Tax Credits (Definition and Calculation of Income) Regulations 2002, reg.4*

With effect from November 14, 2010, reg.5 of the Tax Credits (Mis-cellaneous Amendments) (No.2) Regulations 2010 (SI 2010/2494) amended reg.4(1)(h) by substituting "ordinary statutory paternity pay, additional statutory paternity pay" for "statutory paternity pay". **5.008**

p.428, *amendment to the Tax Credits (Definition and Calculation of Income) Regulations 2002, reg.7*

With effect from November 14, 2010, reg.6 of the Tax Credits (Mis-cellaneous Amendments) (No.2) Regulations 2010 (SI 2010/2494) amended item 21A of Table 3 in reg.7 by substituting "Ordinary statu-tory paternity pay and additional statutory paternity pay" for "Statutory paternity pay". **5.009**

p.456, *amendment to the Child Tax Credit Regulations 2002, reg.2(1)*

With effect from May 5, 2010, art.4 of and Sch.3, para.46 to the Local Education Authorities and Children's Services Authorities (Integration of Functions) (Local and Subordinate Legislation) Order 2010 (SI 2010/1172) amended the definition of "the Careers Service" in reg.2(1) by substituting "local authority" in para.(a) for "local education authority". **5.010**

p.462, *annotation to the Child Tax Credits Regulations 2002, reg.3*

CTC/4390/2004 was not followed, and was criticised, by an Upper Tribunal judge in *CM v HMRC (TC)* [2010] UKUT 400 (AAC) on the issue of whether one party would benefit more than the other party from the relative amounts that may be claimed by the parties. **5.011**

p.466, *annotation to the Child Tax Credit Regulations 2002, reg.5*

In *JN v HMRC (TC)* [2010] UKUT 288 (AAC) the Upper Tribunal considered the meaning of "qualifying young person" before the 2008 amendments in a case where there was a gap in the education of the young person. The case concerned a young person who had left educa-tion in Kenya to come to Britain to continue studying here. The judge noted difficulties in treating the education in Kenya as taking place at a recognised establishment but accepted that the education itself could be recognised. On the facts tax credit was payable during the gap between leaving Kenya and starting a course in Britain. **5.012**

p.493, *annotation to the Tax Credits (Claims and Notifications) Regulations 2002, reg.12*

HMRC advises claimants that it can take up to six weeks to deal with a renewal claim made in this way. It advises claimants who have not heard after six weeks to notify the Tax Credit Helpline. **5.013**

p.497, *annotation to the Tax Credits (Claims and Notifications) Regulations 2002, reg.18*

5.014   HMRC has now revised its procedures for recognising representatives. A claimant can authorise a representative to make a claim by filling in Form 64–8 (authorising your agent) for this and for tax purposes.

p.498, *annotation to the Tax Credits (Claims and Notifications) Regulations 2002, reg.22*

5.015   In *LV v HMRC* (November 10, 2010) an Upper Tribunal judge decided that a mother who had reported by telephone on February 14, 2007 to a DWP office that her son had now been diagnosed as disabled had made a sufficient notification of the disablement for the purposes of regs 22 and 26A for payment of additional child tax credit to be made for the disabled child where, on October 15, 2007, a tribunal had awarded DLA to the child from February 14, 2007. HMRC had argued that the notification had to be to HMRC. The judge decided that this was not required by the definition of "appropriate office" in reg.2. The judge commented that an alternative and narrower interpretation would be unfair because it would penalise the child in connection with the claim for tax credits because of the mistake made by the Secretary of State in handling the DLA claim.

p.528, *annotation to the Tax Credits (Appeals) (No.2) Regulations 2002, "party to the proceedings"*

5.016   It was pointed out in *PD v HMRC (TC)* [2010] UKUT 159 (AAC) that *CTC/2612/2005* was decided under former procedures now replaced by the Tribunal Procedure (First-tier Tribunal) (Social Entitlement Chamber) Rules 2008. Under those rules where one of a joint claim couple appeals a decision, the other is a respondent. The second claimant is therefore a party to the proceedings and should be notified of the proceedings and any proposal to deal with the appeal on the papers. This also applies to the decision in *CTC/2612/2005*. See now Tribunal Procedure (First-tier Tribunal) (Social Entitlement Chamber) Rules 2008, rr.1 (definitions), 5 (case management powers), and 9 (substitution and addition of parties) in Volume III of this work.

p.574, *amendment to the Child Benefit (General) Regulations 2006, reg.1(3)*

5.017   With effect from May 5, 2010, art.4 of, and Sch.3, para.66 to, the Local Education Authorities and Children's Services Authorities (Integration of Functions) (Local and Subordinate Legislation) Order 2010 (SI 2010/1172) amended the definition of "the Careers Service" in reg.1(3) by substituting "local authority" in para.(a) for "local education authority".

p.668, *amendment to the Statutory Maternity Pay (General) Regulations 1986, reg.14(f)*

With effect from May 5, 2010, art.4 of, and Sch.3, para.11 to, the 5.018 Local Education Authorities and Children's Services Authorities (Integration of Functions) (Local and Subordinate Legislation) Order 2010 (SI 2010/1172) amended reg.14(f) by substituting "local authority (within the meaning of the Education Act 1996)" for "local education authority".

p.749, *amendment to the Statutory Paternity Pay and Statutory Adoption Pay (General) Regulations 2002, reg.36(f)*

With effect from May 5, 2010, art.4 of, and Sch.3, para.47 to, the 5.019 Local Education Authorities and Children's Services Authorities (Integration of Functions) (Local and Subordinate Legislation) Order 2010 (SI 2010/1172) amended reg.36(f) by substituting "local authority" for "local education authority".

p.816, *amendments to the Child Trust Funds Regulations 2004, reg.7*

With effect from August 2, 2010, reg.3(2) of the Child Trust Funds 5.020 (Amendment No.3) Regulations 2010 (SI 2010/1894) amended reg.7(1) by substituting "(4B)" for "(4)" (where it first appears), "(2), (4)(a) and (4A)" for "(2) and (4)(a)" and "(3), (4)(b) and (4B)" for "(3) and (4)(b)". With effect from the same date, reg.3(3) of the same Regulations amended reg.7(4) by substituting "Subject to paragraphs (4A) and (4B), where" for "Where".

p.817, *amendments to the Child Trust Funds Regulations 2004, reg.7*

With effect from August 2, 2010, reg.3(4) of the Child Trust Funds 5.021 (Amendment No.3) Regulations 2010 (SI 2010/1894) amended reg.7 by inserting after para.(4) the following new paragraphs:

"(4A) Where a child—
(a) is first an eligible child by virtue of section 2(1)(a) of the Act, and
(b) the commencement date for the child (see paragraph (8)) is after the relevant 2010 date (see paragraph (10E)),
the amount is £50.
(4B) Where a child—
(a) is first an eligible child by virtue of section 2(1)(b) of the Act, and
(b) either—
(i) is born on or after the relevant 2010 date, or
(ii) is first in the United Kingdom (other than temporarily) on or after the relevant 2010 date, or
(iii) becomes an eligible child on or after 3 months (less one day) after the relevant 2010 date,
the amount is £100."

With effect from the same date, reg.3(5) of the same Regulations amended reg.7(7) by substituting "Subject to paragraph (7A), where" for "Where", while reg.3(6) inserted after para.(7) the following new paragraph:

"(7A) Where the child is one to whom section 9 of the Act applies, and the commencement date for the child is after the relevant 2010 date, the amount is £50."

With effect from the same date, reg.3(7) of the same Regulations amended reg.7(8) by omitting sub-para.(b) and the word "and" which preceded it, while reg.3(8) amended each of paras (10) and (10A) by substituting "£50" for "£250". Note that reg.3(8) has effect where the commencement date for the child (within the meaning of reg.7(8) of the Child Trust Funds Regulations 2004, as amended by reg.3(7) of the Child Trust Funds (Amendment No.3) Regulations 2010, is after the day on which reg.3 of those Regulations comes into force in accordance with reg.1(3) (see reg.1(4)). Finally, reg.3(9) inserted after para.(10C) the following new paragraphs:

"(10D) Her Majesty's Revenue and Customs must inform the account provider holding the child's account where an amount is payable to the account under paragraph (10) or (10A).
(10E) In this regulation, "the relevant 2010 date" means—
(a) 2nd August 2010; or
(b) if later, the day on which regulation 3 of the Child Trust Funds (Amendment No. 3) Regulations 2010 came into force."

p.818, *repeal of the Child Trust Funds Regulations 2004, reg.7A*

5.022　　With effect from August 1, 2010, reg.4 of the Child Trust Funds (Amendment No.3) Regulations 2010 (SI 2010/1894) repealed reg.7A (age seven payments).

p.819, *amendments to the Child Trust Funds Regulations 2004, reg.7*

5.023　　With effect from August 2, 2010, reg.5 of the Child Trust Funds (Amendment No.3) Regulations 2010 (SI 2010/1894) amended reg.7B by substituting "the year 2009/10 or 2010/11" for "any year" in para.(1) and omitting para.(4).

p.835, *amendments to the Child Trust Funds Regulations 2004, reg.16*

5.024　　With effect from November 16, 2010, reg.3(1) of the Child Trust Funds (Amendment No.4) Regulations 2010 (SI 2010/2599) amended reg.16 by inserting after para.(2) the following new paragraphs:

"(2A) Where paragraph (2B) applies, a term of an undertaking given in accordance with regulation 14(2)(b) shall not be taken as not satisfied only by reason that the person to whom the Board's approval as an account provider has been given does not accept vouchers.
(2B) This paragraph applies where—

(a) a person does not accept any voucher after a day specified by that person; and

(b) no less than 30 days before the specified day, notice in writing is given to the Board of the person's intention not to accept vouchers after that day."

p.887, *annotation to the Note on leaflets*

In July 2010 HMRC reissued WTC/FS3, *Tax credits formal request for information* and issued WTC/FS9, *Tax credits—suspension of payments.* A guidance note to agents about overpayments was also issued: *How HM Revenue & Customs handle tax credits overpayments.*   5.025

PART VI

FORTHCOMING CHANGES AND UP-RATING OF BENEFITS

FORTHCOMING CHANGES

6.001 This section aims to give users of Social Security Legislation 2010/11 some information on significant changes coming into force between December 8, 2010—the date to which this Supplement is up to date—and mid-April 2011, the date to which the 2011/12 edition will be up to date. The information here reflects our understanding of sources available to us as at December 8, 2010, and users should be aware that there will no doubt be further legislative amendment between then and mid-April 2011. This Part of the Supplement will at least enable users to access the relevant legislation (and usually accompanying Explanatory Notes prepared by the Department) on the Public Sector Information website (http://www.opsi.gov.uk).

REGULATIONS

Employment and Support Allowance (Transitional Provisions, Housing Benefit and Council Tax Benefit) (Existing Awards) (No.2) Regulations 2010 (SI 2010/1907) (as amended)

Most of these entered into force on October 1, 2010 (see "New Legislation" section of this Supplement and the Updating sections of this Supplement). The others entered into force on January 31, 2011.

6.002

With effect from January 31, 2011, reg.25(2) amended reg.144 of the Employment and Support Allowance Regulations 2008 (waiting days) so that the waiting days rule does not apply where the claimant's entitlement to an employment and support allowance commences within 12 weeks of the claimant's entitlement to income support, incapacity benefit, severe disablement allowance, state pension credit, a jobseeker's allowance, a carer's allowance, statutory sick pay or a maternity allowance coming to an end.

With effect from January 31, 2011, reg.24 revoked reg.2(2)(a)–(c) of the Employment and Support Allowance (Transitional Provisions) Regulations 2008, reg.2(2) (claim for an existing award).

With effect from January 31, 2011, reg.26 and Sch.4, para.1A(3) modified the Jobseeker's Allowance Regulations 1996, Sch.1 para.20H (Additional conditions for higher pensioner and disability premium) (see the "New Legislation" section of this Supplement).

With effect from January 31, 2011, reg.26 and Sch.4, para.1A(1) amended the Jobseeker's Allowance Regulations 1996, reg.55 (Short periods of sickness) (see the "New Legislation" section of this Supplement).

With effect from January 31, 2011, reg.26 and Sch.4, para.1A(2) amended the Jobseeker's Allowance Regulations 1996, reg.55A (Periods of sickness and persons receiving treatment outside Great Britain) (see the "New Legislation" section of this Supplement).

With effect from January 31, 2011, reg.26 and Sch.4, para.2 amended reg.2(3) of the Employment and Support Allowance (Transitional Provisions) Regulations 2008 (claim for existing award) (see the "New Legislation" section of this Supplement).

The Social Fund Maternity Grant Amendment Regulations 2010 (SI 2010/2760)

6.003   These regulations came into force on December 13, 2010. They extend the categories of people who may be entitled to a Sure Start Maternity Grant under reg.5 of the Social Fund Maternity and Funeral Expenses (General) Regulations 2005. The new categories are:

- fathers who are responsible for a child aged under 12 months and who are separated from that child's mother;
- people who have been granted an adoption order, a parental order or a residence order in respect of a child aged under 12 months and who are responsible for that child;
- people who have been appointed the guardian of a child aged under 12 months and who are responsible for that child;
- people with whom a child under the age of 12 months has been placed for adoption and who are responsible for that child; and
- people who adopt a child under the age of 12 months under the law of certain foreign countries.

Consequential amendments are made to the rules against double payment.

NEW BENEFIT RATES FROM APRIL 2011

NEW BENEFIT RATES FROM APRIL 2011

(Benefits covered in Volume I)

	April 2010	April 2011
	£ pw	£ pw
Disability benefits		
Attendance allowance		
higher rate	71.40	73.60
lower rate	47.80	49.30
Disability living allowance		
care component		
highest rate	71.40	73.60
middle rate	47.80	49.30
lowest rate	18.95	19.55
mobility component		
higher rate	49.85	51.40
lower rate	18.95	19.55
Carer's allowance	53.90	55.55
Severe disablement allowance		
basic rate	59.45	62.95
age related addition—higher rate	15.00	13.80
age related addition—middle rate	8.40	7.10
age related addition—lower rate	5.45	5.60
Maternity benefits		
Maternity allowance		
standard rate	124.88	128.73
Bereavement benefits and retirement pensions		
Widowed parent's allowance or widowed mother's allowance	97.65	100.70

	April 2010	April 2011
	£ pw	£ pw
Bereavement allowance or widow's pension		
standard rate	97.65	100.70
Retirement pension		
Category A	97.65	100.70
Category B (higher)	97.65	100.70
Category B (lower)	58.50	61.20
Category C	58.50	61.20
Category D	58.50	61.20
Incapacity benefit		
Long-term incapacity benefit		
basic rate	91.40	94.25
increase for age—higher rate	15.00	15.80
increase for age—lower rate	5.80	5.60
invalidity allowance—higher rate	15.00	15.80
invalidity allowance—middle rate	8.40	7.10
invalidity allowance—lower rate	5.45	5.60
Short-term incapacity benefit		
under pension age—higher rate	81.60	84.15
under pension age—lower rate	68.95	71.10
over pension age—higher rate	91.40	94.25
over pension age—lower rate	87.75	90.45
Dependency increases		
Adult		
carer's allowance	31.90	32.90
severe disablement allowance	31.70	32.70
maternity allowance	41.35	42.70
retirement pension	57.05	58.80
long-term incapacity benefit	53.10	54.75
short-term incapacity benefit under pension age	41.35	42.65
short-term incapacity benefit over pension age	51.10	52.70
Child	11.35*	11.35*
Industrial injuries benefits		
Disablement benefit		
aged 18 and over or under 18 with dependants—		
100%	145.80	150.30
90%	131.22	135.27
80%	116.64	120.24
70%	102.06	105.71
60%	87.48	90.18
50%	72.90	75.15
40%	58.32	60.12

	April 2010 £ pw	April 2011 £ pw
30%	43.74	45.09
20%	29.16	30.06
aged under 18 with no dependants—		
100%	89.35	92.10
90%	80.42	82.89
80%	71.48	73.68
70%	62.55	64.47
60%	53.61	55.26
50%	44.68	46.05
40%	35.74	36.84
30%	26.81	27.63
20%	17.87	18.42
unemployability supplement		
basic rate	90.10	92.90
increase for adult dependant	53.10	54.75
increase for child dependant	11.35★	11.35★
increase for early incapacity—higher rate	18.65	19.25
increase for early incapacity—middle rate	12.00	12.40
increase for early incapacity—lower rate	6.00	6.20
constant attendance allowance		
exceptional rate	116.80	120.40
intermediate rate	87.60	90.30
normal maximum rate	58.40	60.20
part-time rate	29.20	30.10
exceptionally severe disablement allowance	58.40	60.20
Reduced earnings allowance		
maximum rate	58.32	60.12
Death benefit		
widow's pension		
higher rate	97.65	102.15
lower rate	29.30	30.65
widower's pension	97.65	102.15

★ These sums payable in respect of children are reduced if payable in respect of the only, elder or eldest child for whom child benefit is being paid (see reg.8 of the Social Security (Overlapping Benefits) Regulations 1979).

	April 2010 £ pw	April 2011 £ pw
Employment and support allowance		
Contribution-based personal rates		
assessment phase—*aged under 25*	51.85	53.45
aged 25 or over	65.45	67.50
main phase	65.45	67.50
Components		
work-related activity	25.95	26.75
support	31.40	32.35
Income-based personal allowances		
single person—*aged under 25*	51.85	53.45
aged 25 or over	65.45	67.50
lone parent—*aged under 18*	51.85	53.45
aged 18 or over	65.45	67.50
couple—*both aged under 18*	51.85	53.45
both aged under 18, with a child	78.30	80.75
both aged under 18, (main phase)	65.45	67.50
both aged under 18, with a child (main phase)	102.75	105.95
one aged under 18, one aged 18 or over	102.75	105.95
both aged 18 or over	102.75	105.95
Premiums		
pensioner—*single person with no component*	67.15	69.85
couple with no component	99.65	103.75
enhanced disability—*single person*	13.65	14.05
couple	19.65	20.25
severe disability—*single person*	53.65	55.30
couple (one qualifies)	53.65	55.30
couple (both qualify)	107.30	110.60
carer	30.05	31.00

NEW BENEFIT RATES FROM APRIL 2011

(Benefits covered in Volume II)

	April 2010	April 2011
	£ pw	£ pw

Contribution-based jobseeker's allowance

personal rates—*aged under 18*	51.85	53.45
aged 18 to 24	51.85	53.45
aged 25 or over	65.45	67.50

Income support and income-based jobseeker's allowance

personal allowances		
single person—*aged under 25*	51.85	53.45
aged 25 or over	65.45	67.50
lone parent—*aged under 18*	51.85	53.45
aged 18 or over	65.45	67.50
couple—*both aged under 18*	51.85	53.45
both aged under 18, with a child	78.30	80.75
one aged under 18, one aged under 25	51.85	53.45
one aged under 18, one aged 25 or over	64.45	67.50
both aged 18 or over	102.75	105.95
child	57.57	62.33
premiums		
family—*ordinary*	17.40	17.40
lone parent	17.40	17.40
pensioner—*single person (JSA)*	67.15	69.85
couple	99.65	103.75
disability—*single person*	28.00	28.85
couple	39.85	41.10
enhanced disability—*single person*	13.65	14.05
couple	19.65	20.25
child	21.00	21.63
severe disability—*single person*	53.65	55.30
couple (one qualifies)	53.65	55.30
couple (both qualify)	107.30	110.60
disabled child	52.08	53.62
carer	30.05	31.00

Pension credit

Standard minimum guarantee		
single person	132.60	137.35
couple	202.40	209.70

New Benefit Rates from April 2011

	April 2010 £ pw	April 2011 £ pw
Additional amount for severe disability		
single person	53.65	55.30
couple (one qualifies)	53.65	55.30
couple (both qualify)	107.30	110.60
Additional amount for carers	30.05	31.00
Savings credit threshold		
single person	98.40	103.15
couple	157.25	164.55
Maximum savings credit		
single person	20.52	20.52
couple	27.09	27.09

NEW TAX CREDIT AND BENEFIT RATES 2011–12

(Benefits covered in Volume IV)

	2010–11	2011–12
	£ pw	£ pw
Benefits in respect of children		
Child benefit		
only, elder or eldest child (couple)	20.30	20.30
each subsequent child	13.40	13.40
Guardian's allowance	14.30	14.75
Employer-paid benefits		
Standard rates		
Statutory sick pay	79.15	81.60
Statutory maternity pay	124.88	128.73
Statutory paternity pay	124.88	128.73
Statutory adoption pay	124.88	128.73
Income threshold	97.00	102.00

	2010–11	2011–12
	£ pa	£ pa
Working tax credit		
Basic element	1,920	1,920
Couple and lone parent element	1,890	1,950
30 hour element	790	790
Disabled worker element	2,570	2,650
Severe disability element	1,095	1,130
50+ Return to work payment (under 30 hours)	1,320	1,365
50+ Return to work payment (30 or more hours)	1,965	2,030
Child tax credit		
Family element	545	545
Family element, baby addition	545	—
Child element	2,300	2,555
Disabled child element	2,715	2,800
Severely disabled child element	1,095	1,130
Tax credit income thresholds		
Income disregard	25,000	10,000
First threshold	6,420	6,420
First threshold for those entitled to child tax credit only	16,190	15,860
First withdrawal rate	*39%*	*41%*
Second threshold	50,000	40,000
Second withdrawal rate	*6.67%*	*41%*